The Decadent Handbook

The ultimate lifestyle guide for those who want to transform the spirit of the age, or failing that, ignore it altogether.

Wayward and debauched advice from the free spirits of our age, including Hari Kunzru, Salena Godden, Maria Alvarez, Michael Bywater, Louise Welsh, Tom Holland, Helen Walsh, Lisa Hilton, Belle de Jour, Joe Boyd, Nicholas Royle and Robert Irwin.

The contributors (those still living by the time of publication) have chosen to be remunerated with La Fée Absinthe, the true spirit of decadence.

The Decadent Handbook

Edited by Rowan Pelling, Amelia Hodsdon
and James Doyle

Dedalus

Published in the UK by Dedalus Limited,
24–26, St Judith's Lane, Sawtry, Cambs, PE28 5XE
email: info@dedalusbooks.com
www.dedalusbooks.com

ISBN 978 1 903517 64 2

Dedalus is distributed in the USA by SCB Distributors,
15608 South New Century Drive, Gardena, California 90248
email: info@scbdistributors.com   web: www.scbdistributors.com

Dedalus is distributed in Australia by Peribo Pty Ltd.
58 Beaumont Road, Mount Kuring-gai N.S.W. 2080
email: info@peribo.com.au

Dedalus is distributed in Canada by Disticor Direct-Book Division,
695 Westney Road South, Suite 14, Ajax, Ontario, LI6 6M9
email: ndalton@disticor.com   web: www.disticordirect.com

Publishing History
First published by Dedalus in hardcover in the UK in 2006
First Dedalus paperback edition in 2007

Printed in Finland by WS Bookwell
Typeset by RefineCatch Limited, Bungay, Suffolk

Contents

CONTENTS

Decadent Drinking

Decadent Anti-heroes

Decadent Culture

Decadent Travel

CONTENTS

Decadent Sex

Decadent Gastronomy

Decadent Death Styles

7

CONTENTS

Rowan Pelling ably assisted by James Doyle and Amelia Hodsdon at an editorial meeting. Photo: Sean Gibson.

The Anti-Contribution

Here is my piece (unpaid) for Rowan Pelling's and Dedalus' book on decadence. Perhaps you could use it as a Z-list celebrity endorsement?

What the fuck does a mummy from Cambridge know about decadence? Doesn't Rowan realise that not believing in the future is the essential mark of the decadent? That the worst of children is that they give you the greatest disadvantage of them all; hope?

Choking hope and being a nappy slave is not decadent. Smoking dope on Jim Morrison's grave is not decadent. Exploiting writers and their petty vanities is also, by the way, not decadent.

Decadence is for heavyweights. You need to possess the resources of character, the resilience of mind and the physical stamina to make of decadence a kind of moral virtue and spiritual strength. It is not for silly lightweight school girls.

HRL. His Royal Lowness. Sebastian Horsley

Introduction

Rowan Pelling

Sebastian Horsley poses a good question in the letters that preface and finish this book, or what we term the anti-contribution: 'What the fuck does a mummy from Cambridge know about decadence?' While I would like to pretend that life in the ancient university town where I reside is a riot of orgiastic, drug-fuelled nihilism, the procession of buggies and Sainsbury's bags outside my window suggests otherwise. I have never seen a velvet-cloaked dandy on the cobbled streets, let alone an aesthete leading a lobster on a string. And despite the proximity to Norfolk, reports of goat sodomy and incest are surprisingly rare.

The truth is what I know about decadence is much the same as your average armchair sybarite. I would doubtless fail the practical examination but might score a few points in the appreciation and theory papers. What would-be hedonist doesn't enjoy the vicarious pleasures and perversions of the decadent movement in the arts? For those readers unfamiliar with the guiding tenets, the decadents were a diverse body of writers, artists and philosophers whose work and ideas flourished in the second half of the 19th century. They were less a formal entity than a loose-linked grouping of collaborators and individuals, whose guiding mantra was 'Art for art's sake.' Their philosophy was typified by pessimism, mysticism, idealism, elitism and, for many of the movement, a certain elaborate artifice in the wardrobe department. Since they had no faith in the future, rationalism or the relentless onward grind of industrialism, the decadents sought extreme sensation or sentiments to save them from the atrophying perils of social convention. The decadent movement was a major force in the evolution of Symbolism and thereby, ultimately, Surrealism.

The guiding lights of the decadent movement are generally held to be the French poet Charles Baudelaire and the German philosopher Arthur Schopenhauer (bards of pessimism, disease and the grave), and amongst the most infamous prophets were the writers Oscar Wilde and Joris-Karl Husymans (both of whose work is represented in this book) and our cover artist, the extraordinary Aubrey Beardsley. Whenever you see a young man with lacquered hair clad in a purple shot-silk suit stroll past you in the street, clutching a bottle of whisky in one hand and a copy of *Les Fleurs du Mal* in the other, you have the decadents to blame. Just look at Pete Doherty and Russell Brand.

The Decadent Handbook is therefore envisaged as an anti-lifestyle guide for people who wish to transform the spirit of the age, or, failing that, ignore it altogether. It's for all those who seek respite from the worst banalities of modern exist-ence: property ladders, yummy mummies, footie daddies, loyalty cards, friendly bacteria, Glade air freshener, decking, Coldplay, The Da Vinci Code and Natasha Kaplinsky. *The Handbook* seeks not to instruct, but to offer diverse inspir-ations – from Tom Holland on the joy of pony girls to Louise Welsh on the hedonistic funeral. And while the spirit of the book is firmly rooted in the decadent movement of the 19th century, its tendrils spread back and forwards in time. We can hardly consider decadence without a glance at the Romans or a word from the Earl of Rochester. Nor can we omit that modern-day heir to the libertine tradition, the rock star. Joe Boyd takes us back to the UFO club in the 1960s, while John Moore remembers the class-A dividends of chart success. If it's sex you're looking for (and who isn't?), one-time call girl Belle de Jour takes a whipping. And I challenge you to find a better piece of writing on the lost days of a bender than Salena

Godden's 'The Last Big Drinky': a story so vividly rendered you can taste the whisky. On a more lateral plane of decadence lurks Jake Polley's sinister tale 'Vermin', a reminder that no force is more callous and amoral than animal instinct. These are just a random selection of the vices on offer.

It seems to me that *The Decadent Handbook* is an apposite book. It's a good time to consider what we mean by 'decadence' in an age where there's much loose talk about 'the decadent West'. Do the inanities of Big Brother, binge drinkers and celebrity hair extensions really signal a new age of Sodom and Gomorrah? Do you see Bacchanalias in Hyde Park? Aren't lazy tags sullying the good reputation of decadence, which requires talent, aptitude and dedication to perfect? Because there's an inbuilt irony in most decadent pursuits (as Maria Alvarez points out in her essay 'Snowball'), which means you cannot become debauched without considerable effort. It takes application to become a drunk, a serial seducer or a drug addict, and more outré excesses take great feats of imagination. Look at the artist Sebastian Horsley, the very model of the modern decadent, whose letters sandwich this volume: he paints, he writes, he broadcasts, he swims with sharks and flies to the Philippines to have himself crucified; all this frenzied activity alongside the drugs, the whores and the pink velvet suit. Truly he is tireless in his pursuit of decadence. I feel exhausted just to think of him. (But it was ever thus; when Byron lived in Venice he spent the hours up to midnight engaged in conspicuous displays of pleasure-seeking, then retired and wrote until dawn.) Occasionally I wonder if it's not a little more decadent to lie here on my Cambridge sofa scoffing Hobnobs and cheerleading Sebastian on his way, than to scale the depths of depravity myself. In our opening chapter 'Decadent Theory' Anne Billson, Hari Kunzru and Nick Groom explore such arguments, while Alan Jenkins' poem 'A Brief History' is a magnificent evocation of art and immorality over two centuries.

No publisher has done more to keep the decadent tradition alive than Dedalus, the originators of this volume. I first encountered Dedalus when I was editing *The Erotic Review* magazine and a friend told me that if I was 'looking for sex, perversion and depravity', I should get hold of their catalogue. I did and was duly captivated by their mix of classic decadent literatures and contemporary fiction that wilfully trampled the boundaries of normality. I was also impressed by the rare and excessively non-commercial devotion to translating Continental writing. As the publisher's manifesto stated: 'Dedalus has invented its own distinctive genre, which we term distorted reality, where the bizarre, the unusual and the grotesque and the surreal meld in a kind of intellectual fiction which is very European.' I swiftly ordered *Torture Garden* by Octave Mirbeau, *Memoirs of a Gnostic Dwarf* by David Madsen and *Prayer-Cushions of the Flesh* by Robert Irwin. It was the beginnings of a decadent library. Some months after that I met two of the founders of Dedalus on a train en route to a literary festival. We bonded over a shared fondness for strong liquor and forceful debate and I accepted an invitation to become one of the company's many honorary directors. This book comes out of that collaboration – and several cases of red wine.

I would like to thank everyone who contributed to this book (spurred on only by the promise of absinthe and a party), but particular praise must go to those who helped in the commissioning and editing of this book: James Doyle, Amelia Hobson and Susanna Forrest. Although the biggest debt of gratitude is reserved for the extraordinary Eric Lane, who has been the engine-room of Dedalus since its inception and is my absolute number one hero (or is that anti-hero?) in publishing.

Dedalus and I hope *The Decadent Handbook* will be a useful companion for anyone hoping to embark on a life of debauchery, aesthetic refinement and their constant shadow companion, terminal ennui; that it will amuse wicked uncles, teenaged Goths, latterday flâneurs and Cambridge mummies. Or, failing that, *The Handbook* aims to further enervate the reader on his or her chaise longue, who is too fatigued for decadence themselves, but nonetheless likes to think that someone, somewhere is still lying in the gutter looking at the stars.

Decadent Theory

A Brief History

Alan Jenkins

Bring me the hypodermics, nurse, that I
Might feel again the riotous joy of youth
Although I may not stir from this divan,
Sequestered from the world by gorgeous drapes
Of organdie and velvet; bring me, from
Their attic prison, two of the youngest boys
That they might entertain me here a while
With re-enactments of old Zeus's rapes
In various guises, bringing to their aid
Such gentle toys as I have furnished them with,
Then have them offer themselves up to me
For the grateful tribute of my sacrifice.
Their visible song, made of perfect sound
And exceeding passion, clothed with the wind's
Fair wings, will soothe me to my needful sleep
Borne on the swansdown billows of that dream
Vouchsafed by thee, divine poppy! O thou
Alone who can bring comfort to my soul
Which else would linger in the world of shades
And everlasting darkness! Summon forth
Such visions as I never hoped to see
On earth, not though I swooned here in the arms
Of pale ambrosia – exquisite embrace:
Rose-petals scattered by the slender nymphs
Who glide in veils diaphanous through glades
On little moonlit feet will be my bed,

Their silken breasts a pillow for my head
As with heavy-lidded eyes they drink the dew
From off each other's maiden lips, and strain
To cool their burning veins. You! Girl, come here . . .

1976

'The clubs are closed now. Most of the old set
Did themselves in, or hopped it – Kenya, Jo'burg,
Brazil, that sort of thing. Not a single debt
Got paid, of course. Then there was that fiasco
With Lucky and the nanny . . . They'll never get him
    though –
Not the newshounds or the police johnnies, oh no.
Christ, that lot are far too thick. I have my own ideas
But what's the point of dredging up old muck?
I still like to play the odd hand now and then
If I can find somewhere . . . congenial. You know, *civilized*.'

'At one time we'd all drive down to someone's place
In Surrey. *Everyone*'d be there. In those days
It didn't matter what you did – the chicks' brains
Were in their boxes anyway . . . I had one once
On a lawn somewhere, she was, like, so far gone
She never even knew . . . Then Brian went in the pool,
The deep six, and the heavies moved in, raids,
Busts, the whole bit. Just think, it could've gone on
And on – that would have been really cool.
Now it's all, like, chains and razor-blades.'

'There were seven of us down at Strangeways
And Diana filmed the whole thing – just turned up
With a camera, little hand-held job' – 'Hand-job? *Sorry!*' –
'And started shooting. What a hoot! After dinner,
Things got pretty hot, and, well, they wanted her

To pack it in at first, but then, *well*, we all got
Into it. We're all there, anyway, for posterity,
What you can see of us – *completely* tonto. I can tell
You, if it got into the wrong hands . . . I mean,
It'd be *no joke*. Jamie's putting it on video.'

'If all the girls here – oh, *come off it*, dears –
Were laid end to end , I wouldn't be at all surprised! . . .'
'He was brilliant at first but now he's not so keen . . .'
'Wasn't her aunt the duchess of something, Saxe-Coburg . . .'
'Problem is, the money's getting burned up . . .'
'*Wonderful* Miranda's got the most *amazing* stuff . . .'
'I'm not sure there's anybody here I'd trust . . .'
'It was more a boff de politesse than a fuck . . .'
'No good when things began to get a little rough . . .'
'That's good – fear in a handful of happy dust . . .'

1856–2006

My life is killing me. It's making me thin,
To sit in this room translating Baudelaire,
My spiritual room, in which the stagnant air
Is faintly tinged with blue and rose, in which I'm lapped
By idleness – the soul's long bath, blueish, roseate,
Scented by regret and desire; where even the furniture
Is prostrate with languor and the draperies speak
A silent language, the language of flowers, of skies,
Of the setting sun. But it's making me thin, not as thin
As the woman who looks eighty – she's eighteen – on the
    street
Begging loose change for some dope, a bar of soap
Or her bag of whippet-bones on a rope; not as thin
As the boys in the AIDS ward on St. Mary's, as the stare
Behind the hand that spray-scrawled *Kill all fairies*
On the wall outside; not as thin as the light

At the end of the tunnel – that's the underpass –
To the heap of rags and plastic bags who lies curled
On its stinking floor, as the page of the *News of the World*
That drapes her, as the arse of the crack-head who rapes her,
As what comes out of it . . . Not as thin as this sort of shit:

> *Wine lends its atmosphere of luxury to even*
> *The filthiest hovel, conjuring the porticos of heaven*
> *From the vaporous red-gold of its bouquet,*
> *Like a sunset in a clouded sky; opium magnifies*
> *Everything, makes boundless space and time, defies*
>
> *Every limit put on the infinite by our feeble senses*
> *And brings a new depth to the pleasures it enhances*
> *And fills the soul to overflowing with a sombre joy.*
> *None of that is equal, though, to the poison that pours*
> *From those terrifying, fatal green eyes of yours,*
>
> *Those lakes wherein my soul trembles, sees itself reversed –*
> *My dreams flock to those bitter depths to quench their thirst.*
> *And none of this equals the prodigal wonder of*
> *Your juices, that gnaw at my unrepentant soul and plunge it*
> *In forgetfulness, vertigo, the brink of death, the pit . . .*

Not as thin as the last-ditch best-shot final pitch
Of the guy whose life's on the skids, going down the tubes
With his job, home, wife and kids; as the understanding in
    their eyes,
As his whisky, as the unpolluted water in his cubes of ice;
Not as thin as the likelihood of truth coming from the lips,
The thin lips of the suits who talk freedom of choice,
As the new white whine, the sound of attitude, as pity at the
    latitude
Of Westminster or Wood Lane, as the thin bat-squeak of a
    voice
In the last book by the latest scribbler to sell himself on TV;
As the presenter's heels, as her words, as what she feels

When she wonders for a moment what they'd look like
    together,
As he'll look one day standing twitching in the wind and rain
Of her inner weather, as the eye of the needle, as the vein;
As the fibre-optic probe that will one day find
My days are numbered, as the stuff that fills my mind:

Strange, dusky goddess, your smell a mix of Havana
And something musky, a voodoo fetish from the savannah
Created by some witch-doctor Faust,
Sorceress with ebony flanks, and long-lost daughter
To pitch-black midnights: the best wine is water,

The best opium harmless compared to your lips
That love dances on; when desire's caravanserai slips
From its camp at dawn and sets out towards you,
Your eyes are the oasis where even boredom drowns;
From those vast rooflights on your soul, shadowed by frowns,

Pitiless, you pour liquid fire. I can't take much more
But neither can I get my tongue around your shore
Nine times, like the Styx, nor can I, hungry Megaera,
Be Proserpine in the hell of your bed, break you
And bring you to heel; and nor can I make you,

Or your loose, heavy hair, a censor in the gloom
Of an alcove, release a less primitive, untamed perfume,
The spell that's cast over the present by the past –
It's the same as when some adoring lover plucks
Memory's exquisite flower from the flesh he fucks . . .

There was a thumping at the door, and a ghost came in –
A bailiff to torture me in the name of the law, an editor's pimp
Wanting more – and he's thin, thin as the smokes
That help me forget the state I'm in, The North, the
    South . . .
Thin as the thin black worm of fear that eats my gut

And secretes a thin sharp taste of loathing in my mouth;
Thin and sharp as the blades with which I cut thin lines,
    already cut
With bicarb of soda, washing powder, worse – to feel sharp, so
    sharp
I could cut myself, and write these lines of verse
In my own blood on my own thin skin.

My Decadent Career

Anne Billson

It all started with a book – *Dreamers of Decadence*, a study of 19th century Symbolist painters by Philippe Jullian. I was an impressionable young art student and horror film buff, and this was the sort of art I fancied: vampires, severed heads, femmes fatales. I decided decadence was right up my street. Shortly afterwards I sold my first drawing – Salome clutching the severed head of John the Baptist, heavily Rotring-inked in Aubrey Beardsleyesque black and white – to a friend. It earned me 50p, and with the money I bought my very first copy of Baudelaire's *Les Fleurs du Mal*, which I liked because it was full of poems about vampires, femmes fatales and spleen. My decadent career was launched.

I soon realised that if I wanted to be truly decadent, I would have to leave home; decadent artists didn't live with their parents. I rented a room in Camden Town, so tiny there was no room for anything other than a wardrobe, chest of drawers and single bed, which meant I was forced to do most things without getting up. I proceeded to live what I imagined was a life of decadence. I covered the walls with pictures from my favourite horror films. I drank crème de menthe for breakfast, ate tinned octopus and Walnut Whips for dinner. I cut my hair like Louise Brooks in *Pandora's Box* and wore Biba green lipstick and dressing-gowns made of Chinese silk. I trawled second-hand shops for black dresses and fake ocelot coats. I read Proust because the illustrations were by my decadent mentor, Philippe Jullian, whose biography of Robert de Montesquieu, model for the character of the Baron de Charlus, was also a mainstay of my library. I devoured

Huysmans, Mirbeau, Wilde, Poe. I listened to Scriabin, because one of his piano sonatas was known as 'Black Mass', and to Roxy Music, because there were name-checks in one of the band's songs to 'the sphinx and Mona Lisa', both featured in the *Dreamers of Decadence* list of symbolist themes. I slept by day and lived by night, when I would build scale cardboard models of black rooms filled with skeletons and rubber snakes. I composed poems about my knees ('Patella Pantagruella') or went for nocturnal walks along the canal to perform elaborate ceremonies that would involve reciting magic spells and flinging stuffed vine leaves into the water.

I didn't know anyone else like me.

I kept a diary, but had nothing to put in it apart from post-adolescent stream-of-consciousness ramblings about suicide, dreams and unrequited yearnings. I was always reading about absinthe and opium, but my personal narcotics intake was limited to Sobranie Cocktail cigarettes (never inhaled), Fribourg and Treyer snuff and, on special occasions, Night Nurse. My attempts at being a femme fatale repeatedly fell at the first hurdle – none of the men I met seemed terribly keen on the green lipstick, and then later, when I switched to more conventional holly red, I found myself with a devoted following, not of the lovelorn writers and artists I'd envisaged, but of schizophrenics, drug addicts and repressed homosexuals who would burst into tears in public places or rub broken glass into their faces when I refused to sleep with them.

Of course, many years and one *fin-de-siècle* later, I look back at my adorable decadent self and realise that I wasn't decadent at all – I was just young, and rather naïve. Now I live in an attic in Paris with a bottle of absinthe in my cocktail cabinet, a real human skull on my bedside table, a faded tattoo on my ankle, two incurable diseases in my system and a never-ending supply of handsome young French men who seem strangely keen to sleep with me. I've written two books about vampires and one about ghosts, Proust is buried in the cemetery just up the road and the Mona Lisa is only a short Metro hop away. Now I am no longer naïve but cynical and cruel. Now I'm decadent without even trying to be.

But I still don't know anyone else like me.

The Flaming Heart becomes a Fount of Tears
Illness and the Modern Decadent Condition

Philip Langeskov

Considering how common illness is, how tremendous the spiritual change that it brings, how astonishing when the lights of health go down, the undiscovered countries that are then disclosed, what wastes and deserts of the soul a slight attack of influenza brings to view, what precipices and lawns sprinkled with bright flowers a little rise of temperature reveals, what ancient and obdurate oaks are uprooted in us by the act of sickness, how we go down into the pit of death and feel the waters of annihilation close above our heads and wake thinking to find ourselves in the presence of the angels and the harpers when we have a tooth out and come to the surface in the dentist's arm-chair and confuse his 'Rinse the mouth – rinse the mouth' with the greeting of the Deity stooping from the floor of Heaven to welcome us – when we think of this, as we are so frequently forced to think of it, it becomes strange indeed that illness has not taken its place with love and battle and jealousy among the prime themes of literature.

Virginia Woolf, 'On Being Ill'

There is almost nothing to be said for the decadent who has not been seriously ill, or at least given the appearance of being

30

so. This should come as no surprise and, if you have come this far, you will, I am sure, be disinclined to argue the point: chances are, you won't have the strength to in any case. No, decadence and illness go hand in hand, and they go, for the most part, merrily. It is a careless, casual relationship, a symbiosis invariably bringing joy to both parties. The decadent has a lust for experience that is all consuming, seeking out new vistas of consciousness, constantly looking for a higher plane; illness, meanwhile, has a lust for bodies whose attentions are elsewhere directed. Were a couple ever so well matched?

There is a famous shot of Verlaine, taken some years before he fell prey to the languorous violence of his final illness, (pulmonary congestion, since you ask). He is sitting in the corner of a café in the midst of an Absinthe-induced stupor. His shoulders are huddled, pushed back, as if in the awful imaginative presence of angels and of devils. One need only look into his eyes to glean that he is not there to seek out the repetitious drudgery of the quotidian Parisian existence. No, he, like all decadents, is looking through life – looking actually *beyond* existence – shaking the nameless void by the lapels and requesting more. Life is life, but a Decadent life is living. Sitting in a café, Verlaine might have said, is all very well, but sitting in a café rapt by hallucinations is infinitely better. It is, though, the great irony of the decadent existence that this very lust for life, this quest for the visionary experience, leaves the decadent prey to the illnesses and diseases that deprive him of the life he wishes so exquisitely to enjoy. It is the diabolic exchange – give me life and I will give you my life – and it is entered into freely but with the accidental certainty of purpose. For the decadent, merely being alive is worthless; it is better to be dead. Yet, in order to live life to the fullest, it is necessary to embrace death.

Rimbaud had it pegged at the very beginning of *A Season in Hell*, where he writes 'my life was a celebration where all hearts were open and all wines flowed', only to recognise a few lines later that, for the celebration to be worth anything, it had to come at a cost: 'I called for diseases, so I could suffocate in sand, in blood.' Open hearts invite illness. Ernest Dowson, too, recognised the bargain. When he 'cried for madder music and stronger wine,' it was the cry – the howl – of the decadent on the point of disintegration. The result for Dowson, both in the poem and in life, was to be 'desolate and sick of an old passion.' But, lest the modern Decadent simper with neglect, it was not simply the *fin-de-siècle* masters who recognised this. Even Lloyd Cole – dear, sweet, Lloyd Cole, with his eighties stubble and his smouldering eyes – saw the scorpion in the flower bed. His lost weekend in a hotel in Amsterdam, which hints, magnificently, at the prodigious consumption of drugs followed by numerous acts of transgressive sex, came at a cost: 'double pneumonia in a single room.' The message is clear: in order to live, the decadent must be careless of life. Yet being careless of life does not – cannot – mean suicide. Suicide is, comparatively, like keeping an appointment or completing a business transaction; it is an action deliberately entered into. And one cannot, of course, be deliberately careless; it implies caring about being careless, and that simply will not do. No, there is a significant distance between taking your own life and allowing your life to be taken because you are occupied elsewhere. If there were not, the gates of Decadence would be open to any whim-struck chancer. For the record, both Rimbaud and Dowson succumbed to illness: Rimbaud was taken, first by greed and then by synovitis of the right knee; Dowson fell at the feet of alcoholism and was scooped up by tuberculosis. Lloyd Cole, the exception proving the so-called rule as it so often does, is still alive.

Some see this carelessness as exhilarating, and they are, movingly, absolutely correct. Others see it as foolhardy. Devotees of this camp succeed in both having *a* point, while utterly failing to grasp *the* point. They will tell you that Oscar Wilde was foolish to sue the Marquess of Queensbury for libel, as such an action could only bring attention to a lifestyle he knew to be wrong in the eyes of the laws of the day. Oscar, if he were here, would probably tell you that he could do nothing else, not because he was backed into a corner, but because the tenets of his soul were such that he could not flee from his exhilaration: it was worth too much to surrender, even if it cost him his life; and, in a round about sort of way, it did. Oscar would also tell you – and this, like all good things, runs counter to perceived opinion – that he did it, not because Bosie told him to, but because he was busy being in love; and, being busy in love, he forgot to put the latch on the back door and, lo and behold, in snuck illness. (A point about Oscar's illness: some say that we will never know what took him; others say that he simply died; others still, Richard Ellman included, say that consumption consumed him. I favour the latter, not least because it fits my argument.) To take sides here, to form a judgement on what is right and what is wrong is, of course, necessary, but to enter into a dispute would be futile: it would be like an atheist arguing with Christ over the existence of God. The point, though, remains sound. And Wilde, whose reputed last statement – 'either the wallpaper goes or I do' – is synonymous with saying 'make my life better or let me die', would have recognised it.

Thinking of Oscar, as you frequently should, invariably brings things round to *The Picture of Dorian Gray*. This is no bad thing. The bargain at the centre of the piece – in short, to be always young at the cost of the soul, while a portrait moulders, as the body might otherwise, in the attic – provides a glimpse into the playground of the Decadent's imagination. It is the equivalent of making the mixture, baking, having and eating the cake, all in the same elegant motion. Imagine, for a moment, that the offer had been made to the real Rimbaud, the real Verlaine or the real Dowson; imagine that they had been offered the opportunity to ravage the body and yet have a body that did not suffer ravages, a body that did not, in short, fall ill. What might they have done? The tragedy for all decadents is that, although they are unrealistic, they are real; Dorian Gray's bargain, however, is simply unrealistic.

Of course, Decadence and illness did not simply arrive hand in hand, just as Verlaine and Rimbaud were not born in the same bed. No, they were brought together by time and circumstance. And, as little is truly original, the example of history played a part. Decadence – or at least the Decadent moment with which we are concerned here – is often seen as the midway point between Romanticism and Modernism, a spiritual way station on the route to our collective contemporary consciousness. I'm happy not to argue. Some might wish to claim, too, that these two movements neatly bookend the high water mark of what is often called 'Modern Decadence', Romanticism at one end, Modernism at the other. (The books, the meat in the sandwich, are provided, of course, by the aesthetic exhortations of the period 1865–1895.) The Romantics gave Decadence the chance to flourish. In dismantling the ornate formality of the second Augustan age, they allowed a little bit of dirt to creep under the fingernails of life. Without the Romantics, Decadence itself would have come as too much of a shock and would, unpalatable as it might seem, most likely have been still born. The Moderns, in their turn, put breath to the sickly embers of Decadence and gave it flame one last time.

The world, by this time, of course, had become almost immune to death, the catastrophe of the Western Front making the Decadent bargain seem little more than the game it always was; the game, however, had become less fun. When the Moderns died, so too did the Decadent moment. The game was up, you see, and the Decadence we have today can often seem little more than a treading of the well worn path alongside the Amazon: it is fun while it lasts, but it brings us precious little that we did not know already. It is cause for alarm, but not undue panic. The Modern Decadent can take courage from the fate of the modern explorer and, although no longer able to be the first, can be just as extravagant, just as elegant and just as incandescent as the great originals.

If Romanticism provided Decadence with the foot stool it needed to reach the stars, it also provided some quite spectacular examples of illness. The early Decadents took note, as, I am sure, will you. John Keats, the greatest of the English Romantics, was also the most ill. The two are not unconnected. There is a case to make that Keats was the Romantic Decadent without equal. Those who dispute this, never saw little Johnny with a glass in his hand. 'Fill for me a brimming bowl, and let me in it drown my soul,' he wrote in 1814, leaving the reader in little doubt where he stood, both mentally and physically. Keats's example did not stop at imbibation, either. (Allen Ginsberg, by the way, who would have liked to have been a decadent, but never quite made it despite his lunging references to tubercular skies, was not the first to trace the influence of Keats on Rimbaud, among others.) No praise, surely, is high enough for the man who, contorted by hunger and fatal illness, could throw, from the window of his Roman villa, a bowl of Spaghetti simply because he thought it could have been better made. If the Decadents needed an example of perfect carelessness in the pursuit of exalted existence they would surely have looked no further. It is a footnote worth noting that, after slamming the pasta to the floor of the Spanish Steps, the food in Keats's house improved considerably, or so Joseph Severn tells us. Another footnote: the glorious gesture did little for Keats's health; he had already been too careless with his life. A few weeks later, Keats coughed blood for the last time.

Keats, of course, lived in an age when tuberculosis – like many illnesses – jumped from host to host with abandon. As the eminent physician, Lord Brock, made clear in his admirably elegiac pamphlet, *The Tragedy of the Last Illness*, to contract tuberculosis in Keats's day was most assuredly to begin the preparations for death: 'The fundamental fact of its infective nature was not known nor could be known or understood until 1882 when the tubercle bacillus was discovered by Theodore Koch'. As Brock also notes, since the Second World War advancements in science and medicine have been such that, in the developed world at least, tuberculosis as a fatal illness has virtually been conquered.

This brings us to the thorny and often posed question of how one can be decadent in the modern age, an age in which it is becoming increasingly difficult to become genuinely ill. Where there are thorns, of course, there are frequently roses to be found. While it has been noted that Decadence in the modern world is, generally speaking, little more than a clamber over fields already muddied by the footsteps of others, this is not the same as to say that Decadence is redundant. And while it must be acknowledged that the Modern Decadent's chances of finding an untouched blade of grass on which to lie are diminished still further by the widespread provision of healthcare; a provision which robs even the poor of many opportunities palely to sicken. Even in acknowledging such considerations one can see a solution. To find it, we must refer back to the opening line of the piece, which, in recognition of general indolence, is repeated below.

'There is almost nothing to be said for the decadent who has not been seriously ill, *or at least given the appearance of being so.*'

The italics are my own, and they are there because it is the second clause of that statement that must interest us here: the suggestion that assuming the characteristics of serious illness is as valuable a decadent experience as actually being seriously ill. Moralists will squirm at the thought – they'll squirm at anything – but, if it should make *you* pause, dear Reader, you have not been paying attention and you should probably return to the beginning of the book, if not the beginning of your life, and start again.

Allow me to explain by considering the case of Ernest Walsh. Ernest Walsh was a poet, an Irishman and an American, but not in that order. He lived in Paris in the 1920s, when the good people were dead and all that remained was to step on it and join them. Ernest stepped on it and, in September 1926, he began what his lover, Kay Boyle, would later describe as 'the terrible process of dying by haemorrhaging.' A month later he was dead, ravaged, at the age of 31, by tuberculosis.

Tuberculosis, as you should by now be aware, is the Emperor of Decadent diseases. The long, slow, wastefulness of its course allows the victim both to wallow in suffering and to create a substantial body of art by which to be remembered. Nor has it any peer in terms of visual effect: the pallid skin, the sunken, sallow eyes, the fevered brow. It is, in short, a look that will never go out of fashion. The symptoms of tuberculosis – the hacking cough, the rasping expectoration of blood, the agonies of sleeplessness – can, like the look, easily be simulated: it requires little more than a dusting of make-up and a night or two of disordered sleep; a red handkerchief – a requisite in any case – would not go amiss. While fakery is, broadly speaking, to be condemned, it has its justifiable moments.

So, let those who were becoming concerned that Decadence had had its day march on; let them march on with renewed confidence, if not vigour. Let them go forth and be ill – but, for God's sake, as Keats might indeed have written, let them do it well. For those who continue to doubt, there is, always, the Lloyd Cole songbook: 'Spin, spin, whisky and gin, I suffer for my art . . .'

Foucault's Smile

Professor Nicholas Royle

Decadence, as its Latin etymology suggests, involves a falling down or falling off (*de-cadere*). Whether it is a question of art or behaviour, the fall is as sure as night. But to whom does it happen? When? And for how long? Decadence is, first of all perhaps, an experience of reading. And of a double fall. Hence the doubling up of art and behaviour, aesthetic and real. It seems to entail, as in the joys of Oscar Wilde, a sense of being beside oneself. No decadence without a witness, even if it is another within the self. This is in part why the academic, even more than the poet or painter, can appear the decadent figure par excellence. The critical or philosophical thinker, in particular, crystallizes the view that decadence, in art or life, is as much a matter of who reads and how, as it is of the purportedly decadent subject or object per se. The pleasure of reading leads irrepressibly towards decadence. At its most extreme (bliss or jouissance), as Roland Barthes says in *The Pleasure of the Text*, the reader 'is never anything but a "living contradiction": a split subject, who simultaneously enjoys, through the text, the consistency of his selfhood and its collapse, its fall.'

It would be possible to demonstrate that, whatever their apparent moral or didactic character, the most decadent works of art are those in which the fall is most critically dramatized and probingly tendered. Here, above all, it would be a question of a fall that has no end, or at least that entails a fundamental derangement of time. Works, in other words, such as Breughel's Icarus (about which Auden writes with such tenderness and dispassion in 'Musée des Beaux Arts') or Milton's *Paradise Lost* (that epic lapse of 'the devil's party', as Blake noted). But, in the limited space available, here are simply a few words concerning the academic who, perhaps more than any other in the past century, has attracted the label of decadent: Michel Foucault. I never met him, but a few years after his death I happened to be in Sweden, teaching at the University of Uppsala, where he had been a lecturer many years earlier.

Two memories specially haunt from my visit to that beautiful old town. Following a talk I gave called 'After Foucault', a group of us were having drinks and, towards the end, I asked if anyone there had any memories of Foucault. An elderly lady who had not spoken until that moment then became animated and recounted her experience of having once been invited to a party at his flat. The nice detail of this night-out was that she was also at this time supposed to be looking after a young woman visiting Uppsala, a cousin of the British Queen. So she took the Queen's cousin along with her. I remember the old lady's expression as she related what happened when a smiling Foucault opened the door: such a scene was revealed, of bodies in action behind the host, that she felt she had no option but immediately to hurry Her Majesty's cousin away. Pressed by others for further details of what exactly she and the other young woman had witnessed that night, she could not be induced to say another word. The other enduring memory is of the university's old anatomy theatre. In order to view this perfectly preserved seventeenth-century edifice it was necessary to get special permission; a woman unlocked the door and left me with the strange privilege of being alone in that remarkable place. Rather like a visual parallel to the ancient Greek amphitheatre where you can sit on the highest tier of seats and hear an actor whisper on the stage far below, so in the old anatomy theatre at Uppsala the circular structure of tiered seats meant that wherever you sat you felt yourself to be right on top of the dissection table. It was an eerie epiphany, as if I were suddenly a witness to the very essence of modern decadence. In a flash I realized that Foucault had been here and also seen this, and that his theory of the panopticon (notions of modern power and all-seeing surveillance based on Jeremy Bentham's essay of 1787) had the anatomy theatre at Uppsala as its primal scene. I was falling onto the very cadaver.

Decadent Outcasts

Nick Groom

I remember a few years ago Ronnie Wood of the Rolling Stones admitting in an interview, 'Yeah, most of the time I am pretty wasted.' Nothing else really needed to be said after that throwaway remark – being 'pretty wasted' seems to sum up the decadence of certain rock bands. It is an image of reckless foppishness, a vision of intoxication, a grand carelessness and ritualistic squandering of genius. Not the Beatles, of course – there's nothing decadent about those four moptops – but the aspirations of Led Zeppelin and the New York Dolls, the Manic Street Preachers and Babyshambles, even Roxy Music and Suede. It's an image that derives from a handful of notorious writers who lived and died some two centuries ago.

The irresistible painting of the poet Thomas Chatterton lying dead on his bed is the degree zero of rockstar suicides. If you want to live fast, die young, and leave a good-looking corpse, you'll never better this pre-Raphaelite icon. The myth of Chatterton – a maverick, outlaw poet who forged arcane verse and, starving to death in a garret, killed himself out of pride – has haunted the imagination of writers and painters since the eighteenth century. English opium eaters such as Samuel Taylor Coleridge and Thomas De Quincey were fatally attracted by Chatterton's self-destructive career and the rumours that fuelled his posthumous celebrity. Chatterton was an opium eater (it may have been an accidental drug overdose that actually killed him), a vegetarian, and radical in his politics; he dressed outrageously, seemed to have a mesmeric effect on young girls, and, like a prototypical French

41

dandy, lived – and died – in a brothel. And amid all this he wrote dreamlike poetry of the most sultry exoticism, of pagan rites performed in fantastical landscapes:

Three times the virgin swimming on the breeze,
Danc'd in the shadow of the mystic trees:
When like a dark cloud spreading to the view,
The first-born sons of war and blood pursue;
Swift as the elk they pour along the plain;
Swift as the flying clouds distilling rain.
Swift as the boundings of the youthful roe,
They course around, and lengthen as they go.
Like the long chain of rocks, whose summits rise,
Far in the sacred regions of the skies;
Upon whose top the black'ning tempest lours,
Whilst down its side the gushing torrent pours.
Like the long cliffy mountains which extend
From Lorbar's cave, to where the nations end,
Which sink in darkness, thick'ning and obscure,
Impenetrable, mystic and impure;
The flying terrors of the war advance,
And round the sacred oak repeat the dance.
Furious they twist around the gloomy trees,
Like leaves in autumn twirling with the breeze.
So when the splendor of the dying day,
Darts the red lustre of the watry way;
Sudden beneath Toddida's whistling brink,
The circling billows in wild eddies sink:
Whirl furious round and the loud bursting wave
Sink down to Chalma's sacerdotal cave:
Explore the palaces on Zira's coast,
Where howls the war song of the chieftan's ghost.

('Narva and Mored')

In Chatterton's lines one glimpses the strange sunless seas of

Coleridge's drug-inspired dream, 'Kubla Khan', and discovers the sources of De Quincey's nightmares:

> I was stared at, hooted at, grinned at, chattered at, by monkeys, by paroquets, by cockatoos. I ran into pagodas: and was fixed, for centuries, at the summit, or in secret rooms; I was the idol; I was the priest; I was worshipped; I was sacrificed. I fled from the wrath of Brama through all the forests of Asia: Vishnu hated me: Seeva laid wait for me. I came suddenly upon Isis and Osiris: I had done a deed, they said, which the ibis and the crocodile trembled at. I was buried, for a thousand years, in stone coffins, with mummies and sphinxes, in narrow chambers at the heart of eternal pyramids. I was kissed, with cancerous kisses, by crocodiles; and laid, confounded with all unutterable slimy things, amongst reeds and Nilotic mud.
>
> (*Confessions of an English Opium Eater*)

With the Romantic poets here we have decadence *avant la lettre*: decadence was not a recognizable aesthetic, and yet already it suffused the imagination. One can see it in the infinite decayed ruins pictured by Piranesi, in the obsessive fascination with tortuous Gothic novels and their barely repressed sexual passion and rampant orientalism, and in the rise of eroto-occultist societies such as the Monks of Medmenham, who slaked their twisted lust in blasphemous orgies where whores were hired and dressed in the habits of nuns. As massive leaps were made in science and technology and the body was increasingly reduced to a sort of biological machine, there grew cravings for a life of sensation rather than of thoughts, and a desire for refuge in what Charles Baudelaire was to call the 'artificial paradises' of drink, drugs, and dreams – such worlds, it was claimed, were the true reality. And it was the writers of the time who imagined this dark and teeming new world into existence.

Poets like Lord Byron seemed to be driven by almost demonic powers. He tossed off the sprawling epic poem 'Don Juan' by dictating to his servant every morning as he shaved; magnetically charismatic and always impeccably turned out, he was a sexually voracious predator on whom the first English vampire novel was based; he fled the country in the wake of truly scandalous rumours about, variously, his persistent adultery, incest with his half-sister, homosexuality, and sodomizing his new wife (the last two at least being capital offences); he toured Europe with an entourage of fellow writers Percy and Mary Shelley and shared their groupies. 'Mad, bad, and dangerous to know', as his lover Lady Caroline Lamb memorably described him, he seemed to be the epitome of the anti-hero: brilliant, beautiful, and deadly.

Byron was also a typical Romantic poet in that, like Chatterton, he died young. There is a fatal inevitability about the whole movement – a pervading sense of loss, failure, transience, and waste, mixed however with a delicious gruesomeness. After Percy Shelley's body was recovered from the Gulf of Spezia where he had mysteriously drowned, his rotting corpse was cremated on the shore. The heart was snatched from the smouldering carcass on the orders of Byron and kept by his 'jackal', Edward Trelawney. After ten years bitter argument it was eventually delivered back to his wife Mary, author of the macabre novel *Frankenstein*. She kept it in her bedside table, wrapped in a copy of a poem her husband had written to John Keats, following that poet's own premature death.

Suicide was also fashionable following the death of Chatterton, and Goethe fuelled the craze with *The Sorrows of Werther*. This intensely dark novel ends with the protagonist, inescapably weary of life, shooting himself, and supposedly inspired some two thousand young men to do the same. Werther was certainly on the mind of the morbid poet Thomas Lovell Beddoes, collector of skulls and author of a grotesque revenge tragedy called *Death's Jest Book*. Beddoes

44

too died in mysterious circumstances – possibly poisoned by his own hand. Others, however, explored mortality in other, more practical ways: the languorous art critic and painter Thomas Griffiths Wainewright was, as Oscar Wilde declared, an artist in pen, pencil, and poison – to fund his connoisseur's taste in engravings and objets d'art he allegedly murdered his mother-in-law and sister-in-law for their life insurance dividends.

These writers entranced the emerging decadent sensibility like the flowers of evil, or the forbidden fruit in the Garden of Eden. They seemed invested with a sort of satanic majesty, free from the restrictions of conventional morality; they revelled in carnality, they were enticingly cruel; they were dazzlingly tempting – to read them was like dining with the damned. Later writers from Alfred Lord Tennyson to John Betjeman – even the fallen poets of the First World War – just didn't have the same heady mix of sensual excess, personal tragedy, and good looks. Hence the reinvention of the image of the Romantic poet by hedonistic rock stars in the sixties and seventies – photos on album covers showed effeminate dandies staring out with rude and belligerent intent, while the rumours that surrounded the recordings and tours created an unholy new trinity of sex & drugs & rock'n'roll. It was essentially a revival of the dark side of the Romantic aesthetic – and, as before, was similarly spiced up with blood, Satanism, the occult, and even death, suicide, and murder.

The sexual exploits of rock bands often went beyond the predictable debauching of impressionable young teenagers and passing groupies around. When the Rolling Stones were busted for drugs at Keith Richards' mansion Redlands, the divinely named Marianne Faithfull, a descendent of Leopold von Sacher-Masoch (the author of *Venus in Furs* who gave his name to 'masochism'), was discovered wearing nothing more than a bearskin rug that seemed to keep slipping off in front of the arresting officers. And then rumours began circulating that Mick Jagger had been arrested while eating a Mars Bar from her pussy (an incident repeatedly denied but nevertheless alluded to in the Donald Cammell and Nic Roeg film *Performance*). Led Zeppelin, in contrast, had a taste for live seafood, using red snappers and octopuses and even sharks to pleasure their lucky girls.

Both bands also became embroiled in tales of diabolical trysts. The Stones' recording of the mad samba, 'Sympathy for the Devil' with lines about piles of stinking corpses, and the rape-and-murder style of 'Gimme Shelter' seemed like a ghastly prophecy when a fan was killed at the Stones' gig at Altamont. Led Zep's guitarist Jimmy Page, meanwhile, cultivated his interests in the 'Great Beast' Aleister Crowley by buying Boleskine, Crowley's house on the banks of Loch Ness, and writing the soundtrack to Kenneth Anger's film Lucifer Rising; likewise, rumours later attributed deaths in and around the band (including that of drummer John Bonham) to Page's meddling in the occult – all of which added to his allure.

But was all this little more than cosmetics and posturing? From Buddy Holly to Jimi Hendrix and Jim Morrison, Marc Bolan to Kurt Cobain, rock has had no shortage of dead boys, but very few that have attained the sacrificial quality of the corpses of Chatterton, Keats, Shelley, and Byron: possibly Brian Jones of the Stones (drowned in mysterious circumstances), Johnny Thunders of transvestite glam band the New York Dolls (possibly murdered, possibly overdosed), and the elegantly wasted Richey Edwards (Manics – disappeared). Neither are there in the rock scene the wanderers, the outcasts, the sinister evil recluses who lurk in the shadows of Gothic novels and the underworld of nineteenth-century London – the nocturnal visitors to clandestine clubs specializing in the perverse and the unutterable that Dorian Gray finds he is unable to resist. Pete Doherty and his crack smoking is rather too refined, rather too knowing in its illegality, and rappers consorting with gangsters and other urban lowlife is neither pretty nor wasted.

But there is a monster who does creep around the fringes of the globe, as if cursed like the Wandering Jew to be hounded from border to border. He was a rock star – once. A magnificent, cartoonish zany in his day who aspired to supreme decadence. He didn't find it in the rococo costumes he flounced about in, or in the homo-erotic yobbo anthems to which he strutted and fretted his hours upon the stage. He found it as he aged, when he began to yearn again for the adulation of prepubescent boys and girls. Since then, Gary Glitter has been vilified. His crimes and secrets – like the hideous crimes and secrets that lie at the heart of Gothic novels – are indefensible, inexplicable to all right thinking people, and so he is condemned to carry this crime, this terrible notoriety wherever he goes. Like Satan, his hell goes with him, and burns with the ferocity of the law – a law that seems ever more eager to exterminate him. He, perhaps, has most in common with the archetypal Romantic decadents, now that Jimmy Page has received an OBE, Mick Jagger has been knighted, and even the eerily immortal Keith Richards has invested some £60,000 in a trendy beach hut on an exclusive part of the English coast. Byron's friends certainly feared that as successive scandals broke, he risked being lynched by a mob if he ventured out in London and, of course, Wilde was convicted and sentenced to hard labour, ruined and ultimately destroyed by his ordeal – his imprisonment was effectively a death penalty. Was the public outcry against these two as vociferous as that against Gary Glitter? Whether you like it or not, he is a true outcast – and may be the most decadent rock star on the planet.

Memories of the Decadence

Hari Kunzru

At the beginning of the Decadence things were easy. Although we were bored, and though everything had been done before, we were seized with a peculiar sense of potential. Our anomie had something optimistic to it. It was the golden age of our decline.

During the Decadence we went for promenades in the poorer quarters of the city, pausing to examine choice deformities, examples of disease or dementia. Soon we began to imitate them, at first only in mannerisms, later using make-up, drugs, prosthetics, or surgery. At length it became impossible to tell the fashionable from the afflicted. We thought this a salutary moral lesson, and took great delight in ignoring it.

During the Decadence we ate and drank to excess, until a point came when excess went out of fashion. Then we would revert to an extreme frugality. Mathematicians told us the attractor governing our consumption was a simple period which, though occasionally disrupted by shifts elsewhere in the libidinal economy, was reasonably easy to map. Manufacturers of luxury foods and the proprietors of health farms, spas and colonic irrigation parlours learned to track the so called Bulimia Cycle, and for a time such businesses became extremely profitable. Soon however, activity became so intense that the pattern was disrupted and our predictions went awry, setting in motion a wave of bankruptcies, suicides and social ostracisms.

During the Decadence we gave up sexual intercourse, substituting for it various kinds of fetishism. We refined our tastes, narrowing their range and fantastically increasing their complexity. Certain people became interested in abstraction, concentrating perhaps on household objects or patterns of light and shade. Such citizens were known to climax spontaneously at the sight of a safety pin or a line of red tail lights stretching forward along a dual carriageway. One celebrated roué took his pleasure entirely from the contemplation of lipstick stains on the rims of Waterford crystal champagne flutes. He claimed this stemmed more from an appreciation of colour and texture than any displacement of the presence of a woman onto the glass.

During the erotic phase of the Decadence, combinations of time, place, mood and the presence of physical objects became ever more specific. An increasing percentage of resources were dedicated to sexual research and organisation. Orgasms began to require corporate sponsorship, a trend which reached its apogee in the meticulously-planned bacchanals at Nuremberg, Jonestown and Hyde Park. The latter, in which an estimated two hundred thousand people participated in a ritual designed solely to produce the little death in a middle-aged software billionaire, was considered the highpoint of the movement. A cluster of massively-parallel processors were connected to a variety of front-end delivery devices. When triggered they instantiated patented pleasure-algorithms in the crowd, causing runaway positive feedback which was gathered into a series of giant cells, amusingly styled to represent luminous *linga* and *yoni*. When the charge had accumulated to a sufficient degree it was fed back via a fibreoptic core to the Park Lane hotel suite where the entrepreneur lay, bathed in the glow of his hi-res monitors. The crowd themselves, devotees of the influential cult of auto-erotic consumption, financed the event through ticket sales and the purchase of various items of merchandising. The energy generated by their activity produced a small quantity of almost-clear seminal fluid on the raw silk sheets of the billionaire's bed, and augmented his bank balance by an estimated twelve and a half million pounds. It was thus considered a success and plans for a two-hundred date world tour were drawn up, only to be scotched by his premature death from skin cancer in a Hawaii tanning dome. Soon afterwards, a fashion for feverish masturbatory interiority gained favour, inaugurating a rage for Keats, broom closets and antique printed pornography. Boarding schools were set up throughout the country. The days of the megabacchanals drew temporarily to a close.

The involvement of large numbers of people in organised sexual experimentation necessitated the development of information networks, directories and algebraic search engines dedicated to matching those of compatible tastes. Nymphets were put in touch with elderly professors, cyborg freaks with the manufacturers of Japanese industrial robots, those interested in coercion with those who wanted to be coerced. This last category caused some problems among purist dominants, for whom the desire to be coerced disqualified some candidates from consideration as slaves, concentration camp inmates or members of religious orders. A standard disclaimer form was quickly developed. Willingness to sign meant automatic barring as an involuntary submissive. These questions of consent were handled by the Society of Sadean Solicitors (SSS), whose obsessive fascination with the Byzantine complexities of this area of law never once led them to waive their exorbitant fees.

During the Decadence, eroticism itself was only a passing fad. The information network which grew up to enable efficient sexual contact became itself the object of our interests. Connoisseurs of classifications, indices and filing systems paid astronomical sums for rare databases. We became collectors of objects, not from any particular interest in the things themselves, but simply for the opportunities they presented us for cataloguing. Some citizens rejected computer automation altogether, taking great pride in feats of card-indexing. Cross-referencing by hand became an art as much appreciated as sculpture or the programming of combat games.

We soon developed an acute awareness of taxonomy. Classification according to phylum, genus and species became *de rigueur*, not just for biological material, but in many other fields as well. Televised public debates were held over the correct designation of common phenomena. They were conducted along the lines of mediaeval theological disputations, and took place in a studio mocked up to represent the cloisters of the twelfth-century University of Bologna. The only anachronism was the pair of bikini-clad girls who operated the digital scoreboard.

We engaged in a passionate love affair with hierarchies, all the more intense for our awareness that they were meaningless, even ridiculous as tools for understanding our distributed, networked world. As the ebbs and flows of our frenzied culture became more extreme, we turned to the verities of dead, static systems to comfort ourselves, soothing the ache of the data pumping faster through our bruised, red-raw flesh. We relearned Abulafia's Caballah and studied the circular taxonomies of the Catalan, Ramón Lull. We rejected Watson and Crick for Paracelsus and John Dee, embraced Galen and the four humours, studied the Tree of Knowledge, the Body Politic, the Great Chain of Being and the angelology of the Scholastics. We wept at the beauty of the Metaphysical Grammarians, and yearned to know the true Hebrew God spoke to Adam before the flood.

Eventually the cult of learning collapsed altogether and with it, the preoccupation with self-definition which had driven the entire early period of the Decadence. Citizens no longer cared to record or understand the minutiae of their personal experience. They left themselves unexplored. After the collapse of all extant systems of knowledge, a feature of the early decadent period, subjective experience had become the only reference point for establishing meaning or value.

Ceasing even to ask what one wanted thus became considered the most advanced form of transgression. Embracing this we conducted the pursuit of pleasure in a lacklustre, half-hearted way. If we stumbled on something we liked, it was purely by chance. Maybe we would return to it. More often than not we would limp off somewhere else. There were many casualties. Service industries suffered dreadfully. Aesthetics collapsed as a discipline.

During this critical period of the Decadence, we did whatever we could to avoid the act of choice. We chose our political leaders via a lottery, and organised our social lives by an ingenious system of random number generation. Many citizens abandoned even their most basic body functions to chance. Gambling disappeared as a pastime, since none of us were interested in beating the odds.

Pure randomness soon fell into decline. Some definition returned, though our codes were still fuzzy, unclear and imprecise. The *vague vogue*, as it became known, lasted some time, though the inexact measuring systems in use during this phase render impossible any accurate statement of its length, impact, or intensity. It was a time of rumour, myth, superstition and nameless fear. Certain revisionist scholars have accordingly refused to recognise it as a historical entity, since it seems in so many ways continuous with the rest of our troubled, fluid times.

Having exhausted the most arcane possibilities of body and mind, having become bored with boredom itself, we began to adopt postures of total commitment. Ideologies were formed, wars fought, and causes died for, all in a spirit of absolute hedonism. We believed because it pleased us to believe. Our crusades and jihads were as bloody as any in history. We performed breathtaking acts of self-sacrifice and exacted violent retribution on our enemies. Bizarre monotheisms arose, whose fiery ill-worded theologies afforded ample opportunity for schisms, heresies and apostasy. There were public crucifixions. Young men with faraway eyes held their hands in flame rather than sign documents of recantation. Soon totalitarianism swept through our cities, bringing tanks and napalm in its wake. We covered the earth in ashes. The devastation ushered in a period of mourning, during which we wept rivers of tears, planted trees and erected monuments whose poignancy matched the vastness of our remorse. Joy followed hard on the heels of our mourning. Lassitude followed joy. Our prophets and scientists ran simulations to predict the next lurch of our communal whims, but each time their code was outdated as soon as it was compiled. The cycle ran faster, cults and movements swarming like flies on a carcass, paradigms blooming and withering like exotic cancers. Soon there was only speed, a sensation of pure intensity.

Then one day the Decadence ended. We began to be moderate in all things. Our decisions were considered, the product of sound judgement. Our institutions stabilised and prepared themselves for steady growth. We quoted maxims to each other. 'A little and often'. 'Mens sana in corpore sano'. Now our economists have quelled the speculators, advocating co-operation and a sound industrial base. We believe in the family, in community and an undefined spirituality, though if you asked us we could not tell you why. Debating is of no interest any more. We want a quiet life. 'All to the good', as we often say to our neighbours. We are content. And yet . . . And yet there is something stale in the air. Citizens whisper in the social clubs. They say that it cannot last.

Scotland and Decadence

Stuart Kelly

Decadence, like most artistic phenomena, is easy to recognise and hard to define. To account for its lack is even harder, even though its absence may be just as conspicuous. And it should be stated at the outside: Scottish decadents are as elusive as a certain Loch's putative plesiosaurus.

Ironically, according to the *Oxford English Dictionary*, the word 'decadence' enters the English language thanks to a Renaissance text, *The Complaynt of Scotland*. Published in 1549, and sometimes attributed to the Dundee-born Protestant scholar Robert Wedderburn, *The Complaynt* is a fierce and witty polemic, pressing Scotland's claims as an independent, sovereign country. The word occurs in a passage where Dame Scotia is, as one might expect from the title, complaining: 'my triumphant stait is succumbit in decadens, ther can nocht be ane mair vehement perplexite'.

Is there a glimpse here as to why the phrase 'Scottish Decadence' seems ever so slightly oxymoronic? At the opening of *The Complaynt*, the narrator argues that 'the varld is neir ane ende', and the eschatology of the Reformation stressed the imminence of the apocalypse. Decadence could be understood, if not actively enjoyed, as one of the 'signs of the end of the age'; a quite literal *fin-de-siècle*. 'Carpe diem' took on a different meaning – not 'gather ye rosebuds while ye may' but 'repent: for ye know not the hour'. Although it failed to usher in the Great Reckoning, the Reformation radically reshaped the Scottish mindscape. On the ecclesiastical level, church décor bypassed the baroque and headed straight to minimalism – the almost kitsch redeployment of Catholic iconography present in works by Gustave Moreau, Swinburne and Dowson was far less feasible in Scotland. Industriousness, restraint and gravity became the cardinal virtues; fecklessness, self-indulgence and frivolity the mortal sins. Most importantly, however, the Reformers had won.

The success of their theology left a crusading imprint on writers who ostensibly rejected the Protestant work-ethic: even a writer as dismissive of conventional mores as Alexander Trocchi still launched a 'revolutionary' programme, Sigma, 'the Invisible Insurrection in a Million Minds'. The idea that the world could be changed, and that there was an artistic duty to do so, unites such diverse writers and thinkers as Geddes, Buchan and MacDiarmid. Art for art's sake was never sufficient. Scottish forms of rebellion – most notably, drunkenness – reacted against 'Calvinist' austerity, but, by self-consciously behaving 'badly', left its moral dominance intact. Take, for example, James Boswell, whose every sexual escapade was immediately followed by earnest bleats for forgiveness. Even the characters in such contemporary works as *Trainspotting* and *Morvern Callar*, who are sexually and chemically explorative, have a sense of moral code. Their escapes are desperate, not decadent.

Many of the themes associated with decadence were similarly stymied by the Kirk. There's more than an element of truth in the old joke that the Church of Scotland disapproves of sex standing up for fear it might lead to dancing. Scotland did have a nascent theatrical tradition – indeed, John Knox himself saw a play where an actor played Knox – but a Puritan element found fault even with a play as numbingly moral as the Rev. Home's *Douglas*. The revival of theatre in the 20th century conformed to the crusading ethic; with politically explicit works such as 7:84's *The Cheviot, The Stag and the Black, Black Oil*, or *Communicado's Jock Tamson's Bairns*. For an aspiring poet of the 1890s, there were very few chorus girls to woo.

Certain 'ostentations', such as cosmetics, gourmet foods and dilettantism, were indubitably frowned on by the Church; but, as importantly, the Scottish economy was such that there were fewer opportunities for conspicuous consumption. A Marxist reading of the curious absence of decadence might suggest the notion that both fiscally and by moral inclination, Scotland had no leisure class.

Across this predominantly dreich landscape, a few isolated figures gleam. Thomas de Quincey (1785–1859) may have been the 'English Opium Eater', but he spent more than half his life in Edinburgh: usually, it must be said, impecuniously. He contributed to *Noctes Ambrosianae*, the irreverent satire in Blackwood's Magazine; a highlight of which is the description of James Hogg's experimentation with opium. Another, briefer, guest was the 'Great Beast', Aleister Crowley (1875–1947), who quit Welwyn Garden City for a retreat on the banks of Loch Ness before relocating to Sicily.

Indigenous Scots, if they were inclined to bohemian pursuits, tended to explore this fascination outside of Scotland. John Davidson (1857–1909) is known now, if at all, for 'Thirty Bob a Week', which inspired T S Eliot. He was, however, a contributor to *The Yellow Book*, a chronicler of the demimonde in Fleet Street Eclogues, and the author of a series of remarkable, rebellious Testaments. The gloriously hedonistic Norman Douglas (1868–1952), author of *South Wind*, is most closely associated with the Mediterranean, not his Aberdeenshire birthplace.

Perhaps the closest – close, but no cigar – Scotland came to producing a genuine 'decadent' was Robert Louis Stevenson (1850–1894). He was, of course, profoundly affected by his Calvinist upbringing, and, despite his ill-health, no one could deny the vigour of his travels in the Cevennes, the United States and Samoa. It is in his aesthetic and critical writings, especially his contretemps with Henry James, that his stake in a decadent sensibility lies. Art, for Stevenson, was unreal. It was illusive, artifical, self-contained and perfect, in contrast to Life's messiness, open-endedness, actuality. With more sunlight, a different doctrinal inheritance and more money in his pocket, he might have been a Caledonian Huysmans.

Snowball

Maria Alvarez

If debauchery is the Don Juan of vices, then decadence is Count Dracula. True decadence of spirit is seldom what it appears.

Sometimes it's mistaken for addiction – hardly a vice, much though censorious types confuse it as such. The excess of depravity is a vice, but one that requires far too many copious exertions to be properly decadent. It takes determination, cash and sheer dedication to be a debauchee. Guzzling four bottles of Krug for breakfast is hard grind; not to mention all those sexual acrobatics with partners of both genders on a daily diet of old Bolivian marching powder. In fact, the whole thing smacks of one of Satan's practical jokes: an interminable X-rated territorial army drill.

Decadence hovers above all this, in its own shadowy realm of perfumed rottenness, sucking the life-blood of the other vices for its death-in-life existence.

Many moons ago, I was an idle part-time graduate McJobber. My companions were a pair of young unemployed actors. Our afternoons were invariably whiled away in a backwater pub in west London, followed by bottles of whisky back home pilfered from the (absent) landlord's cache.

We took to wondering what it would be like to have enough money to be really debauched. As poor people, we began with banal visions of an apocalyptic cornucopia of drink, drugs, oysters, and orgies in Claridges.

Yet after a while, this imaginary surfeit grew tedious. It all seemed a mite too much bother. One more line of coke . . . yawn . . . one more threesome with Torvill and

Dean . . . yawn. (Evidently, we were growing dangerously twisted.)

We invented an imaginary butler, Mr Snow – Snowball for short. An impeccable gentleman's gentleman, Snowball resembled Sir Ralph Richardson in his dotage. Apart from the usual domestic duties, polishing our trainers and so forth, Snowball was required to indulge in all the debaucheries and pleasures we had grown too tired and bored to enjoy ourselves. Our amusement consisted in making up tasks for Snowball to do. 'Snowball, will you orgasm with Ms Sharon Stone for me, I'm too tired to carry on.' Or 'Snowball, there's a case of exquisite Armagnac in the cellar. Do drink it all in one day, there's a good chap.' Or, 'Snowball, could you watch this *Horny Housewives Go Deep Throat* nonsense for me, I need a nap?'

Needless to say, Snowball always set about his duties with exemplary solemnity and efficiency no matter how trivial the request: 'Snowball, will you choose a diamond cock-ring from Aspreys and send it to the nice farmer from the Archers "with best wishes on your birthday from your greatest fans" etc etc.'

We had moved beyond cheap vicariousness to the austerely decadent satisfaction of knowing that the business of enjoyment was being enacted for us – by proxy.

At the time, however, being young, greedy and irreverent, we were not given to the examined life and took little notice of the implications of our game, the fact that in our comic fantasy we'd chanced upon the very nucleus of decadence: its sensual and moral atrophy.

Time did not stand still. Unfortunately, we had to let Snowball go. The actors got work; I moved to a trendy area of London and found myself in a boho environment whose tentacles spread here and there to wealth and privilege.

I began to be intrigued by the reputation of one particular individual, Diego, who gave infamous parties in his

Chelsea home and whom I'd yet to meet. A felicitous birth mixture of Eurotrash, aristo and oil-rich Middle East, he had serious dosh. The stories abounded. He had set off on holiday to Sardinia only to return a day later due to the excessive heat. Another time he'd chartered a yacht and promptly left it moored somewhere full of revellers while he removed himself to a hotel. More often than not he'd order sumptuous meals for a whole group of people, invariably leaving for a mysterious meeting before the starter – but always having taken care of the bill. Though only 28, he owned a Bentley, which was rusting in the garage and employed a butler.

Diego sounded like Snowball's rightful master. In retrospect, it was the prospect of experiencing our dutifully debauched butler scenario in actuality that excited me most.

Diego's parties were reputed to be glitteringly louche affairs. Out of sheer bad luck, I was always absent when any of my friends attended. After several months the longed-for calling-card arrived. As was Diego's laid-back wont, someone got a call around eleven o'clock about a party at his place. The troops were assembled in several cabs to descend on SW3.

Languid beauties flopped around on sofas spilling ash on Aubusson carpets. I couldn't see the host. I enquired excitedly about the butler. I learned to my disappointment that the latter had done his job ordering the drink from Harrods and had been sent away to his obscure granny flat for a good night's sleep.

Finally the host appeared, apologising for being late for his own party. He'd been dining somewhere near Whitehall. Impeccably dressed in an unflashy Saville Row suit, he had, also, impeccably modest manners. His wife was Swiss and tortuously silent. Tall and reed-thin, she brought to mind the kind of fragile nineteenth-century beauty who used to take the waters at Baden Baden. Neither of them seemed the slightest bit tipsy, though they appeared faintly fatigued, in that way that people who've never enjoyed a chip butty do.

It took no more than one of the languid beauties to ask Diego to summon 'Sooncome' and – hey presto – a huge hamper of class A drugs was ordered. They were to arrive with the intriguing 'Sooncome' in a black BMW (courtesy of the man's earnings from Diego and his retinue). Sooncome had derived his nickname from his trademark response on the phone when asked for a delivery, which was 'yeah soon come, blood.' Naturally, he took great delight in spinning out his arrival over several hours.

Once Sooncome had been called everyone, except our hosts, grew fidgety and fractious during the long wait. If any-thing, Diego increasingly assumed the role of a benevolent monarch. Sooncome arrived to much general jubilation. He was of Jamaican origin and sported a gold tooth and a dia-mond incisor. But in a ceremonial way, he was Snowball, fulfilling his function – if not terribly promptly. Fuelled by Sooncome's wares, the party guests listened with rictus grins to the dealer's non-stop right-wing orations on moral phil-osophy, comparative government, the psychology of policing, and the most economic way of inflicting knife-damage on 'the enemy'. Little wonder this lot liked him. He must have reminded them of their fathers. It took me a while to realise that our hosts had disappeared some time before. In fact, Diego had greeted Sooncome with affable courtesy, paid him, and absented himself. I imagined him holed up with a mini Himalaya of powder in his bedroom. In the spirit of socio-logical research, I sneaked off down the corridor to investigate further. The door was slightly ajar; I peeped through it into a vaguely Oriental-looking bedroom. The host was seated on an armchair, talking quietly to his wife and a friend. They were all drinking tea. This, I gathered was what he invariably did as soon as Sooncome arrived. Or retired straight to bed. From time to time he might condescend to take a line; but the problem was that he simply loathed sticking things up his nose.

I was also informed that at the end of these soirees, Sooncome would disappear with a blue-blooded gal or two. Sometimes expensive escort girls were summoned to the mix (usually, courtesy of Diego's wallet.) They too would often end up with Sooncome. Whether because he held out the promise of more drugs or because he was possessed of physical stamina to equal his verbal one, I never found out.

All those years earlier in our daft imaginings we had stumbled on the essence of decadence. A falling off from vitality (as the dictionary puts it), in spiritual terms it's the bastard child of ennui: a state of aestheticised satiety, an attenuating decay. No wonder it has always been associated with aristocracy and idle riches – the sinister lustre of *Götterdämmerung*. Hegel pointed out that the master classes depend on their 'slaves' to do the business of functioning and existing for them, thus making the exchange a paradoxical one in which the master's role is rendered psychologically slavish. I'd elucidate on this interesting theory further except, reader, I can't be bothered. (It's catching this decadence lark. Thank God Snowball never existed.)

Postcript

Several years later I learned that Diego had 'fallen.' Unable to stand the excessive noise of the parties and averse to nasal penetration, he hit on the idea of injecting smack with a tiny coterie. Anything to die for real, I suppose.

Decadent Lifestyle

The Decadent Household

Lisa Hilton

Location

Whether caducious castle or corrupt cottage, the location of your decadent pad is of crucial importance. The Sussex coast is to be avoided at all costs; since it is principally inhabited by earnest middle-aged women writing whimsically earnest novels about middle-aged couplings in whimsical beach huts. Whitstable and Brighton are similarly unsuitable as being packed with irritatingly cool media types, but Whitby has potential, as do the bleaker marches of Lancashire. Provincial towns are a no no, and the bible de decadence, *A Rebours*, warns of the terrifying consequences of locating to suburbia; dcadent domiciles must be either intensely urban ie inner London, or profoundly rustic. Not even Baudelaire would have been capable of behaving louchely in Clapham or Surrey. Decadent homes must be either rented or inherited (mortgages are for the weak), and should be selected entirely on aesthetic grounds, with no reference to convenient tube stops, gyms or primary schools. Everyone you want to see will come to visit anyway, and the neighbours are bound to move.

Decorating Tips

Decadent decor is considerably more challenging nowadays than a red light bulb and a skull on the bureau. Only women's magazines think red velvet is decadent. The architect Lutyens is rarely considered a degenerate fellow traveller, but he insisted that the drawing rooms of all his homes be painted glossy black. Pistachio lends a summery touch to the ceiling, as gold is much too obvious, and there should be plenty of low, inviting upholstery, preferably featuring obscure and endangered species. Zohar on Via Brera in Milan will make you anything in zebra, proper baby-calf vellum or galuchat (gossamer fine ray skin),but if you can't run to the real thing, Peter Jones fabrics department has a great selection of fakes. Before you splutter, Peter Jones is a very decadent place to go shopping. Think about it – it represents everything people who want to be cool claim not to aspire to. Just never, never, resort to leopard; it is as imaginative as Jade Jagger. Get your grape cutters and corkscrew in gloriously vulgar solid silver from Tiffany and have your candles imported from Diptyque on the Boulevard St. Germain. In an inversion of William Morris's principle, have nothing functional that is not beautiful, a dictum which should be extended to visitors and spouses.

Around the Home

If you are a drug user, be houseproud. There's nothing more distressing than snowy surfaces and skanky teaspoons cluttering up the place. A small Venetian mirror can be designated for snorting, and cut-up sari silks, available inexpensively from Southall market, make colourful and attractive tourniquets for guests who may have forgotten their own. A crème Brule torch (Peter Jones again), is easier on the eye and the fingers than stumps of putrid candle. Other kitchen equipment can be minimal, unless you are seriously proposing to cook something (see Clapham above), but you might want a refrigerator to keep bottles and rose petal jam at the correct temperature. If you ever feel up to eating, many companies now deliver oysters and foie gras fresh to the door. Piles of Caravagesque fruit look charming, and may also be consumed for vitamins, though bananas are rarely attractive. Lobsters are an excellent food for children as they are very time-consuming to eat, combining essential nutrition and instructive play.

Your home should contain none of the following: house-plants, television sets, anything from IKEA, recipe books or framed prints from art galleries, photographs of happy family moments, scatter cushions and nubbly organic soap with bits of bouquet garni sticking out, copies of *Elle Deco*.

Entertaining

'Wisdom,' wrote the libertine philosopher St Evremond, 'is given us principally that we might learn to handle our pleas-ures'. Proper debauchery requires planning, and with a little forethought, you and your guests should be able to despoil one another in a pleasant and relaxing atmosphere. A servant is useful, preferably one with no legal status or command of English to minimise the risk of complaints to the police. When you entertain, the twee anxieties of placement may be avoided by shaping each guest's initial on a black plate in their drug of choice. Dressing for entertainments is de riguer, though it is customary for the hostess to be served naked on a silver platter with the dessert course. Children, lightly painted in gold or silver body make-up, may be used as plate holders or andirons, but don't put the little dears too close to the fire lest they burn and scream disagreeably. A variety of cocktails should be offered, though absinthe is no longer smart. Very good vintage champagne, adulterated with Guinness or slivovitz, is delightful when poured from a china teapot. A chamber pot should be provided beneath the table for the gentlemens' use, rinsed first with pure orange flower water to avoid odours. Floral arrangements are a dif-ficulty – lilies are simply too Edgar Allen Poe, and red roses remind one of cheap package holidays to Agadir. Garish plastic flowers can be wiped clean easily and provide an original touch, so give the servant a tenner and ask it to buy something nice.

If your house is large enough for Saturday to Monday parties, the convention is that the host should first fuck the lady with the bedroom on his right.

The Decadent Mother

Rowan Pelling

Vanessa always loathed the very thought of children. 'They're creepy, like dwarves,' she said to her hairdresser. She was tricked into motherhood at the age of thirty-nine after her Harley Street gynaecologist told her, 'One more abortion and you'll need a hysterectomy.' Even so, she knocked back gin in a scalding hot bath every night for a week – all to no effect. 'What do old wives know,' she muttered, 'they probably all had ten kids.' The brat stuck fast through the vodka martinis, the all-night raves, the cocaine brunches and thirty Gitanes a day. Even her drug dealer's startlingly large cock, ramming her hard as she stared in bored silence at the wall, failed to dislodge the brute.

'The baby seems small,' said the technician who carried out the five-month scan, her mouth pursed tight as a cat's arse. 'Good,' said Vanessa, 'the smaller the better. Who wants to squeeze a stuffed turkey out of their cunt?' Not that she had any intention of squeezing. She told her young, tanned obstetrician, 'I'm not too posh to push, I'm too rich.' 'Too much of a bitch, you mean,' he said with a vulpine smile. Three minutes later they were both on his couch.

Vanessa told no one she was pregnant except the doctors and her dull, industrialist husband. 'How foolish he looks when he's pleased,' she thought, 'and the child's not even his.' When, at five months, a vulgar mound swelled beneath her concave ribs, she sent an email to friends saying: 'Going into rehab; back in a while.' She would rather die than wear a maternity frock in public. So she abandoned her West End flat, the Soho basements and Brixton lovers, and went by cover of night to Surrey.

She had never known ennui like the marital home. Her husband emptied the drinks cabinet and halved her allowance. In listless silence, all day and most of the night she watched the procession of corpses on Sky News and CNN, looking for clues – would death be better than this? At regular intervals she jabbed her stomach viciously to make the baby stir. 'If I'm sodding awake, you should be too,' she shouted at her belly.

As Vanessa would later boast, she was tipping out the Para-cetemols when the new couple at the Grange asked her to 'drop by for happy hour.' 'Linda and I like to get to know the neighbours,' said Keith, a hire-van magnate, the tip of his pink tongue visible between his laser-white teeth. He served large gins from the bar in his lounge.

'A small one won't harm the babby,' Keith said.

Two hours later they were in the hot tub playing 'truth or dare'. The next Thursday Vanessa dropped by for 'home movie night' and in the weeks to come she would marvel at Linda's versatility. Sometimes the party was joined by Elaine, a blonde WPC, who dispensed Es from a phial labelled 'multi-vitamins'.

At eight and a half months pregnant, Vanessa was driven by her husband to the Portland Hospital, where her obstetrician groped her once for luck before performing an elective cae-sarean. 'Don't hand it to me!' she shrieked as a tiny, mewling, blood-stained bundle was thrust at her face. 'And don't think,' she said looking directly at her spouse for the first time in months, 'that I'm going to let that thing suck my nipple.'

A big-boned maternity nurse was hired; her face as smooth and ugly as one of the plastic trolls that had sparked a brief playground craze in Vanessa's childhood. (She would later prove to be a kleptomaniac with a severe personality disorder. Her replacement, a pretty Serb, would leave the child in his cot, day after day, until the wood was gnawed to splinters round the top of the frame.) Nurse and child were dispatched to the attic floor, where Vanessa couldn't hear 'all that bloody wailing'. She hired a personal trainer, Mark, and bought amphetamines and coke from Elaine, and in under four weeks she was back in her jeans. To celebrate, she fucked Mark in the master bedroom. 'He could barely string two words together,' she told her hairdresser, 'but even his cock had muscles.'

Vanessa returned to her Mayfair flat six weeks after giving birth. She visited a 'brilliant, cut-price' dermatologist Linda had tipped her off about. The tall, chalk-white Estonian peered at her face and agreed there were faint lines around her eyes and the corners of the mouth. He warned her that some people had 'issues' with his treatment, which involved injections with 'animal-based fillers'. It transpired, with gentle probing, that the animals in question were foetuses, purchased from Russian abortion clinics. Vanessa looked at him and smiled: 'Bring it on.'

She didn't see her child again until the christening. 'Oh, you hold him,' she said to her dull husband's dull best friend, the banker, who was to be his godfather. That night she opened her child's presents. She took the claret back to London and swapped the Tiffany cufflinks for a pendant.

Vanessa's visits home grew more sporadic over the years. When her son was five her husband felt forced to divorce her. 'Thank God he's finally shown some backbone,' said Vanessa to her lawyer as they dined in the Garrick Club. A year later her former husband married the pretty Serb nanny. 'Some men cannot be cured of their foolishness,' said Vanessa at the news.

Vanessa's son was later to write: 'People joke about a mother who is rarely there. You know the sort of thing: "All I remember of mama is the swish of her silken gown and the faint scent of lavender as she left for the ball." But my mother was truly absent. I only met her three times after the divorce, and on one of those occasions she left me for the day with a musician who was later jailed for keeping child porn on his laptop. The second time she appeared unexpectedly at a school founder's day; she was visibly drunk and kept saying in a loud voice, "Who's that little creep over there?" On my final visit, to her London flat, she couldn't disguise her boredom and asked if I'd mind if she watched TV.'

He showed this passage of his memoir to his mother on the fourth and final occasion of their meeting. She read it swiftly and nodded dismissively, as if it were a shopping receipt presented for her approval. 'Poor, poor diddums,' she mocked, 'do you think you'd have anything to write about if your childhood had been happy?' You're hardly the most imaginative of people."

He stared at her silently.

'No,' Vanessa said, pouring a large whisky and exhaling a smoke circle into his face, 'I don't think so either.'

Her son returned home and ended his book with these words: 'Some women should probably be sterilised at birth.'

Vanessa laughed when a friend told her what he'd written.

'Frankly, it's hard to disagree,' she said.

The Fashionable Side
Living in Shoredietrich

Xavior Roide

One's address is always a matter of concern to those who are concerned with the fashionable. The fashionable is the spell cast over the fictitious 'now', a literary invention which Taoist fellows fondle and with which nostalgic narcissists tackle. Being ahead of the game however, fashion turns the 'now' into the 'next' with cunning sleight of hand-in-marble. With fashion we are never meant to feel that we are truly in the moment, that we have arrived, but rather that we are somehow nostalgic for this moment, an absurd situation indeed! As a result, we are never really there nor ever nearly here, though we assume otherwise. Fashion deludes us, it deliberately causes discontent. To fashion something out of marble is to see more than the marble, we always have to fiddle with what is given; we never relax; our marbled hands tremble with sensitivity. Given this shaky state of affairs it is no surprise to realize that secondary qualities are the concern of Art. Art is always a secondary concern. To make it a primary one is an act of decadence.

Currently, I have the most fashionable address in London. Sitting near the top end of Columbia Rd, I am a grateful glance towards the scruffy street walkers on Hackney Road, a simple stone's throw from the George And Dragon, a brief walk to Curtain Rd's 'Ball Music Hall', a mere five minutes cycle to Bistrotheque (for to walk down Hackney Rd would be to pose as a local, and I'm an internationalist), and a frenetic sprint from Brick Lane (the locals still enjoy a good chase).

My address sits at centre of where the four humourless boroughs meet: sanguine Hoxton, choleric Shoreditch, melancholic Hackney, and phlegmatic Bethnal Green. Never-theless, as a *transcultural* I see no traditional borders and I take no traditional sides. Where I live used to be called Hockney (Hackney meets Hoxton), when canvas art was the fashion, but now I have fashioned this place Shoredietrich because being a cabaret star is oh so au courant.

It used to be said of Hockney, 'Where there is dereliction today there will be an art gallery tomorrow.' Now, in Shoredietrich, due to the sheer amount of nonsense produced by postmodernists posing as artists, or rather decorators-but-never-painters™, it is truer to say: 'Where there is an art gal-lery today there will be dereliction tomorrow'. On the ruins we will build makeshift theatres and dance The Adoration of the Earth.

Hoxton Square is increasingly gathering a terrible reputa-tion for becoming plebeian. The White Cube is surrounded by tepid bars and doomed music venues that seem to be designed to look like an Australian's living room. These are the places that draw the cocky mockney boys in crummy monkey suits; why, one can scarcely parade around Hoxton Square in full regalia without having some raggedy comment being flung onto one by these creatures. Shoreditch is equally full of ugly bars and pubs that play urban music. I want urbane music. As soon as middle-class boys and girls who work in offices come to an area to drink beer it is all over. You can spot these creatures by their haircuts, always five years out of date. As a result, Hackney and Bethnal Green are becoming the preferred places for the *Artistocracy* to parade in, but how long will it last? The streetwalkers on my corner have begun to charge more and smile less.

I'm terribly lucky to live in none of these places. I live in Shoredietrich. On Sunday the famous Columbia Rd Flower Market is still the perfect place to buy lilies for one's button-hole before cycling off west to meet one's fellow Teaists at The Wolseley in St James. Cream tea is all the rage you know.

Hearts of Darkness

Vanora Bennett

Don't bother with caviar if all it suggests to you is a few tremulous black eggs, wobbling pitifully on a cracker, at the kind of indifferent polite soirée where you also get one glass of champagne-on-the-cheap, bow ties and insipidly grown-up conversation. There's no point in eating it if you don't do it right; and right, when it comes to caviar, means revelling in its fascinatingly expensive wrongness.

Caviar comes from the wanton slaughter of a rare fish, the sturgeon, in the remote Caspian Sea – an illicit trade that, since the collapse of the Soviet Union, has kept a generation of poachers and dodgy businessmen in money. It has also brought the biggest and rarest of the three kinds of sturgeon in the sea, the beluga, to the brink of extinction. Hardly an eco-sustainable party snack, then – but the caviar baddies are showing no signs of regret that their hunger for instant big bucks is destroying the environment their children and grandchildren will inherit. Any caviar you eat today, even if it comes from a tin virtuously labelled 'produce of Iran' (where post-Soviet smugglers do not operate), is likely to be the evil stuff, stolen from the sea, produced at minimal costs, canned and fraudulently labelled by murderous crooks and smuggled on to Western markets at a mark-up of many million per cent.

That background of danger and distress puts the consumer under a decadent obligation. By eating caviar – by being will-ing to part with a king's ransom for a taste of something so rare, ambiguous and endangered – you are signalling that you're the kind of person who is also willing to countenance thrillingly improper relationships between all pleasure and all payment. Behave accordingly.

First, don't bother listening to gourmet-talk about the quality of beluga, or sevruga, or osietra: the taste you're after is the taste of misused power and cruelty, and every bowl of sturgeon eggs will be full of that.

Second, think quantity. Remember that one tiny, mean-spirited mouthful is never going to be enough. You're after excess, glut, extremes – the head-rush feeling that comes from shovelling glistening dollops of the stuff into your mouth; the live-for-the-moment euphoria of not giving a damn how much it costs.

If you can't get that at the polite soirée, even by helping yourself to entire trayfuls of respectable caviar canapés, there's only one thing to do: leave and source a better supply else-where. Either pay the full whack for the full plate at a legit sales outlet, or, more entertainingly, go hunting for the other sort.

It's not hard to find. Britain is full of whispering, cheating, alluring caviar salesmen. Some are the genuine Caspian kind, with long southern eyelashes and gold teeth, operating out of organic butchers' shops and open-all-evening emporia in high streets near you. Others are apparently virtuous part-timers: Russian sailors in town for a few days with a bagful of swag to offload; chess players moonlighting between tour-naments. Dozens are reputed to make their way every month to every big food hall in London, trying to flog their dirty wares to shocked sales managers; you could do worse than to catch them on their crestfallen way out, and strike a private bargain.

If you want the real deal, though, you'll have to travel further. Reclining on a despoiled sofa from the Hermitage, quaffing vodka with Mafiosi as the snow falls outside, singing depraved songs as you lick up fish-eggs with your fingers will give you a first inkling of the sinister pleasures to be got from this underworld delicacy. But it's only when you reach the oily southern shores of the crime-infested Caspian itself, and are invited by a gun-toting poacher hanging out his nets on the driftwood to share his 'power food' breakfast – a gutful of stolen eggs on a great slab of white bread – that you will truly appreciate the heart of the darkness that is caviar.

Pissing in Space

Medlar Lucan & Durian Gray

Medlar and Durian, astronauts

Ever since, as schoolboys, Durian and I huddled together at
Lucan Lodge on that distant July night in 1969, watching
Buzz Aldrin and Neil Armstrong bounce like sedated trampo-
linists across the moon, I have nursed a deep longing to go
into space: to don that puffy white regalia, to climb, waving
like Liberace, into the tiny cockpit at the top of a Titan rocket
– then to be flung in a torrent of fire towards the stars!

Alas, neither of us have the physique, never mind the men-
tality, for the job. NASA require their astronauts to be A1
specimens. As representatives of the F class ('totally unsuitable
material, lacking in endurance, know-how and moral character') we were never likely to make the grade – although our
names are held on file in Brussels as volunteers, should the
Kingdom of Belgium ever wish to start a space programme.
We remain at full readiness, awaiting the call.

In the meantime we content ourselves with imaginary
journeys into space. We have tried various forms of 'virtual
reality' (a concept, like 'virtual orgasm', which fails to deliver
on several fronts). Films are a help, of course, as are flight
simulators, and a certain amount of 'flying ointment' (i.e.
henbane).

By far the most effective method we have found is to sit in a
darkened room with a small reading-lamp, a glass of plum
brandy, and a copy of that classic of space literature, *Carrying
the Fire*.

Its author is Michael Collins, a test pilot and astronaut

with an unusual view of existence (due partly, no doubt, to a working life carried out at an average speed of 22,000 miles per hour). He was the man, in Apollo XI, who stayed in the command ship orbiting the moon while Aldrin and Armstrong flew down for a stroll among the boulders. Call him an observer, a voyeur, what you will – his lonely position gave him the leisure to contemplate the mysteries of their task. This was beyond his companions – they were too busy with the practicalities of fuel consumption, angle of descent, and not smashing into rocks. Collins was something of a poet – he put into words the sensations, thoughts and emotions of an earthling who is suddenly shot into space. His account is splendid. It earns him an honoured place in the Temple of Decadence.

His gifts first caught our attention when he described the cramped Gemini 10 spacecraft as 'an orbiting men's room'; and again when he spoke of the medical examinations at the School of Aerospace Medicine in Texas: 'no orifice is inviolate, no privacy respected.' (Suddenly, space travel took on exciting new possibilities in our minds.)

One of the finest moments in the book is an account of urinating in a space-suit. It is, apparently, something that everyone wants to ask an astronaut. He quotes the technical manual in full.

Operating Procedure
Chemical Urine Volume Measuring System (CUVMS) Condom Receiver

1. *Uncoil collection/mixing bag from around selector valve.*
2. *Place penis against receiver inlet check valve and roll latex receiver onto penis.*
3. *Rotate selector valve knob (clockwise) to the 'Urinate' position.*
4. *Urinate.*
5. *When urination is complete, turn selector valve knob to 'Sample.'*

6. *Roll off latex receiver and remove penis.*
7. *Obtain urine sample bag from stowage location.*
8. *Mark sample bag tag with required identification.*
9. *Place sample bag collar over selector valve sampler flange and turn collar 1/6 turn to stop position.*
10. *Knead collection/mixing bag to thoroughly mix urine and tracer chemical.*
11. *Rotate sample injector lever 90 degrees so that sample needle pierces sample bag rubber stopper.*
12. *Squeeze collection/mixing bag to transfer approximately 75 cc. of tracered urine into the sample bag.*
13. *Rotate the sample injector lever 90 degrees so as to retract the sample needle.*
14. *Remove filled urine sample bag from selector valve.*
15. *Stow filled urine sample bag.*
16. *Attach the CUVMS to the spacecraft overboard dump line by means of the quick disconnect.*
17. *Rotate selector valve knob to 'Blow-Down' position.*
18. *Operate spacecraft overboard dump system.*
19. *Disconnect CUVMS from spacecraft overboard dump line at the quick disconnect.*
20. *Wrap collection/mixing bag around selector valve and stow CUVMS.*

This is less a set of instructions than a prose poem! Step 4 (*'Urinate.'*) has the simplicity of a sketch by Ingres. One can almost feel the sense of relief as this brusque command cuts through the tangle of formalities that precede it ... And instruction 19, I feel, has a similar cadence to some of the finer verses of Allen Ginsberg

Mad Monday 8.55 am, Liverpool

Helen Walsh

While the bulk of the country forlornly builds itself up for the five-day drudge, Liverpool is putting on its glad rags ready to crank the party mood up another gear. In my city, the start of the orthodox working week signals the mother of all closing parties – Mad Monday. Liverpool has always gone its own skewy way when it comes to hedonism. When London went skiffle mad, we had Merseybeat. When punk took over the U.K, Liverpool veered towards an unhinged amalgam of Warholesque art-rock and gay disco. And when unemployment battered the nation into a state of inertia in the early 80s, Liverpool reacted by slotting another twenty-four hours on the weekend. Keen to keep the punters in the pubs rather than allowing them to waste precious pennies on such fripperies as rent, food and so forth, minehosts came up with the brilliant notion of a) cashing giros through their pub tills and b) slashing all drink prices to 50p on a Monday. The city has wrested itself cockily back from the wretched 80s, but the tradition remains – even if the bevs are a whopping 99p a throw these days.

How gloriously liberating it feels to leave one's house to carouse while the rest of the country is at work. Michelin star cuisine? Hip Hotels? Deviant sex? None of these esoteric delectations even come close to a Mad Monday in town. Forget the Docks and its avant-garde bars. Forget the trendy Hope Street restaurants and the cheap and cheerful lap-dancing clubs, where the girls work Sundays just so they can Mad Monday it. If you want a real slice of Europe's newest Capital of Culture then follow the shrill clamour of

81

malingerers, OAPs, students and lapdancers as they boulevard the boozers' circuit each Monday.

Mad Mondays are as much about communal revelry as they are about solitary drinking and that's what makes these sessions so special to me. I love to indulge in solitary drinking – I absolutely fucking love it. It's a great way of discovering yourself, of breaking the ice with yourself, falling in love with yourself all over again – and occasionally falling out with yourself. You can learn more about the inner you over the course of one unflinching binge than a six-week stint with a shrink will ever reveal – and it's a hell of a lot more fun.

When I finished Uni I spent an awful lot of time walking up mountains trying to figure out what job I wanted, where I was going and suchlike – but my long, cold peregrinations yielded nothing more than wind-slapped ears and blistered soles. My Scouse boyfriend, Kevin gave me some priceless advice – spend a day on the ale. On Monday. In Liverpool. That'll sort your noggin out for sure.

So in a dark remote corner of The Roscoe Head under a thick plume of smoke, I took my first sip of bitter and my first step towards enlightenment. By my second pint, my tongue loosened, my thoughts emboldened, I began to open up to myself. By my third, these introspective probings had segued into full-blown debates about the meaning of life with fellow tipplers (all of whom, I might add, were over 70 and wiser – if younger – than judges). By my sixth and final pint the road to wellness was complete. True happiness stood within an ace. All it would take was a job that allowed me to solitary drink, here, every Monday. I called my newfound guru from the pub's ancient phone to ask his advice. Easy, he said, lapdancer or writer – you'll excel at both.

Mad Mondays and solitary drinking have since become a brilliant and necessary diversion for me. Not the least of it is that, in prolonging the weekend it means I can postpone the inevitable – writing. Any novelist who claims to spring out of bed and race to their PC first thing Monday is either lying – or crap. The reality is ten per cent inspiration and ninety per cent perspiration. Nine days out of ten I'm looking for a legitimate excuse to body swerve my computer. Roll on Monday!

The Wheeled Dance of Death

Robert irwin

'Safe skating is fun skating! Be considerate to pedestrians, as
well as to your fellow skaters. Obey the traffic laws. These
handy dos and don'ts will make your day all the more enjoy-
able.' Few people now remember how horrible it was in the
80s, how when the parks were crowded with clean-limbed,
sparkly-eyed young people getting fit while having fun and
making new friends and the whole ghastly scene was presided
over by benevolently patronising skate-instructors in silver
helmets and white t-shirts. Everybody used to look as though
they cleaned their teeth regularly. The horror. The horror . . .
All of a sudden, as I was penning this, it became more than a
matter of words on the page, for it did indeed come back to
me in brightly visualised detail how it was in those days and I
could see the clear-eyed and friendly skate-instructor loom-
ing before me in a vision out of nightmare and I had to rush
out to the bathroom and gaze down the lavatory pan and wait
for the fierce surge of vomit. For a moment I had the sense
that the skate-instructor was kneeling beside me and holding
my head down in the pan. But I know him of old as an illusion
and I am better now.

For good or ill those days are now past us. (For ill, I hope.)
But back then in the 80s it was usually in the twilight that I
used to venture out to skate. I have a skin condition and, if I
was to be admired, I preferred that it should be as the silhou-
ette of a extreme skater moving in the dark with lethal speed,
rather than as the bearer of roses of corruption on my cheek.
And besides I am very old. In my time, I have talked with
Alex Sanders, the King of the Witches, about the uselessness

of the backstop, the superficial flashiness of the grapevine manoeuvre and blood sacrifice. Going further back, I can remember Josephine Baker dancing on skates in front of the Trocadero. But it was my nocturnal encounter with the Ars Moriendi Skate Chapter that gave me confidence to roll out in daytime. As their name may suggest, the Ars Moriendi skaters are unusual in their antiquarian and morbid interests and they are primarily interested in reviving *fin-de-siècle* techniques of skating. Lithographs, engravings and old photographs are pored over as we struggle to recreate the costumes and skate techniques of Paris's apaches and cocottes before the slaughter of the Great War.

Even so I have also learnt a lot of practical things from the Ars Moriendi, some of which is unprintable, but I suppose I could pass on a few tips. First, relaxation is the key. If you set out on your wheels and you are stone-cold sober and stiff and you fall, you are likely to do yourself a serious injury. SO KIDS, HERE IS A REALLY USEFUL SAFETY TIP! As part of the warm-up, get very drunk and, if possible, smoke a joint as a health-conscious preliminary to your skate routine. That way, if you fall over, you are much much much much less likely to injure yourself. Much less likely. I should know. Very little chance of getting hurt. These days I never put on my skates, except when I am pissed and, God knows, I fall over all the time, but I rise from the tarmac scatheless. People look at me strangely, but I am smiling as I reassume an upright position. It is as if God, or, more likely, someone other than God, is looking after me. Tripping on LSD on skates is, if anything, even more relaxing and, as I say, relaxation is the key to good skating. It is better to be quite relaxed and laid out flat on your back on the road than to be some teetering dwork who is to be seen frantically waving his arms and bending his knees in a pathetic attempt to stay upright. It just is a style thing.

Music also helps you to relax on your wheels. When I first met the Ars Moriendi gang, I was an uncultured thug who thought that the height of skate art was dancing on wheels to the Velvet Underground or Guns and Roses, but Ars Moriendi introduced me to the fiercer delights of Strauss's *Salome*, Scriabin's *Poème de l'extase* and Syzmanowski's *Song of the Night*.

NEXT TIP. You need to learn how to stop. Now don't use the brake at the back of your skate. It is almost completely useless. Unscrew it and throw it away. The easiest and most comfortable way to stop is to crash into someone. But you need to be thoughtful about this. Don't crash into any old body. If you are a man, it is much nicer to crash into a young woman, the plumper the better, and to wrap your arms around her, as if steadying yourself for support. A well-executed rolling clinch can bring you as close to ecstasy as this lower world allows. At her best a young woman is more than a skater's airbag, as she offers a pneumatic, perfumed bliss. If you are a female skater, you will doubtless prefer the reassuring hardness of a young male body to serve as your stop.

NEXT TIP. Always be aware of non-skaters – the pedestrians, cyclists, drivers, skate-boarders, small dogs, assorted vermin. Watch out for them and learn to hate them. They get in the way. Often deliberately. On a good stretch of tarmac they are a waste of space. Sometimes a pedestrian will try to play chicken with you. If you get a sense that is happening, you owe it to yourself not to veer an inch from your determined course and you should accelerate. You may also clap your wrist guards together in order to startle the obstructive fellow. Any skater who is any good has murder in his heart. Never try to talk to a skate-boarder. It is a waste of time as all those Morlocks can manage is grunts. You may be sure that not one of them has heard of Syzmanowski. Small dogs can be a pest. Practice the side-kick with your wheels.

FINAL TIP. It is well worth seeking tuition and advice from more experienced skaters. In London, they are hard to find and they keep themselves to themselves, preferring to meet in deserted warehouses and abandoned aerodromes. But there is one place where you can be sure of meeting most of the leading figures in decadent roller-blading. (I know that you are supposed to call it in-line skating, but we don't.) In the months of April and May the great chapters of skaters assemble before the shrine of Our Lady of Fatima in northern Portugal and there they confer and pass on new movements. The Ars Moriendi attends regularly. I have never actually been inside the shrine, but I gather it is dedicated to the Virgin, who sometime before the Great War appeared before some local shepherds' kids and scared them witless with apocalyptic prophecies before vanishing. But who gives a shit about all that? The point is that the beautifully laid white marble expanse leading up to the shrine is a truly great skating space. What is more, by mid-morning, there is usually a steady trail of old peasanty-type people making their way on hands and knees towards the shrine, kissing the ground as they do so. It is great to leap over them. To clear one of these folk is easy, but sometimes if you attempt to leap over three or four at once, things can go wrong and so be relaxed as you fall and, obviously, if possible, find someone to cushion your fall. Another thing, and here you may think me a bit weird, is that on the edges of the skating space are stalls selling votive objects for people to present to the shrine – wax babies and severed arms, legs and ears of wax. These stalls, summoning up images of injury and death as they do, furnish a perfect back-cloth to my skating stunts. Without the risk of injury, the adrenalin rush, the wheeled dance with death, skating is noth-ing. As I get older, I accelerate, speeding towards my end. I ask myself if, this year when I make my eagerly anticipated appearance at Fatima, and, tanked up with vodka from the hip flask, begin to make my moves, is there any chance that I may behold a vision of the Virgin calling me to the righteous and sober life? And how would it be to collide with her?

Decadent Girl About Town

Catherine Townsend

My week of living dangerously started after my ex-boyfriend showed up the day before Valentine's Day brandishing a bag of treats. Candy and flowers? No, it was my stuff, in a bin bag.

But in his haste to get back to the petite blonde from his office who he had always insisted was 'just a friend', he forgot his American Express platinum card.

I probably should have done the mature and responsible thing and returned it right away. But what can I say? Karma's a bitch, and that week, so was I.

So after spending one night crying into my Ben and Jerry's – and giving my mobile to my girlfriend Victoria to avoid drunk dialling – I headed to Selfridges for a bit of shopping therapy. I wanted to look like a punk rock version of Audrey Hepburn, so within half an hour, I scored myself a pair of Christian Louboutin gold snakeskin peep-toe stilettos, a Gucci handbag and a Vivienne Westwood little black dress.

Then, I cleaned out my handbag in anticipation of the one-night stands to follow, replacing my journalist's notebook with a silver clit-stimulating vibrator, an array of condoms, and mini bottle of lubricant.

I also grabbed some make-up remover cloths (so that I could handle post-coital cleanups gracefully, and would not wake up at some random man's pad looking like a dishevelled raccoon!)

Despite my current sexual dry spell, I decided that only fabulous underwear should be allowed to grace my skin – that is, when I am wearing any at all! So I pick up a beige leather corset, plus a gorgeous bra, knickers and 40s-style hold-ups with seams up the back from Agent Provocateur. The total bill was £500 – almost a month's rent, but so worth it.

On Valentine's Day, I treated myself to a huge bouquet of roses, even though the florists, sensing men's desperation, had jacked the price up to £7 per flower.

When the urge to test my ex hit, I rushed to the gym, skipping the treadmill in lieu of a gruelling half-hour session in the steam room. Screw detoxing, I was planning to work off the extra calories through sex.

Speaking of dieting, as a true gourmande I ditched Atkins and South Beach after realising that strict adherence to the SEP (Somebody Else Pays) diet is the only way forward. Which is brilliant when I get loads of offers, but once I didn't eat for almost 48 hours this way – but it did wonders for my waistline!

On the new regime, breakfast is either two massive lattes at The Electric with an editorial contact in possession of an expense account, or swanning into the Hummingbird bakery to lick the icing off a pink cupcake [fairy cake].

Normally, I skip lunch – unless it's a Bloody Mary, the cocktail that should be its own food group.

Midweek, my girlfriends took me out to drown my sorrows in goldfish-bowl sized mojitos at the Light Bar and lavender martinis at the Sanderson, but since this was the dreaded V-Day week they all had late dates.

So I took myself to Nobu, card in hand, for black cod and yellowtail tartare with jalapeno sauce and a lovely Gewürztraminer. I savoured each bite of the moist paper-thin fish and licked my lips afterward, ignoring the pitying stares of the woman on my right holding hands with her boyfriend. Guess she didn't catch him checking out my cleavage when she went to the loo!

I soon realised that the sweetest moments in my solitude happen when I am doing nice things for someone else, not plotting revenge. In Hyde Park, I helped an old woman and her dog across the street, and became the Robin Hood of pastries when I bought boxes of giant sugar cookies to give to the homeless guy on my block.

On Friday night, I boarded a plane to Geneva to meet a six-foot-five male friend, and complete womaniser, who's had a crush on me for ages. He escorted me to a dinner party, where we dipped chunks of bread into huge vats of melted cheese fondue. Then we slipped into the hot tub and sipped champagne while watching the sunrise.

Finally, we retired to the bedroom for dessert. 'I want dark chocolate and pistachio ice cream,' I tell him, 'but blended together into a milkshake.' He obliges, and I slurped the syrupy mixture as he slid his hands down my body.

But before we went any further, my conscience sobered up and got the better of me. So I dialled my ex, admitted that I had been using the card and offered to pay him back. 'Don't worry about it,' he said adding, 'It's not you, it's just that my emotional problems that made it hard to connect to anyone on a deep level. Anyway, how much could you have put on there in five days? Two hundred quid?'

I couldn't help giggling as I put the phone down. Then I went back into the bedroom and fucked Richard, digging the five-inch heels purchased with my ex's credit card into his back.

The Players' Lounge

Mark Mason

Eh, Ash – *Ash – ASH* ! Cop for this, will ya? There, stick it
down there. Odge up. Give us yer glass . . . there you go . . .
get that down yer. Fuckin' good stuff that, mate, not yer house
bollocks, that's 'Poll – Rodjay', that is . . . Bloke at the bar told
me to get it . . . Yeah, good, innit? Eh, Lee – *LEE* ! Put her
down for a second, have a gobful of this . . . look, you can go
back to yer Stella in a minute, just try it . . . yeah, blindin',
innit? Eh? Nah, I know I ain't, just thought I'd try it . . . Yeah,
that bloke – over at the bar – hang on . . . where's he gone?
Can't see him. Anyway, interesting bloke . . . Had a good chat
with him.

Weird geezer he was . . . wearing this sort of scarf thing
round his neck, I mean, fuck me, even Becks wouldn't wear
one of 'em . . . 'krevat', he said . . . thought they was summat
to do with those Serb geezers? Anyhow, don't get me wrong,
like, he was a good bloke . . . you know, sort of . . . I dunno,
sort of *interestin'* . . . Used big words and that . . . he clocked
me, soon as I got there, you know, he was just sort of sittin'
there, I thought, here we go, usual bollocks, autograph, 'wot's
that manager of yours really like ?', blah blah fuckin' blah . . .
but he wasn't, didn't do none of that, said he was . . . wot was
it? . . . yeah, 'fascinated' to meet me, cos he reckons we're . . .
hang on, he wrote it down for me . . . where is it? Thought it
was on that twenty . . . nah, hang on, it's this fifty here . . . he
reckons we're . . . 'the very pers- . . . perso- . . .' wot
the fuck's this say? . . . 'pers-on-if-ic-ashun' . . . yeah, that's it,
he was going on about that . . . 'personificashun of decadence
in the modern era'.

Eh? I dunno. Sounds like a perfume, dunnit? D'ya reckon I should get some for Charmaine? . . . Hang on, wot's this? . . . He's written summat else . . . hang on . . . 'drain of re- . . . re- . . . re-sauces away from re- . . . re- . . . re-in-vest-ment in the game' . . . yeah, hang on, I've heard those geezers from the posh papers saying that on Five Live . . . hold up, let's finish this . . . 'drain of re-sauces away from re-in-vest-ment in the game straight into Ferraris and Slippery Nipples.' Wot's that all about? I've got a Lambo.

Hold up, this 'decadence' thing . . . he was going on about that . . . trying to explain it, you know . . . here, look, he's done us some notes . . . 'Nero' . . . wot's Ash's dog gotta do with it? . . . 'Rim-bord' . . . Eh? 'Rim-bord'? Who's he when he's away from home ? . . . *Nah,* hang on, he mentioned him, it ain't Rimbord it's Rambo . . . stupid bastard can't spell . . . anyway, wot's boxing gotta do with football? . . . Wot else has he put? . . . 'Oscar Wilde' . . . Fucked if I know . . . Is he Kim's dad ?

Tell you what, though, Lee, I mean I know he can't spell, and I know he dresses like a twat and all that, but he was interestin' . . . Nah, I know I didn't get it all . . . All right, I didn't get any of it, but he told me about this stuff and it's fuckin' good, innit? So he must know a thing or two. Reckoned one of the big clubs is gonna go tits up sooner or later . . . Wot, *us*? Nah . . . He must mean the other lot. Anyhow, he said when it happens we'd . . . hang on, let's get this right . . . he said we'd 'reap the rewards of our own decadence' . . . Eh? Christ knows . . . Ere, Lee, d'ya reckon we could get 'em to stick this stuff on tap in the players' bar ?

Vermin

Jacob Polley

Matthew Byrne. He and I plan to parachute from the outhouse roof using bed sheets held by their corners. His extravagant curly hair's so unlike my own, and so like my own father's, that I wonder if we haven't been mixed up, he and I.

We both stand on the slates above the outhouse gutter, the white sheets trailing from our shoulders like capes. We bend our knees. We count to three. We stand on tiptoe, staring out across the yard. We count to three again. We stand.

Neither of us will step off into the air and eventually we climb down, ashamed.

After her bath, I spy the mole just below my mother's ribs. She tells me it must never be picked. She says: 'It was left over from when I was made.'

That night, I dream I pick the mole off and find it's attached to a thread of skin that won't stop unravelling from my mother's side. I'm shocked awake by her laughter.

Sheds, pigsties. The brown-kneed sisters from next door who lead me between loose planks into the hovel where the workbench sits, its wooden top gouged and scattered with corkscrews of drilled steel. There they stretch me out and insist I be still and dead and numb in heaven, my arms stiff at my sides. Then they strip and examine me all over, their eyes and their little teeth glittering. From the road outside I can hear the cows like a low tide, coming in to be milked.

The sisters' father walks with his gun broken over his arm: his low-slung beagle's the only innocent around here. His master hangs two drawn rabbits naked in the shed, their skin the skin of his daughters' hips when they lift one another's dresses and ask me, smiling: 'Do you think it's wrong?'

Do I think it's wrong? They know it is, but they wait. Their ears are four delicate locks. I realise then that to speak is to never say anything new.

'I don't think it's wrong,' I say. The sisters know that I think it is, but pretend to find me utterly convincing. In the old pigsty the four oil-spots of their pupils bloom.

We pull ourselves into the derelict loft space where the farm implements lie, abandoned to us, their iron wickedly cast and their wooden handles smooth as bobbins: who wouldn't touch them, wouldn't urge that they be touched, wouldn't feel them infused with honest sweat and sweat themselves to imagine them put to stranger use?

Chains and bridles; a saddle cracked and furred with dust; the damp webbing of milky stains that only prove we're the same as those who were here once, then died: that despite us the work of history will happen in the shadows beyond the circle of our burning single-mindedness.

And how deep in the woods we hold our palms to a fire-place, ringed with black stones, and feel remnant heat like a body's while the branches pluck lovingly at our clothes!

And how the duck pond's unfathomable green induces us to look with awful concentration!

And how in a meadow scabbed with old cowpats, the grass growing higher from them and more emerald, we turn up a trove of sweet-smelling magazines and sit sorting through them, the sisters and I, insatiably separate, the exposed roots of the oak they were pushed between now darkly, erotically interior as rain starts to fall and lacquer the bark and the women holding themselves open come apart in our hands.

This countryside's for hiding in; is full of holes and lovely burrows, their bone-strewn entrances spicy and damp. We never consider the city, its chimneys and alleyways, for the fields and the hedgerows are world enough: the dusty leaves like filthy tongues; the hedgehog fizzing with lice when we lean in close to test its prickling with a stick; the rusty stream dribbling through the reeking undergrowth: such imperfection!

The puddles are dieseled with the shades of our mothers' eye-shadows, the evening sky flawed with intimate pinks.

Summer, and our science is to take turns peeing in the water trough and then to return, week after week, to see the water thickening with piss-weed. The excitement of the life lodged within us, inaccessible but for our blood and our piss, which must swarm invisibly to grow what it has in the sunlit trough!

And there's itchy skin if we handle the fresh corrugated stems of the cow parsley, and earwigs to be shaken out later when the same stems brittle. There are wet beds if we taste the milk squeezed from a dandelion stalk. There's ringworm like a brand on the first sister's temple, that I can't help believing is punishment, and fear for myself in the night.

And her father catches us, far from the village. He comes upon us in a tumbledown place with hay on the floor (for everywhere we newly discover has already been found and neglected). And it's not what we're doing but the way that we jump. He drives his daughters on ahead of him, over the barbed-wire fences and up the rutted lanes, his mysterious, canvas hunting bag swollen at his side.

I'm left alone out there with the wind pouring South all around me. He's said nothing to help me configure my crime. He's given me no name I might call myself while resolving to never be called it again; so my crime becomes loneliness, and the accusatory wind finds its way into my head. I carry it all the way home.

Now the sisters will not leave their garden. They have a new friend with a nose like a pig's and the three of them throw stones at me over the hedge. I lurk in the field behind the house, at the foot of the rookery where I find bald, stringy chicks thrown down from their nests.

There's murder, too, on my mind, and as if it's simply enough to be thinking it, the farmer hails Matthew Byrne and I one Sunday from high in the cab of his tractor. We're walking past his hay barn. He'll pay us twenty pence, he says, for every mouse or rat he turns out from the haystack with his forklift and we kill on the floor of the barn. He gives us a length of black plastic pipe each. We spend the afternoon chasing around the vast, airy hall as it echoes to the forklift's groaning hydraulics and the crack crack crack of our sticks on the dusty cement. We arrange the small corpses for the farmer to count, nudging them into line with the toes of our boots. They hardly seem dead, there's so little blood.

Later, my mother asks me what I've been doing all day. I lie to her quickly. I'm already a different person to the one I believe she sees, standing in my clothes.

Matthew Byrne will soon call at my door and take me down the back lanes where he'll point to a colossal turd, curled at the edge of a nettle patch. He'll make me admit that it's mine, and we'll never speak again.

The sisters' mother will die in the winter, on the bend outside the village. I'll go looking for her blood among the cubes of broken windscreen scattered over the road.

One morning afterwards, as if nothing's happened, the sisters will invite me to stand with them on the ice covering the cistern behind their house. The ice will creak and we'll look down at the bubbles frozen into it and the dark water, as deep as we're tall, still liquid far below.

Decadent Drinking

The Last Big Drinky

Salena Godden

Wednesday

It started when she finished the radio show last Wednesday, now seven days later there are lines of empty bottles, eighteen vodka, six gin, various wine and champagne bottles, Bailey's and Schnapps, in a row by the bin along the kitchen wall by several plastic bags of crumpled beer and cider cans. She shows me her tongue it's furred green. She washes towels and bed sheets; coated in pizza, booze, fag ash, blood and come. She shows me a note the neighbour upstairs left asking if everything was alright, he saw the ambulance the other night. It was an accident, the girl with golden hair fell, they were trying to get her to sleep it off a bit in Saliva's bed and she fell face first and smacked her forehead open. It looked like a second right eyebrow; the gash pissed blood everywhere, we had to keep the photographer's dog from licking it and you could see deep inside, something like skull-bone or matter.

'I am having a bit of a drinky from this week's radio show through to next...' We heard Saliva announce on air and that was that. Now Saliva doesn't remember where she put each end of the piece of string, it comes in flashes, could be the beginning or the middle or the end of the story, but I was there and one thing is for sure she was in the pub everyday. I also know that really was the last big drinky.

It was a laugh, like when the boys were dressed in her underwear and swimming goggles and they ran out into the street in February's first falling snow, it fell in lovely flakes and we all danced barefoot in the road, holding our tongues out to catch snowflakes. Another neighbour came out and said something about being quiet. We apologised, tried to quieten down, but then we forgot about that and opened another bottle of frozen vodka playing that song we love. Saliva got new poems out and Carcass read aloud in his booming Shakespeare voice and we all fell about laughing. It was a wild week, a carefree careless full moon, a lawless restlessness. I kept throwing lemons and tomatoes at Babyblue's head until I was sick. I peuked in the bathroom sink and Saliva looked after me, I was going to try and sleep on the toilet but she called me a lightweight whilst pushing my sick down the plug hole with her finger.

Thursday

'What are we drinking? BBC?' Carcass asked

' No, I sold a poem.'

'Nice! So which poem are we drinking then?'

' "I Don't Do Love" . . . they paid cash into my account, thirsty?'

Saliva orders another round of black sambuca and pints to chase

'Here's to "I Don't Do Love" Carcass bellows 'You don't do love, loves does you.'

'I don't do love, love does me, now lets have a drinky...'

It was winter dusk light when she awoke wondering if she had slept all night or all day and then she didn't know which day or time it was. Saliva woke up twitching, she has vodka orange whilst she brushes her teeth, she says the mint toothpaste would make the orange taste shit so she brushes her teeth with vodka. She washes her face in ice-cold sparkling water from the bottle. She wears yesterday's suit with tomorrow's shirt and stops at the off-licence to pick up vodka, cranberry, couple of bottles of champagne and two packets of cigarettes on the way to the pub, so she wouldn't miss closing on the way back. She sat at the bar and talked to the barman holding her pen erect. She had her notebook open on a blank page to write, but the barman talks to her and she keeps answering him. She wanted to write about this dream she had about the rose petals she has been collecting in pint glasses in rows around the skirting boards of her flat, but instead all she scribbled in large curly letters is a new word she's made up – Vodrosekapetal.

'It's funny! Taste this Malibu, tastes like suntan oil.' She smirks dirtily, she says it tastes like sun tan lotion and drinks it ordering doubles for us all because it tastes like holidays. That was the night Saliva invited the golden haired girl back with everyone else, including me, Babyblue and Carcass; Saliva invited half the pub back to hers, as usual everybody back to Saliva's. The photographer, the barman, Buddhist lady, the butcher, the baker, the candlestick maker, there were loads of us in the apartment. The golden girl, poor thing, she fell and had to have eight stitches, we found out in the pub the next day when we were all having brunch-time pints of Bloody Mary.

People came and went that week; it was like Paddington Station, but timeless and continuous. Sleep? I remember passing out when the room was a haze of grey smoke and that violet light of dawn was seeping through a crack in the curtains. Babyblue and Saliva went to bed together to have sex they won't remember. She likes it, though, because Babyblue is her favourite. He's a beautiful six-foot-six, twenty-year-old boy with the colouring of honey and summer hay bales, and he loves Saliva. He lives in what she calls the treats and surprises compartment of her head, the good times chamber in her life; they only do good times together, nothing heavy. They hook up, have a laugh, have a fuck and drink and that suits them both fine.

Friday

Someone puts Iggy Pop 'I wanna Be Your Dog' on nice and loud, I had crashed with Carcass at my feet like a wolfhound. We take a pinch of snuff, pour morning vodka oranges down us and spring back into a new drinky. That was the day we went drinking around Camden all afternoon and on leaving The Good Mixer near closing time I watched Saliva in the market on Inverness Street. There were rotting peaches, apricots in the gutter and decomposing grapes and squashed tomatoes. She shouted to the night sky, said it was merely an old black blanket with moth holes of sunlight, 'We are not even as clever as ants, we are tiny human bacteria, even the stars are distinguishing, the stars are distinguished,' she laughed out loud to herself, saying she meant to say extinguished and on the other side of the street I saw a little girl in a red coat tugging on her mothers hand,

'Mummy look at the funny lady.'

'Don't stare dear.'

Back at Saliva's we fall out of a cab none of us remember getting into. That was when Saliva got us to lay on the bed and she threw those pints of rose petals all over us. I looked up and saw it snowing outside and inside with rose petals, it was beautiful, glass upon glass of soft fresh rose petals. A petal soaked in vodka on your tongue that's a vodrosekapetal, Saliva kept saying, vodrosekapetal, vod-rose-ka-petal . . . and then somebody made noodles. They are half eaten in fistfuls but mostly thrown around, they stick to your face, splat your cheek and the ceiling, there is a weird smell as the light bulb fries noodles, the wooden floorboards are covered in a carpet of wilting petals and ripped open fruit like the market on Inverness Street whilst the windows are battered with heavy snow. Mushrooms and rose petals, they taste good together, we eat Mexican liberty caps wrapped in rose petals.

Me and Saliva start sucking noodles off his belly . . . Kissing me and Saliva kisses him and then we three kiss and there is that electricity of anticipation and so we say shall we? Then we say why not? Kissing and stumbling into the bedroom to roll around the bed until daylight's a sodden blur of breathy exchanges and then we pass out exhausted covered in a fog of drunken sex with the first shards of sunlight streaming through the wide open window.

Saturday

Waking up he lifts the white sheet to see it was not a dream, entwined and naked, we are a six-legged animal. Saliva gets up and says, 'I think this calls for a drinky! Coffee is what normal people drink in the morning!' she laughs, naked and swigging the best part of a litre of Bailey's,

'Nice, try it, it's a bit like coffee and drinky . . .'

Saliva is in the middle . . . I can feel both fingers slipping in and out together . . . three fingers slide inside...we look into our eyes and faces and we nod and are in this together . . . and we are . . . and we take it in turns, curling tongues around the skin . . . as if underwater . . . and in slow motion . . . we are an octopus and we move over and under each other . . . we become a pit of snakes . . . it sounds like feeding time at the zoo . . . we are greedy . . . filled . . . filling . . . at the same time . . . and on all fours but on six legs . . . feeling it slapping softly against fingertips . . . a timeless place . . . the possibilities and pleasure endless . . . we are three . . . rolling over each other, under each other and into each other's arms . . . legs thrown over shoulders and mouths open and gasps until . . . ah . . . rub it in . . . belly and breasts . . . splutter and laugh . . . and its time for a little smoke and a little drinky.

Sunday

We talk sitting upright cross-legged in a triangle under the sheet like a white tent . . . daylight passed into night and then dawn was rosy lighting up pinkish snow outside . . . a feathery place . . . glasses of frozen vodka and orange . . . a careless white underworld . . . we smoke blue smoke . . . caked in wet and petals and outside it snows again and fat snowflakes fly onto the bed and we peek out from the covers into the court-yard at the flurry, at the white trees and rooftops and we find the white world outside is inside and it's a beautiful place . . . we are in love there and then . . . in that very moment . . . we decide to get married . . . the three of us and then . . . we discuss sticking a lemon up there . . . pinned between them . . . squealing and ticklish and wriggling whilst they take it in turns to . . . kissing each other at the same time . . . we put on fishnet tights which are ripped at the gusset . . . sighing and holding hands . . . taking it in turns slowly . . . we tie him up . . . he ties us up . . . we are handcuffed together and we'll lose the keys . . . we laugh and kiss . . . he watches . . . it's ridiculous . . . it's twister and hysterical . . . she is coming . . . I am com-ing . . . we are laughing . . . blind-folded . . . he is delirious . . . we are cock-drunk . . . he is cunt-blind . . . he kneels in front of a spaghetti of ripped fishnetted legs in a snowdrift . . . four legs in a meringue . . . three tongues catch snowflakes . . . two cunts held open by thirty fingers . . . one cock crowing in the dawn and coming over a million hairs.

Monday

It's chronic daylight and Saliva and I drink cold tins of cider and the phone won't stop ringing. She lights a fag, takes a deep breath and answers, it's a one-day workshop, its been cancelled. Saliva doesn't care, she is not convinced she will be able to tell kids how great a poet's life is, not today, let them find out for themselves. The phone rings again, it's a bit of telly, they want an interview and a poem. Saliva says she won't do it for free, I am smoking a fag listening as she pulls faces and hand gestures 'wankers' at the phone receiver . . .

'What is it with you Media types anyway? I know how this goes, first you will tell me that its just a little chat and a poem, then you edit my shit so I fill your polemic and tokenism AND you'll try to justify your salary by getting creative on my shit but ask me to do it for free . . . don't tell me it's good for my CV . . .'

Saliva is a tiger, pacing she pounds the floor stretching the phone line and says,

'CV? I am my CV. I'll have to suffer you crudely cutting my work, the good lines will be edited out because they are too RUDE! Why do you people persist in coming to me in the first place? You should go get Pam Ayres – she's clean. Why come for me when you know my work and have seen me live! SOMETIMES I CAN BE A RIGHT DIRTY BITCH! GO GET PAM AYRES! PAM AYRES IS DAYTIME FAMILY FUN . . . WHAT? What do you mean? You people treat poetry like ordering pizza, you say you like it but instead of cheese can you have custard? I will tell you custard and pizza don't work but you think you know all about poetry and you'll argue armed with the bit of Hughes and Plath you had to do in school, you say instead of cheese lets have custard on pizza! Having lured my starving arse out to dinner on expenses at Soho House, you'll sit there thinking you are now a poetry editor. Then you will film me somewhere humiliating like an open-top tourist bus in Oxford Circus at rush hour dressed like a chicken and wonder why it doesn't reson-ate with the same delivery as when you saw me read in the Colony Rooms. To add insult to injury you will spell my name wrong and you'll phone me with insipid, ridiculous suggestions at all hours, you'll suggest using toffees instead of mushrooms and buttons instead of olives and shampoo instead of tomato sauce, like now all of a sudden you know all about pizzas? Now you know all about poetry? And I get to do all this for free? You've got the commission right? Are you doing YOUR job for free? Is the camera-man free? Is this BBCharity? I bet there is money in the budget for your colonic irrigation, your Christmas in Goa, but the monkey on the screen, ME I do it for ZERO . . . then I get stopped and frankly harassed in the pub by some smart ass saying have you ever tried using pepperoni on pizza because they saw ME on telly using pennies for pepperoni sausage and I will have to tell them it was YOUR stupid idea and YOUR editing that used PENNIES instead of PEPPERONI . . . but its ME on the idiot box flipping over like the funny monkey . . . so throw me a peanut, why don't you peel me a banana? And? Yes please do, you do that, you check the budget . . . pennies instead of pepperoni I don't think so chump . . . check your budget and then you get back to me . . . thank you.'

'Was I a bit rude to me me me me-dear . . . meeja lady?' Saliva asks, we walk having left the house abruptly before the phone can ring again. 'I think saying I am a dirty bitch, go get Pam Ayres was a bit strong.'

'Ha ha! Look!'

We split a mushroom and it tastes muddy, we swig cider to wash it down and walk, sniggering about custard on pizza, pennies for pepperoni.

The job centre is noisy with queues of non-activity and Saliva goes in wearing a purple bowler hat, swigging a tin of cider. We fit in, covered in handprints, bruised love bites, we are twins with dreadlock bed clumps at the back of our heads. It's in part both hilarious and terrifying now the magic mushrooms have worn off, or are they coming back up? We look like crack whores, we stink of booze and sex, we cannot walk upright or straight, when we look at each other we keep cracking up. The woman behind the desk gives Saliva a grilling; she made a mistake wearing the purple hat, the fur coat and the idiot grin. It's too hot, we are sweating profusely, we shift in our seats nervous to get out of there. The woman is officious, she asks,

'What have you done to seek work in the last two weeks?'

Saliva tells her she is waiting for her agent to get back to her publisher to get back to her manager who is waiting to get the contracts from the lawyer.

'And?'

'Oh and . . . and I have been sending out my CV and . . . reading newspapers, checking the Internet and stuff . . . I got a telly offer today actually, BBC, I am waiting for them to get back to me . . . regarding pizza . . . I mean budget . . .' Saliva squirms unconvincingly. The New Deal Advisor sniffs and she taps the keys of the computer with her talons and we know she knows, she knows we know she can smell the good time we had on us.

We head into the first pub we pass, it stinks, dark and creepy, the barkeep looks odd and unfriendly. We get a pair of halves just to give us the strength and energy to get to the nice pub. A urine drenched, peuk covered old man with a red face sits opposite us and won't stop laughing. We laugh with him for a minute, he laughs and says something and we nod pretending to understand and he laughs again repeating himself. Snot comes out of his nose in a bubble then he coughs up something like a chunk of cottage cheese. Saliva downs the remainder of the half, stands and hurriedly leaves the pub to retch in the gutter with sheer repulsion.

'You OK?' I ask lighting her a fag

'I felt the tramp, its surreal, like I felt his soul, his life force or some vibe . . . it was disgusting.'

In the nice pub we watch the snow outside and it's warm by the fire. We have a laugh and a drinky, pints of spritzer are followed by vodkas and sambucas and lots of joking about the faces we pull and the noises people make when they have sex. Random people, strangers come and sit with us and join in making fucking noises so Saliva gets them drinks too. London is thirsty, good because we are having a drinky, Saliva keeps saying, let's drink I don't do love, love does me. She tries to drink without using her hands and accidentally bites the glass. I stand ready to mop blood, Saliva's mouth is full of glass but she isn't hurt or cut. She grins at me and picks chunks and shards of glass out of her mouth, rinses her mouth out with sambuca and spits it on the pub floor.

Tuesday

In the Lock Tavern a mad woman is sitting with us, she has been in prison three times. She has the remains of two black eyes where police beat her up in the back of a van. She has been abused all of her life she says. Saliva gets her a large whisky. The mad woman says she has two beautiful daughters and she went inside because one of her daughters married a wife-beater and she nearly killed him for it. You don't hurt my girls and get away with it she says. She says she is violent; she says she is always angry. Saliva catches a glance with me and we wonder if she is about to turn nasty, I am ready to grab the ashtray and lump her if it kicks off, she spits as she speaks, lurching and leaning over us. Her arms are tattooed and her teeth broken, she says nobody takes the piss out of me and gets away with it and she points one of her fat tobacco stained digits in our faces. Saliva suddenly stands up and forces the woman to cuddle her, there in the middle of the pub, she hugs this frothing mad woman and she kisses her face. Saliva won't let go of the rigid woman, she holds her telling the mad woman over and over that she is magic, a lovely and special lady and the mad woman crumbles and starts weeping, Saliva licks and wipes her tears, telling her she is a brilliant person with a twinkle in her eyes and the mad woman breaks down sobbing and says nobody has said a kind word like that to her ever before.

'Can you see the rainbows around the street lights?'

We are walking in the snow down the middle of the road, the street lights make everything orange. Once we are home we manage the best part of another bottle of vodka and pass out in our clothes. Saliva writhes in terrible nightmares, she screams in her sleep, says she has thick syrup for blood. She says there are faces of people looking over the bed, knocking at the windows. She tries to sleep but she says all she can hear is her heart struggling to beat, we twitch, flinching in and out of consciousness trying to remember to breathe. We are both aching all over inside and covered in black, purple bruises and cuts from all the rough and tumble, the bundles and the play, and the love bite fights. Drenched in cold sweat, acrid and fearful. She says she is unable to move, if the monster comes she won't be able to fight it. In a tiny voice she mumbles weakly that she is dying, she says this is what dying feels like. She says she feels like she is falling off the world and she begs me to never let go of her hand while it is still dark, we share the fear. Holding my hand she is convinced she will stop breathing. She says vodka and cock will kill her in the end and she feels as though she is rotting.

Wednesday

By lunchtime we manage to get out of bed, clothes damp with night sweat and there are still three bottles of vodka in the freezer. The walls and floors are sticky, caked with booze, food fights, candle-wax and used condoms, spilt puddles of noodles, brown petals. We both get hot flushes trying to clean up and my tongue is kind of bleeding. I make her eat a boiled egg and run us a bath, hearing her peuk and piss shit. Terrible panic, paranoid to go outside and afraid to meet the devil that is here inside, she jumps at shadows and her own reflection. She curls in a ball on the sofa covering her face with her hands and says she is waiting for it to stop, her heart keeps speeding

109

up and stopping, she vomits a pint of water and jokes weakly that it's like a stomach rinse, we are still hallucinating.

'I don't want to be Saliva anymore, its crap, I want to go to church and work with the needy and play tennis, roller-skate, do yoga, eat pulses and wear white dresses . . .'

'Yeah right! Here . . .' I light two fags, pass her one and we giggle nervously.

Now she has to go and do the radio show in a few hours, its already getting dark.

'I promise that was the last big drinky, that was the last big big drinky. Seven days straight, from radio show to show, back to back, that was the last . . .'

Saliva repeats to herself, putting records into her box for the show.

'That was the last big drinky . . . but . . . hey the Full Moon boys are my guests this week. I guess I'll have to have a wee sherry with them, before tonight's show, just to warm up a bit, won't I? Just a wee sherry or two before the show, not a drinky though, just a sherry. Just a sherry, or maybe a port. You coming with me? Fancy a wee sherry? Or a little port maybe? Take the edge off. You have to come with me because . . . because that's not like a drinky is it? That's just having a sherry and that's a different story altogether.'

Paul Verlaine in the Café Procope, inkwell and absinthe in front of
him. Photo copyright Bibliothèque Nationale.

Absinthe

Phil Baker

Gaston Beauvais, the doomed absintheur of Marie Corelli's
Wormwood, is a man with literary aspirations: he has even written a short study of Alfred de Musset. Musset was among the
first of the major French poets to fall victim to absinthe,
although it comes to look like an occupational hazard as the
nineteenth century goes on. Musset is a melancholy writer,
whose work is often about lost love. His first published book
was a self-expressive translation of Thomas De Quincey's
Confessions of an English Opium Eater, full of personal digres-
sions and even 'improvements'; Musset re-unites De Quincey
and Anne, the lost child prostitute, in a sentimental happy
ending, as if he found the original unbearable.

Musset drank for some years at the Café Procope, and at the
Café de la Regence, on the corner of the Rue Saint-Honoré
and the Place du Palais Royal. There is a second-hand
account of him in the Goncourt journals:

> Dr. Martin told me yesterday that he had often seen
> Musset taking his absinthe at the Café de la Regence, an
> absinthe that looked like a thick soup. After which the
> waiter gave him his arm and led him, or rather half-
> carried him, to the carriage waiting for him at the door.

Musset's absinthe drinking was well known. Nearly sixty
years after his death, when absinthe was about to be banned, a
politician with vested interests named Alfred Girod (from the
absinthe manufacturing district of Pontarlier) did everything
he could to defend it. It was ridiculous to endanger such a

successful French industry. The anti-absinthe lobby claimed it turned men into ferocious beasts, he said – but he had a glass every day, and did he look like a mad dog? Finally, in desperation, he said it had inspired the poetry of Alfred de Musset. How could they possibly ban that?

In his lifetime Musset was made a member of the Académie Française, but he often missed their meetings. When somebody remarked that Musset often *absented* himself, Villemain, the Secretary of the Academy, couldn't resist a bitter pun: you mean to say, he said, that he *absinthes* himself a bit too much.

There is a poem dedicated to Musset by another poet of the time, Edmond Bougeois, about the thin green line between being inspired and being washed up.

Anxious and grieving, in the smoky enclosure
Of a café, I dream, and, dreaming, I write
Of the blue tints of the sun that I love
When I see its light in a glass of absinthe.

Then the mind scales the highest peaks
And the heart is full of hope and the scent of hyacinth,
I write and write, saying; absinthe is holy
And the green-eyed muse is forever sovereign.

But alas! A poet is still just a man.
With the first glass drunk, for better writing,
I wanted a second, and the writing slowed.

The tumultuous waves of thought dried up
And deserted, my brain became hollow:
It only needed one glass, and I drank two.

Musset's younger contemporary, Charles Baudelaire, the author of *Les Fleurs du Mal* (The Flowers of Evil), became fixed in the public mind – particularly on the other side of the channel – as vice incarnate. He was more complex than that, and Christopher Isherwood has tried to pin down some of his contradictions. He was a religious blasphemer, a scruffy dandy, a revolutionary who despised the masses, a deeply moral individual who was fascinated by evil, and a philosopher of love who was ill at ease with women. In his *Intimate Journals* Baudelaire writes, "Even when quite a child I felt two conflicting sensations in my heart: the horror of life and the ecstasy of life. That, indeed, was the mark of a neurasthenic idler."

Baudelaire was a great explorer of the new sensations of urban life, of early 'modernity' and what we might now call alienation and neurosis, extending the domain of art and poetry to cover previously taboo subjects and find a new, strange beauty in them. He was a great exponent of dandyism, considered as an attitude or a philosophy rather than just a matter of clothing. He was also completely unimpressed by the idea of 'progress', hated the banality of modern life, and was inclined to believe in Original Sin. Late in his life he began to fear madness. He tried to give up drink and drugs and took up prayer with a new intensity, praying not only to God but to Edgar Allan Poe (whom he revered, and translated into French), as some people might pray to a saint to 'intercede' for them.

Isherwood writes, "Paris taught him his vices, absinthe and opium, and the extravagant dandyism of his early manhood which involved him in debt for the rest of his life." Baudelaire also translated De Quincey's *Confessions of An English Opium Eater* and wrote his own classic accounts of hashish, opium and alcohol in *Les Paradis Artificiels* and in his essay 'Wine and Hashish Compared as a Means for the Multiplication of the Personality'. Jules Bertaut's *Le Boulevard* includes a picture of Baudelaire rushing into a café, the Café de Madrid, and moving the water jug: "the sight of water upsets me", he says, before sinking two or three absinthes with a "detached and insouciant" air.

The Lost Art of the Bender

Erich Kuersten

The bender. The very name brings to mind drama and danger, tragedy and determination. That strange and forbidden part of town you always wanted to explore but don't because society and common sense tell you you might not come back, and if you do come back you might not be the same person.

It seems that in these allegedly more enlightened days, the bender is all but forgotten as a legitimate form of self-exploration and abuse. Now when people talk of destroying themselves through consumption of alcohol, they generally mean overdoing it one night, getting sick later that same evening or early the next morning, then repenting for the remainder of the weekend. This cycle of loathsome behavior is okay if you simply wish to embarrass yourself in front of your friends, but what if you have a deeper, darker wish? What if you long to escape, to disappear from sight and drink unrepentantly and alone for a long period of time, to vanish off the face of the earth for a long 'lost' weekend? What then? Then you are aiming to go on a bender.

Defined in the lexicon of drinking slang, a bender is a period of at least three days of continued drunkenness. Why three? Because the weekend is two days long. It's that third day (quite possibly a workday) that all bets are off, when eyebrows start to raise, when tongues start to cluck, when the amused laughter turns into whispers of concern.

Times past, the bender was saluted as a period when good men went bad, usually for excellent reasons. Maybe the love of their life betrayed them, maybe a loved one passed away, maybe they were laid off, maybe there wasn't a good reason at all except that natural human desire to see how far you can take something without killing yourself, then walk away relatively unscathed. Being able to say, with all honesty, 'Yeah, I went on a real bender after that happened,' is akin to casually mentioning you parachuted behind enemy lines.

The typical recipe for a bender is as follows: 1) Begin drinking within five minutes of waking up, 2) continue drinking, 3) pass out, 4) wake and repeat. Continue this process until a) you're hospitalized, b) dead or c) you come to your senses and realize you must stop.

The root of a bender is simply one drink, perhaps at a Friday happy hour. It then multiplies and finally ceases to be mere recreational drinking when one wakes up the next morning and, as a hangover cure or simply for breakfast, starts the day fresh off with another drink. As morning drinks lead to brunch drinks and lunch drinks eliminate the need for lunch, one's grip on reality is relaxed to the point that it slips completely away and with the aid of a television, a VCR, drawn curtains, and lots of privacy, the petty world of normality and all its tedium . . . evaporates. And the bender is underway.

Sound good? Here's what you'll need to do:

1. Score a handful of good movies because cable is too uncontrollable. You want something nice and familiar. Howard Hughes used to watch his favourite movie *Ice Station Zebra* over and over again, for years on end. Wouldn't you like to be that deranged? You will be when you're on a legitimate bender. So rent, own or borrow a collection of favourite movies. Ideally ones with lots of inspiring drinking scenes.

2. Invest heavily in the alcohol of your choice. Variety is a good idea, as your moods and tastes may shift mid-bender. You should always have more than you need. Stock up. It won't go bad, it'll get better.

3. Turn your phone off and the volume down on your answering machine. In between moments of clarity, you may think you have the ability to talk coherently on the phone. This can lead to trouble as you have to explain your words later and can't remember them. And never mention you're actually on a bender. Make the mistake of cavalierly mentioning the fact to the wrong person and you'll have a teary-eyed bunch of interventionists at your door. The bender is a very personal journey, keep it that way.

4. Close the curtains and lock the door. Think of yourself as a vampire, sunlight and visitors are the bender's natural enemies.

You're all set. Start drinking! I like to start with red wine, then shift to vodka cocktails and cheap American lager, then charge ahead with Jack Daniels on the rocks. Rhythm and pace are essential. Start guzzling hard liquor right off the bat and the binge is over before it started. On the other hand, you want to paddle fast enough to get past the breakwater and into the wide sea that is the bender.

After a while you may realize you've been passed out on the couch for some time. The tape in the VCR will have rewound and the ice in your drink will have melted. Perhaps you will even realize it is 3 in the morning. That's quite okay. Just slowly get up, make yourself another drink and press play on the VCR remote. You are in bender-land and there's no time frame to dictate your actions, no place to be, and video knows no schedule. You can simply let the miasma of day/night duality drift away. There's no worries about social activities, current events, food, sleeping schedule maintenance, etc. All you need is another drink to make everything smooth like a slow passing cloud on a hot summer's day.

Turn inward. Unlike a single night of hard boozing, you will fluctuate between moments of complete madness and perfect clarity. Why? During a typical night of pounding booze your psyche tends to go into hiding, it will hold its breath and try not to inhale the madness you would expose it to. But during a bender it will realize it has to come up for air, leaving you in a unique condition to examine the brightest and darkest memories of your life. Enjoy the fresh if somewhat grimmer perspective, you will come away with an understanding of concepts you never even caught glimpse of.

Examine the bottle in your hand. Read the label. Did you know Jack Daniels was invented by a 16-year-old minister? Commute with your demons, it is your co-conspirator of the moment. Soon it will be your brother.

Wander the room. See things you never noticed before, the way a lamp hangs, the way it throws noir light on an ashtray left by a long forgotten girlfriend. You realize you've gotten to know the surface you so well you've neglected the inner you. Bring light to all those dark corners you forgot about, remember what you used to be, what you still are. Pull books from shelves you haven't read in years, remember what they did to you. You're also in the perfect state to browse old photographs, to get back in touch with old emotions. Also revel in the nihilistic notion that all these fine feelings will most likely be forgotten until the next bender.

Have a seat. Refresh your drink, have a cigarette. Outside your room you can feel forces moving against you, do not check your messages, do not answer the door. This is your world now, you are sovereign and have no need of counsel. At this moment comes the realization that no one owns your time but you. As long as the booze holds out.

Sooner or later, however, things can begin to crumble. You may find yourself in bed wondering how you got there, and if you will be able to get a glass of water to your lips without vomiting. You may hyperventilate, suffer heart palpitations, sweat, shake, hallucinate and lose circulation in your face and limbs, but mainly you will vomit – vomit – vomit! Just remember to rehydrate, force some bland food down and drink some more alcohol as quickly as possible. You may keep throwing it up, but damn you, force it down.

You will find at this juncture that it takes more alcohol just to lose your shakes than it used to take to get you wasted. Now you are truly, 'Leaving Las Vegas'.

Days will melt into nights and back into days and you may lose track of time. Don't turn on the news, it's hoarse shouting will depress you. Now you may start wondering how long you should keep it going. Some people, famous and other-wise, have kept benders going for years, especially British theatre actors and American writers. Stephen King claims he wrote his best novels while on one long bender, drinking a case of 16-ounce tallboys a night while cranking out bestsell-ers he barely remembers writing. Now he's in AA and writes pap he does remember.

Of course, long term benders do not always work out for the best, poet Dylan Thomas' exit being one of the more famous examples. Dylan culminated a decade-long bender on a New York sidewalk where, on his knees, he told a young woman: 'I have just drunk 18 straight whiskies. I think that's the record. I love you.' He promptly died of what the autopsy called 'insult to the brain' (and a compliment to the lady).

I know nothing about dying, unfortunately, but I can explain how to stop if that's the option you choose. 1) Utilize every hangover cure you know. 2) Keep moving; clean your messes, do the dishes, shower, exercise, take a long walk, etc. 3), Drink beer. As Albert Finney says in *Under the Volcano*, 'Theresh nething bedder t'sober wunnup, thin beeah.' Open the shades, listen to your answering machine messages and vow never to drink again. Around 5 or 6 pm you may need some form of sedative – preferably a Valium but Advil will do in a pinch. Wait until most of the booze is out of your system before taking anything heavy, as it could easily cause death, or worse, more vomiting.

If all goes well, you will be a shattered mess by the next morning. Force yourself out of bed, take a long, cold shower, and start drinking Gatorade. Maybe you will have to stay home from work. If you're lucky, maybe you don't even have to work, maybe you've already been fired. Regardless, by late afternoon, you will feel good enough to eat some lunch.

So what, you may ask, are the benefits to such self-destructive behaviour? Well, none really. Or . . . are there? Think back to the height of your bender. Everything was numbed, timeless bliss. You let yourself go, utterly. You became swept into the sea. You practically drowned and you miraculously returned. You could have kept going, but you turned back. On the slow raft ride to eternity, you sailed long enough to relax, but not long enough that you couldn't get home. You caught a glimpse of heaven and a glimpse of hell. You drank of what lies beyond pleasure, pain and petty mortal striving.

Decadent Anti-heroes

The Debauchee

Earl of Rochester

I rise at eleven, I dine about two
I get drunk before seven, and the next thing I do;
I send for my whore, when, for fear of a clap
I fuck in her hand, and spew in her lap;
Then we quarrel and scold, till I fall asleep,
When the jilt growing bold, to my pocket does creep;
Then slily she leaves me, and to revenge the affront
At once both my lass and my money I want.
If by chance then I wake, hot-headed and drunk
What a coyl do I make for the loss of my punk?
I storm, and I roar, and I fall in a rage,
And missing my lass, I bugger my page:
Then crop-sick, all morning I rail at my men,
And in bed I lie yearning till eleven again.

Phrases and Philosophies for the Use of the Young

Oscar Wilde

The first duty in life is to be as artificial as possible. What the second duty is no one has as yet discovered.

Wickedness is a myth invented by good people to account for the curious attractiveness of others.

If the poor only had profiles there would be no difficulty in solving the problem of poverty.

Those who see any difference between soul and body have neither.

A really well-made buttonhole is the only link between Art and Nature.

Religions die when they are proved to be true. Science is the record of dead religions.

The well-bred contradict other people. The wise contradict themselves.

Nothing that actually occurs is of the smallest importance.

Dullness is the coming of age of seriousness.

In all unimportant matters, style, not sincerity, is the essential. In all important matters, style, not sincerity, is the essential.

If one tells the truth, one is sure, sooner or later, to be found out.

Pleasure is the only thing one should live for. Nothing ages like happiness.

It is only by not paying one's bills that one can hope to live in the memory of the commercial classes.

No crime is vulgar, but all vulgarity is crime. Vulgarity is the conduct of others.

Only the shallow know themselves.

Time is a waste of money.

One should always be a little improbable.

There is a fatality about all good resolutions. They are invariably made too soon.

The only way to atone for being occasionally a little over-dressed is by being always absolutely over-educated.

To be premature is to be perfect.

Any preoccupation with ideas of what is right and wrong in conduct shows an arrested intellectual development.

Ambition is the last refuge of the failure.

A truth ceases to be true when more than one person believes in it.

In examinations the foolish ask questions that the wise cannot answer.

Greek dress was in its essence inartistic. Nothing should reveal the body but the body.

One should either be a work of art, or wear a work of art.

It is only the superficial qualities that last. Man's deeper nature is soon found out.

Industry is the root of all ugliness.

The ages live in history through their anachronisms.

It is only the gods who taste of death. Apollo has passed away, but Hyacinth, whom men say he slew, lives on. Nero and Narcissus are always with us.

The old believe everything: the middle-aged suspect everything: the young know everything.

The condition of perfection is idleness: the aim of perfection is youth.

Only the great masters of style ever succeed in being obscure.

There is something tragic about the enormous number of young men there are in England at the present moment who start life with perfect profiles, and end by adopting some useful profession.

To love oneself is the beginning of a life-long romance.

Against Nature

J.K. Huysmans

More than two months passed by before des Esseintes could immerse himself in the silent repose of his house at Fontenay; purchases of every kind compelled him to walk the streets of Paris again, to scour the city from one end to the other.

And what researches he had undertaken, what meditations he had given himself up to, before confiding his house to the decorators!

He had long been expert in the sincerities and deceptions of colour. In days gone by, when he still entertained women at his home, he had constructed a boudoir in which, amid dainty pieces of furniture carved from pale Japanese camphor-wood, and beneath a kind of tent of rose-tinted Indian satin, bare flesh blushed delicately under the prepared lighting filtering through the material.

This room, in which mirrors on the wall echoed each other and reflected a whole series of pink boudoirs as far as the eye could see, had been celebrated among whores, who took delight in immersing their nudity in this bath of warm rose, made aromatic by the scent of mint given off by the wood of the furniture.

But, even putting aside the benefits of that artificial atmosphere, which seemed to transfuse new blood into skin tired and worn by heavy make-up and by nights of dissipation, he savoured particular pleasures on his own account in these languorous surroundings, pleasures which somehow energised memories of past afflictions and old anxieties and made them more intense.

Thus, out of hatred and contempt for his childhood, he had

suspended from the ceiling of this room a small, silver wire cage in which a captive cricket sang, as they had amid the ashes of the fireplaces at the Château de Lourps; when he listened to this sound, so often heard in the past, all the constrained and silent evenings spent next to his mother, all the neglect of his suffering and repressed boyhood stirred up within him; and then, to the jerkings of the woman he was mechanically caressing and whose words or laughter would break into his fantasies and rudely recall him to reality of the bedroom, a tumult would arise in his soul, a need to avenge the miseries he'd endured, a rage to defile the memories of his family by shameful actions, a furious desire to lie panting on cushions of flesh, to drain to their utmost dregs the most violent and the most bitter of carnal frenzies.

Again, at other times, when in the grip of depression, when, during rainy autumn days, he was assailed by a hatred of the streets, of his home, of the muddy yellow sky and the macadam-black clouds, he would take refuge in this retreat, setting the cage lightly in motion and watching it endlessly reflected in the play of the mirrors, until it seemed to his dazed eyes that the cage was not moving at all, but that the whole boudoir was reeling and turning, filling the house with a rose-coloured waltz.

And in the days when he had felt impelled to draw attention to himself, des Esseintes had designed marvellously strange furnishings, dividing his drawing room into a series of alcoves, each decorated with a different wall-hanging that related by a subtle analogy, by a vague harmony of joyful or sombre, delicate or crude colours, to the character of the Latin or French books he most loved. He would then seclude himself in whichever of these recesses the décor of which seemed to him to best correspond with the essence of the work which the caprice of the moment had led him to read.

And lastly, he had had constructed a high-ceilinged room, intended for the reception of his tradesmen; they would enter, sit themselves side by side on church pews, and then he would climb up into a magisterial pulpit from which he would preach sermons on dandyism, entreating his bootmakers and tailors to conform, in every particular, to his briefs in matters of style, threatening them with pecuniary excommunication if they failed to follow, to the letter, the instructions contained in his monitories and bulls.

He acquired a reputation as an eccentric, to which he gave the finishing touch by wearing suits of white velvet and waistcoats embroidered with gold thread, by inserting, by way of a cravat, a bouquet of Parma violets in the open neck of his shirt, and by giving notorious dinners to men of letters, at one of which, inspired by the eighteenth century, he organised a funeral repast to celebrate that most trivial of mishaps that can afflict a man.

In a dining room hung in black that opened onto the garden of the house, now transformed with its paths powdered with charcoal, its little pond bordered with basalt and filled with ink, its shrubberies laid out with cypresses and pines, dinner had been served on a black tablecloth, adorned with baskets of violets and black *Scabiosa*, and lit by candelabra from which green flames blazed and by chandeliers in which wax tapers flared.

While a hidden orchestra played funeral marches, the guests had been waited on by naked black women wearing slippers and stockings of silver cloth sprinkled with tears.

From black-bordered plates they had eaten turtle soup, Russian rye bread, ripe olives from Turkey, caviar, salted mullet roes, smoked black pudding from Frankfurt, game with sauces the colour of liquorice and boot polish, truffle gravy, chocolate cream, plum-puddings, nectarines, grape preserves, mulberries and black-heart cherries; from dark glasses they had drunk wines from Limagne and Roussillon, from Tenedos, Val de Peñas and Oporto; and after coffee and walnut brandy, they had savoured kvass, porter and stout.

'A farewell dinner for a temporarily dead virility' was what he had written on the invitation card, which looked just like a burial announcement.

But these extravagances in which he had once so gloried burned themselves out in due course; now he was filled with contempt for such puerile and outmoded displays, for his abnormal clothes and his bizarrely embellished apartment. He dreamed simply of composing, for his own pleasure and no longer for the astonishment of others, an interior that would be comfortable, albeit decorated in a rare style, of fashioning for himself a unique, calm setting, adapted to the needs of his future solitude.

When the house at Fontenay was ready, appointed according to his plans and desires by an architect, when all that remained was to determine a scheme of furnishing and decoration, he devoted himself afresh to a lengthy review of the whole range of colours and shades.

What he wanted were colours whose expressiveness would be enhanced by the artificial light of a lamp; it little mattered to him if, by the light of day, they were insipid or crude, for it was at night that he lived, feeling that then one was more oneself, more alone, and that the mind only grew animated and active with the approach of darkness; he found, too, a peculiar pleasure in being in a richly illuminated room, the only person up and about amid shadow-haunted and sleeping houses, a kind of pleasure in which an element of vanity entered, perhaps, a wholly singular satisfaction known to late-night workers, when, drawing aside the window curtains, they perceive that everything around them is extinguished, that all is silent, that all is dead.

Slowly, one by one, he selected the colours.

By candlelight, blue tends toward an artificial green; if it is dark, like cobalt or indigo, it turns black; if it is light, it turns grey; if it is a soft true blue, like turquoise, it grows dull and cold. So, unless it was combined with some other colour, as an auxiliary, there could be no question of making blue the dominant note of a room.

On the other hand, iron greys look gloomier and heavier still; pearl greys lose their azure and metamorphose into a dirty white; browns become lifeless and cold; as for dark greens, such as emperor and myrtle green, they have the same properties as deep blue and merge into black. There remained, then, the paler greens, such as peacock green, vermilion and lacquer, but there again light banishes their blues and preserves only their yellows, which in turn have a false tone, a hint of cloudiness, about them.

There was no need to spend time thinking about tints of salmon, maize and rose, the effeminate natures of which were contrary to all ideas of isolation; and finally there was no need either to consider violet, which loses its colour, only the reddish tones holding their own at night, and what a red! a viscous red like the dregs of cheap wine. Besides, it seemed to him pointless to use this colour, since by ingesting santonin in the right dose everything looks violet, and this way it was easy to change the colour of his hangings without even touching them.

These colours disposed of, only three remained: red, orange, yellow.

Of these, he preferred orange, thus by his own example confirming the truth of a theory which he declared had an almost mathematical exactitude: that a harmony exists between the sensual nature of a truly artistic individual and the colour which his eyes see in the most unique and vivid fashion.

Disregarding entirely the generality of men whose gross retinas perceive neither the cadence peculiar to each colour nor the mysterious charm of their gradations and nuances; and disregarding, too, the bourgeois, whose eyes are insensible to the pomp and splendour of strong, vibrant tones; considering, therefore, only people with refined pupils, cultivated by literature and art, he was convinced that the eyes of those among them who dream of ideal beauty, who demand illusions, who prefer shades in their bedroom, are generally caressed by blue and its derivatives, such as mauve, lilac and pearl grey, provided always that they remain soft and do not overstep the bounds where they lose their personalities and are transformed into pure violets and blunt greys.

By contrast, men who affect a military bearing, plethoric, red-blooded, sturdy males who disdain rules of decorum and half-measures and charge unthinkingly into things and immediately lose their heads, these types, for the most part, delight in the striking gleams of yellows and reds, the clashing cymbals of the vermilions and chromes that blind and intoxicate them.

Lastly, as for the eyes of the enfeebled and the nervous, whose sensual appetites crave foods that have been smoked or pickled, as for the eyes of the over-excitable and the hypochondriac, almost all of them adore that irritating and morbid colour with its sham splendours, its acidic feverishness: orange.

Des Esseintes' choice could not, therefore, be in any doubt; but unquestionable difficulties still presented themselves. If red and yellow are enhanced by candlelight, the same doesn't always hold true of their compound, orange, which flares up and often transmutes into a nasturtium red, a fiery red.

He studied all their nuances by candlelight and discovered one shade which would not, he felt, lose its stability and disappoint his expectations; these preliminaries completed, he also determined not to use, in his study at least, fabrics and carpets from the Orient, which, now that rich merchants can buy them at a discount in large department stores, had become so boring and so common.

He decided, in the end, to bind his walls like books, with smoothed *gros-grain* morocco, and with skins from the Cape that had been flattened by strong steel plates under a powerful press.

Once the wainscotting was finished, he had the mouldings and high skirting boards painted a dark indigo, a lacquered indigo like that which coach-makers employ for their carriage panels; on the ceiling, slightly domed and also lined with morocco, like an enormous round skylight framed in orange-coloured skin, was a circle of the heavens in royal blue silk, embroidered for an old ecclesiastical cope by the Cologne guild of weavers in days gone by, in the middle of which ascended silver seraphim with outstretched wings.

In the evening, when the arrangments were done, everything harmonised, blended and settled: the wainscotting conserved its blue, sustained and warmed by the oranges, which, in their turn, preserved their colour unadulterated, invigorated and fanned into life, as it were, by the insistent breath of the blues.

As far as furnishings went, des Esseintes didn't have to spend long searching, the room's sole luxury consisted of books and rare flowers; later, he planned to decorate the remaining bare panels with a few sketches or paintings, but for now he limited himself to putting up ebony shelves and bookcases around most of the walls, spreading the pelts of wild beasts and the skins of blue foxes on the parquet floor, installing, next to a massive fifteenth-century counting-table, deep winged armchairs and an old church reading-stand of forged iron, one of those antique lecterns on which the deacon formerly placed the antiphonary and which now supported a weighty folio edition of du Cange's *Glossarium mediae et infimae latinitatis.*

The casement windows, the blue, fissured glass of which was dotted with gold-flecked bottle-bottom bosses that intercepted the view of the countryside and allowed only a faint light to penetrate, were draped in their turn with curtains cut from old ecclesiastical stoles, the sombre, smoky golden thread of which was stifled by the almost dead russet of the weave.

Finally, on the mantelpiece, the cloth of which was also cut from the sumptuous fabric of a Florentine dalmatic, between two gilded copper monstrances of Byzantine style originally brought from the old Abbaye-au-Bois at Bièvre, was a marvellous church canon with three separate compartments delicately wrought like lace-work, containing, under its glass frame, three pieces by Baudelaire, copied onto real vellum in wonderful, splendidly illuminated missal letters: to the right and left were the sonnets bearing the titles *La Mort des amants* and *L'Ennemi*; and in the middle was the prose poem entitled, *Any where out of the World. N'importe ou, hors du monde.*

Cuttings from Torture Garden

Octave Mirbeau

Being perfect artists and resourceful poets, the Chinese have piously conserved the love and devoted cult of flowers: one of the rarest and most ancient traditions to have survived their decadence. And, as flowers have to be distinguished from one another, they have used graceful analogies, dream images, pure or pleasurable names which perpetuate and harmonise in our minds the sensations of gentle charm and violent intoxication which they inspire in us. This is how the Chinese honour their favourite flower, the peony, according to its form and colour with such delightful names that each one is a complete poem or novel in itself: 'Young Girl Offering Her Breasts' or 'The Water Sleeping Under The Moon' or 'The Sun In The Forest' or 'The First Desire of the Reclining Virgin', or 'My Dress is no longer completely white because the Son of Heaven left behind a little of his rosy blood when he tore it', or how about 'I have swooned with my Lover in the Garden'?

And Clara, who recounted these charming things to me, cried indignantly as she stamped the ground with her small feet in her little yellow slippers.

'And they consider these divine poets who call their flowers "I swooned with my Lover in the Garden" to be apes and savages!'

The Chinese are right to be proud of their Torture Garden, perhaps the most absolutely beautiful in all China where there are many marvellous gardens. The rarest and the most delicate and robust species of flora are collected from the mountain snow line and the parched furnace of the plains as well as

137

those mysterious and wild plants which hide in the most impenetrable forests and which popular superstition considers as being the souls of evil genies. From mangrove to saxatile azalea; from horned and biflorous violet to distillatory nepenthe; from voluble hibiscus to stoloniferous sunflower; from androsace invisible in its rocky fissure to the most wildly tangled liana – each species represented by numerous specimens which, gorged upon organic food treated to the rituals of gardening experts, assume abnormal forms and colourings, the wonderful intensity of which, with our sullen climates and insipid gardens, we are unable to imagine.

Clara pointed out strange plants growing in the ground across which water gushed forth from all sides. I approached. On high stalks, scaly and stained black like snakeskins were enormous spars, kind of funnel-shaped cornets with the dark violet of putrefaction inside, and the greenish-yellow of decomposition outside, like the open thoraxes of dead animals. Long, blood-red spadices, imitating monstrous phalluses, came forth from these cornets. Attracted by the corpse-like odour that these horrible plants exhaled, flies hovered in concentrated swarms, swallowed up at the bottom of the spar which was adorned from top to bottom with silky projectiles that enlaced the flies and held them prisoner more effectively than any spider's web. Along the stem, the digitalised leaves were clenched and twisted like the hands of men under torture.

'You see, darling,' declared Clara. 'These flowers are not the creation of a sick mind or a delirious genius – they're of nature . . . Didn't I tell you that nature loves death?'

We had now entered into bamboo palisades along which ran honeysuckle, odorous jasmine, begonia, mauve tree ferns and climbing hibiscus that had not yet blossomed. Moonseed wrapped itself around a stone column with its countless liana. At the top of the column the face of a hideous divinity grimaced, its ears stretched like bats' wings, its hair ending in fiery horns. Incarvillea, day-lilies, moraea and delphinium nudicaul concealed the base with their pink bells, scarlet thyrses, golden calyxes and purple stars . . .

Here and there in the indentations of the palisade, appearing like halls of verdure and flower-beds, were wooden benches equipped with chains and bronze necklaces, iron tables shaped like crosses, blocks and racks, gibbets, automatic quartering machines, beds laden with cutting blades, bristling with steel points, fixed chokers, props and wheels, boilers and basins above extinguished hearths, all the implements of sacrifice and torture covered in blood – in some places dried and darkish, in others sticky and red. Puddles of blood filled the hollows in the ground and long tears of congealed blood hung from the dismantled mechanisms. Around these machines the ground had absorbed the blood. But blood still stained the whiteness of the jasmines and flecked the coral-pink of the honeysuckles and the mauve of the passion flowers. And small fragments of human flesh, caught by whips and leather lashes, had flown here and there on to the tops of petals and leaves. Noticing that I was feeling faint and that I flinched at these puddles whose stain had enlarged and reached the middle of the avenue, Clara, in a gentle voice, encouraged me:

'That's nothing yet, darling . . . Let's go on!'

We reached an avenue leading to the central pond and the peacocks, which hitherto had followed us, suddenly abandoned us and scattered with a great noise through the flower-beds and the garden lawns.

The broad avenue was bordered by dead trees on both sides – immense tamarinds whose massive bare branches interlaced in hard arabesques across the sky. A recess was hollowed out in every trunk. The majority remained empty but some

139

enclosed the violently contorted bodies of men and women subjected to hideous and obscene tortures. Some sort of clerk dressed in a black robe stood gravely in front of the occupied recesses with a writing-case on his chest and a police register in his hands.

'It's the avenue of the accused,' Clara told me. 'And these people you see standing here come to take the confessions which only prolonged suffering could tear out of the wretches . . . It is an ingenious idea. I really do believe they got it from Greek mythology. It's a horrible transposition of the charming fable of the wood nymph trapped in the trees!'

Clara approached a tree in which a woman who was still young was growling. She was hanging by her wrists from an iron hook and her wrists were held between two blocks of wood clasped with great force. A rough rope of coconut thread covered with pulverised pimento and mustard and soaked in a salt solution was wound around her arms.

'That rope is kept on,' Clara was kind enough to explain, 'until the limb is swollen to four times its usual size. . .'

Shadows descended across the garden, trailing blue veils that lay lightly over the bare lawns and more thickly over the flower-beds whose outlines had clarified. The white flowers of the cherry and peach trees – whose whiteness was now moon-like – had elements of slippage and wandering, the strangely stooping aspect of phantoms. And the gibbets and gallows raised their sinister casks and black frames in the eastern sky that was the colour of blue steel.

Horror! Above a flower-bed, against the purple of the dying evening, endlessly turning on the stakes, slowly turning, turning in the void and swaying like immense flowers with stalks visible in the night, I saw, endlessly turning, the silhouettes of five tortured men.

'Clara! Clara! Clara!'

Ah yes! The Torture Garden! Passions, appetites, personal interests, hatreds and lies, along with laws, social institutions, justice, love, glory, heroism and religion. These are its monstrous and hideous flowers – instruments of eternal human suffering. What I saw that day, what I heard, exists and cries out and yells outside that garden, which for me is no more than a symbol of the whole earth. I have vainly sought a lull in crime and a rest in death, but I have found them nowhere.

Decadent Culture

UFO Club

Joe Boyd

John 'Hoppy' Hopkins and I opened the UFO Club in Mr Gannon's Irish dance hall in Tottenham Court Rd in December of 1966. It soon became the epicentre of London's psychedelic revolution. Pink Floyd were the resident band for the first few months, succeeded as crowd favourites by Soft Machine, Arthur Brown, Tomorrow and the Bonzo Dog Doo-dah band. By the summer, Hoppy was in prison on a trumped-up charge and UFO had been run out of the West End by the police at the urging of the *News of the World*. But for a few months in the spring of 1967, it was glorious place to be of a Friday night.

Besides the Floyd, we booked The Exploding Galaxy dance troupe, avant-garde jazz outfits such as Sun Trolley, and ten-minute comedies by The People Show. Yoko Ono cast her *Bottoms* movie mostly from UFO audiences, who signed up for it in a book by the door. One night she asked for a contact microphone on a long lead, an amp and a stepladder. When the place was packed we cleared some space in front of the stage for the ladder, taped the mic to a pair of scissors, plugged it in and cranked up the volume. Yoko emerged from the dressing room leading a beautiful girl in a paper dress who smiled serenely atop the ladder as Yoko cut the garment off her, the amplified scritch-scritch of the scissors booming across the club.

A uniformed bobby turned up one night, asking to be allowed in to collect clothes left behind by a man being held in custody. This made sense: half an our earlier, a naked guy had bolted past me up the stairs and disappeared into the night. Hoppy and I agreed that an exception could be made, so I told the audience we were going to let the fuzz in to look for the clothes and turn on the overhead lights (murmurs and booing). As the crowd spread out in a wide circle, some garments could be seen scattered around the floor. The young bobby seemed to blush as he glanced at the crowd, a vivid cross-section of 'London Freak' circa May 1967: long hair on the boys, flowered dresses on the girls, Arabian or Indian shirts, a few kaftans, jeans, even a few white shirts and khaki slacks. Many were tripping; most were laughing or grinning.

The laughter grew as it became clear that his hastily-gathered armful contained more than was required to make his prisoner decent: two or three pairs of underpants (gender undetermined), a couple of shirts, a bra, several socks etc. As he made his way to the door, the working-class constable regarded us with amazement, not hatred. We, in turn, regretted that he could not grasp why we took drugs and danced in the lights, lived for the moment and regarded our fellow man with benign tolerance, even love. That was the theory, anyway. Tested, it would come undone in the ensuing years, even as the bobby's mates donned kaftans, rolled joints, and joined the crowds at festivals.

The first man I knew to take hallucinogens was Eric Von Schmidt. (You can see Eric's photo on one of the record jackets beside Sally Grossman on the cover of 'Bringing It All Back Home' and hear Dylan blurt 'I learned this song from Ric Von Schmidt' on his eponymous first LP.) Mail-order packages of peyote buds from Moore's Orchid Farm in Texas arrived periodically at the Von Schmidt apartment near Harvard Square. He would cook them up in a pot and invite friends over to drink the soup. They would stack some LPs on the record player – Ali Akhbar Khan, Lord Buckley, Chopin, The Swan Silvertones, Lighting Hopkins – then drink the potion and try not to be sick. If you couldn't keep it down you weren't, in Eric's view, calm enough ('centred' had not yet been used in this context) to deserve the high. It was an experience meant for an intellectual and spiritual elite, not the masses (although he certainly would never have put it that way).

The market is too efficient, of course, to limit transcendence to people who can stomach peyote. Down the street from Eric's flat in 1962 was the laboratory of Professor Timothy Leary, who advertised in the Harvard Crimson for volunteers to take LSD at $1 an hour and was determined to become the Johnny Appleseed of hallucinogens. By 1967, pure, powerful LSD tabs were still available while adulterated, amphetamine-laced concoctions were starting to be widely distributed. Few bothered about how elevated the experience might be.

In June that summer, a *News of the World* reporter tipped off Scotland Yard about a 'drugs-and-sex orgy' at Keith Richard's place and was rewarded with a ringside seat at the raid. It has become the stuff of legend: Mars bars, threesomes, Marianne Faithfull naked under a fur rug etc., a symbol of out-of-control decadence. The media stopped winking and grinning about 'Swinging London' and started wallowing in horror stories about teenagers being led astray. 'Sgt Pepper' was the world's soundtrack that month and powerful Establishment figures were horrified by the implications of influential pop stars' open fondness for drugs.

For the UFO audience, the Stones' bust represented the sinister collusion of circulation-seeking editors, treacherous grasses and killjoy drug squads. Jagger and Richards may have been wealthy superstars, but they were counter-culture heroes, too. Hoppy had also been busted that spring (after a plainclothesman reached, conjuror-like, behind his sofa and pulled out an evidentiary plum) and had just been sentenced to eight months in Wormwood Scrubs. Ads and editorials in the *International Times*, posters around UFO and grafitti in Notting Hill Gate reminded everyone of the injustice. A bucket was passed at the club, the money going to a legal defence fund for drug busts.

On the last Friday of that momentous month just before Tomorrow took the stage, I found myself in conversation with Twink and a few others. Hoppy's jailing outraged us and the behaviour of the NotW seemed like the last straw. We decided to close the club after the first set and parade through the West End, finishing off with a protest in front of the *NotW* building in Fleet St. The West End at 1am on a Friday night was nothing like as busy as it is today, but there were quite a few 'normals' about, and they gaped as we rounded Picadilly and headed for Leicester Square, then down through Covent Garden towards Fleet St. Our destination was a letdown: the News of the World building was dark and silent. Firebrands among us started planning a blockade of the Sunday paper and an assault on their vans the next night.

The long walk in the night air, the hostile stares from the 'straights' and the threats from the police had energized everyone, so the club was packed and buzzing when Tomorrow hit the stage about 4am. The unity of spirit between audience and musicians was tremendous: Twink had been at the head of our 200-strong column. Tearing into 'White Bicycle', they had never sounded tighter. At some point Skip from the Pretty Things took over on drums as Twink grabbed the microphone and plunged into the audience. Howe's playing moved to another level of intensity, sending the dancers leaping into the cones of projected light as Twink crawled along the floor, hugging people and chanting 'revolution, revolution'. Everyone was high – on chemicals or adrenalin or both. You really did believe in that moment that when the mode of music changes, the walls of the city shake. The tide of history was with us and music was the key.

The bill for this glorious moment came due a month later. The *News of the World* may not have known who we were before that weekend, but they certainly did afterwards. The fruits of their plotting burst forth the last Sunday in July: beneath a grainy, out-of-focus shot of a bare-breasted girl, the front-page screamed that she was fifteen years old and that the photograph had been taken at the 'hippy vice den' known as UFO. Our normally stoic landlord buckled under police pressure and evicted us.

A good recording may preserve elements of a great musical moment, but bottling the energy of social and cultural forces is impossible. Without realizing it, we had started on a down-hill slope that was mirrored in New York and San Francisco. The agape spirit of '67 evaporated in the heat of ugly drugs, violence, commercialism and police pressure. In Amsterdam, people began stealing and repainting the white bicycles.

Performance

Mick Brown

Performance is a film that, as Marianne Faithfull memorably put it, 'preserves a whole era under glass,' freeze-framing London at the tail end of the Sixties: the London of the Rolling Stones and of the Kray twins, of newly found sexual freedom, drug-drenched hedonism and psychopathic violence. Superficially a 'crime movie about rock and roll' – which is how the idea of the film was first sold to Warner Bros – *Performance* is a multi-textured feast for the mind and the senses; a film which simultaneously explores the nature of identity, the relation-ship between violence and creativity, sex and death, organised crime, amorality, power, drugs and rock and roll. As Turner, the rock-star anti-hero (played by Mick Jagger), says at one point in the film: 'The only performance that makes it, that really makes it, that makes it all the way, is the one that achieves madness.'

Even before its opening in Britain in January 1971 the film had acquired its own peculiar mythology. Shot in the summer of 1968, *Performance* sat on the shelf for more than two years while Warner Bros deliberated on whether or not to release it, so disturbed were they by the film's treatment of drugs-use and sexuality. And just as *Performance* is a film that seems, in some curious way, to leave an indelible mark on everyone who sees it, so it is also a film that seems to have forever changed those who were associated with it. James Fox, then a rising star in Britain and Hollywood, was allegedly so dis-turbed by the events of the film that shortly afterwards he retired from acting altogether and took to Christian evangel-ism. He did not work again for ten years. Anita Pallenberg left the set of *Performance* addicted to heroin. Michèle Breton fell into a life of drug addiction, destitution and mental break-down. Mick Jagger emerged apparently unscathed, but within a year unleashed the demon that was Altamont. For Donald Cammell, *Performance*'s writer, co-director and presiding alchemist, the film would cast a baleful shadow over his life and career that would come to horrific fruition some thirty years later

'The film is simply about an idea,' Donald Cammell told the film critic Derek Malcolm in an interview published in the *Guardian* in 1970, shortly before the British release of *Performance*. 'It's a movie that goes into an allegorical areas and it moves from a definition of what violence is to an explan-ation of a way of being. It is an attempt, maybe successful and maybe not, to use film for exploring the nature of violence as seen from the point of view of an artist. It says that this crook leads this fading pop star to realise that violence is a facet of creative art, that his energy is derived from the same sources of those as the crook. And that that energy is always dangerous, sometimes fatal.'

Performance took its spirit from the London milieu of which its director and principal players were all a part: the inter-section at which the worlds of rock music, the new aristocracy – and crime – collided. Marianne Faithfull would describe it as: 'An allegory of libertine Chelsea life in the late Sixties, with its baronial rock stars, wayward jeunesse dorée, drugs, sex and decadence.' It's the film's dazzling integration of themes – shaped by the cultural and sexual obsessions of Donald Cammell and by his prodigious intelligence and imagination – which makes *Performance* so extraordinary; and it is the circumstances which surrounded the film – the story behind the story – which make it the cult movie nonpareil.

It was a film galvanised by the relationships, both on and off screen, of its principals. Cammell, Fox and Jagger were all close friends. Cammell had lived in ménages à trois, at different times, with both Anita Pallenbergand Michèle Breton. At the time of making the film, Pallenberg was the lover of Keith Richard, Jagger's fellow Rolling Stone and closest friend. It is this intermingling of relationships that has led to *Performance* being described, with some justification, as 'the most expensive home movie ever made.'

The film was sold to Warner Bros on the basis of a skimpy treatment about a chance meeting between a rock star and a gangster. There was no proper script. Cammell hadn't written one. He began the film not knowing how it would end, and would later claim that even halfway through shooting he had no clear idea who would live and who would die. Cammell had scripted two films before *Performance* but had no experience as a director. Nor did his co-director, Nic Roeg, although he was an experienced and highly respected cinematographer.

Only after filming had begun did Warner executives begin to express doubts about the film's volatile contents, their nervousness increasing almost by the day, to the point where filming was actually halted and the fate of the project hung in the balance. When, at last, the film was delivered to the studio it was received with shudders of apprehension. At a test screening in Santa Monica members of the audience walked out of the theatre in protest. Legend has it that the wife of one studio executive actually threw up. Warner Bros refused to release the film without substantial cuts and re-editing, and it was to be two years before it was eventually released for public exhibition. By that time its cult status was already assured.

Performance was given its world premiere in New York on 30 July 1970, heralded by an advertisement in the *Village Voice* showing pictures of Jagger in rock-star and gangster guise, alongside copy which read: 'Somewhere in your head there's a wild electric dream. Come see it in *Performance*, where underground meets underworld.'

The film was greeted by cries of bewilderment and outrage

from critics. John Simon, writing in the *New York Times*, wondered if it wasn't 'the most loathsome film of all,' while Andrew Sarris in the *Village Voice* described it as 'the most deliberately decadent film I have ever seen.'

Extraordinarily, the intervening years have done nothing to diminish the impact of *Performance*. It remains as dazzling, provocative and thought-provoking now as it did thirty years ago – a film which traps 'a whole era under glass' certainly, but which transcends the age in which it was made by virtue of its singularity and its brilliance, and which has continued to exercise a powerful fascination on successive generations as one of the greatest British films, of any kind, of all time.

Footnote: Donald Cammell killed himself on 23rd April 1996 with a gun-shot wound to the top of the head, in an eerie re-enactment of Turner's fatal shooting in *Performance*.

Decadent Cinema

Isabelle McNeill

Cinema is arguably the most decadent of art forms. A group of strangers come together in a darkened room, not only to lose themselves in fantasy, but also to indulge in communal sensory stimulation. Then there is the seductive passivity of much cinematic viewing pleasure: we lie back and let images and sounds do things to our minds and bodies. We are moved to tears, we are quiveringly frightened, we are convulsed with laughter and we are turned on – all in a public place. Some would argue that watching films is inherently perverse. Scopophilia, voyeurism, narcissism and masochism have all been used by theorists to try to describe and understand the nature of film spectatorship. Whichever perversion – or neurosis – you opt for however, it is undeniable that cinema creates a strange space in between a public sphere of shared experience and a private realm of inner yearnings. Whether or not we are aware of it, we get a kick out of the cinematic spectacle, and that thrill taps into our most secret fantasies and desires.

Pleasures of the Senses

One of the reasons that cinema is so exciting is that it is a multi-sensory experience. Although it only acts directly upon two of the senses, it can evoke others. The sound made by skin touching skin or the smacking of lips around a tasty morsel, a close-up of fingers moving across a textured surface – such visual and sonic clues connote taste and touch in very powerful ways. There is a deeply indulgent pleasure to be had in films that revel in sensation. Many filmmakers have exploited this, from Jean Renoir lingering on the slippery silkiness of water in *Partie de Campagne* (1936) to cinematographer Christopher Doyle's luminous fabrics, shiny surfaces and glowing light in films such as Wong Kar Wai's *2046* (2004). Few however have devoted such obsessive and perverse attention to the tactile as Polish filmmaker Walerian Borowczyk. Recurrent in his work is a fetishistic displacement of the sexual act onto the sensual experience of other things in the world, with the result that the erotic seeps into unusual places. A close-up image of a white-skinned foot pawing wet mud on a shiny, black rubber boot in 'La Marée' (the first segment of *Contes Immoraux*, *Immoral Tales*, 1974) is unexpectedly arousing, and after gazing at repeated shots of large yellow snails sucking like salivating mouths over all kinds of surfaces in *La Bête* (*The Beast*, 1975), you will never again see gastropods in quite the same light (or at least not until you watch Peter Greenaway's *A Zed & Two Noughts*, 1985). Borowczyk's oddest exploration of the eroticism of objects is perhaps the rare short *Une Collection Particulière* (1973). First shown as part of a 'work-in-progress' screening of *Contes Immoraux* in 1973, this collector's cabinet curiosity puts on display an assortment of sexual objects, toys and images. Borowczyk presents the collection (which he himself owned) with lavish attention to touch and rhythm, suggesting an appealing tactility in spite of the often humorous and crude nature of the curios. The creaking and ticking of vintage mechanical toys and old records generates a rhythm that echoes thrusting of a more carnal kind, as well as the movement of film itself (perhaps the ultimate fetish-object for a cinephile). At the same time the camera lingers on the textures of wood, cloth, paper and engravings, from the silk and lace clothing of a masturbating doll, to the ultra-soft velvet case of a smooth ivory dildo. The sense of touch is heightened by the presence, in close-up, of fingertips touching and holding these erotic relics, stimulating our tactile desires as we watch.

Excess

Sensuous cinema can target any erogenous zone, but oral pleasures can be especially debauched in their mingling of touch and taste, sex and food, each indulgence augmenting the other. Perhaps the definitive exploration of decadent devouring is *La Grande Bouffe* (*Blow Out*, Marco Ferreri, 1973), which depicts the suicidal gastronomic orgy of four disillusioned friends. Holed up in an opulent villa with plenty of expensive ingredients, they embark upon a culinary extravaganza with the express aim of dying in the most luxuriously gourmand manner imaginable. The randy (but impotent) Marcello (Marcello Mastroianni) wants to add sex to the menu, but the skinny prostitutes he sends for are soon sickened by the endless consumption of succulent meats, creamy purees and rich puddings. Enter local schoolmistress Andrea (Andréa Ferréol): a voluptuous redhead with pannacotta skin and insatiable appetites, she seems happy to ease their woes as they gorge themselves to death. The grotesque abundance of food finds a luscious counterpart in her ample body and the two are increasingly intermingled. Her bottom forms the mould for chef Ugo's last supper, while Philippe's final mouthful is of pink blancmange breasts Andrea has concocted for him. The real decadence of this film is in its mise-en-scène, feeding the viewer a veritable binge of richly sumptuous colours and elaborate décor. But even if you are drawn to the characters' decadently nihilistic philosophy, you will probably want to eschew overeating as a suicide method.

Ferreri's film shows that in the lascivious excesses of decadent cinema the forces of eros and thanatos are never far apart. This idea permeates the work of Peter Greenaway, whose explorations of corporeal decadence also privilege mise-en-scène, combining the attention to detail and warm milky light of Vermeer paintings with a wealth of luxurious food, fabric and flesh. Greenaway never shirks from probing the absurdity of bodies programmed for sex and death. Perhaps the most violently gastronomic of his films is *The Cook, the Thief, His Wife and Her Lover* (1989), which whips up an impressive grande bouffe of its own, its action unfolding among the kitchens, toilets and groaning tables of a gourmet restaurant. The suspense is almost unbearable as the eponymous thief, a brutal thug, catches on to his wife's fervent affair with a quietly bookish lover. But the narrative dwindles before the outrageous and disturbing set pieces, the frame crammed with comestibles and rampant or mortified flesh. Stomach-turning in the extreme, and seen as an allegory for Thatcherism, the film reveals the chaos of unbridled appetites, be they for power, sex or cuisine.

Performance and Spectacle

If décor has so much potential for decadence in cinema, it is in part because of the fantastical possibilities created by setting a scene. From Marlene Dietrich's glittering sequins and top hat in *Der Blaue Engel* (*The Blue Angel*, Sternberg, 1930) to the elaborate masks in *Eyes Wide Shut* (Kubrick, 1999), theatrical props provide liberation from our everyday identities as well as the vicarious thrill of exhibitionism. Nicolas Roeg and Donald Cammell's *Performance* (1970) brings the theme into its title and enacts the dizzying possibilities of role-play in its narrative. Chas (James Fox) is a violent gangster who takes refuge in a room belonging to the charismatic Mr. Turner (Mick Jagger), a former rock star in need of new excitement. The two men seem poles apart but Chas becomes drawn into Turner's drug-fuelled, chaotic world and in experimenting with the androgynous wigs and blouses of rock 'n' roll style his sense of self begins to waver. Forget the explicit sex scenes with Anita Pallenberg, the climactic moment of audio-visual pleasure for the viewer is the performance of *Memo from Turner*, which combines a fabulously cool rock song with the dreamlike – or nightmarish – blurring of the two men's identities.

Dressing up is not only about freedom from the self, it can also be relished as sheer spectacle. Nowhere is decadence more spectacularly explored than in Max Ophüls' 1955 film *Lola Montès*. Forced by circumstances and a mercenary ring-master to act out the scandalous and titillating tale of her life as dancer and courtesan, Lola endures the lecherous gaze of the audience as she bares her soul in a lavish acrobatic show, complete with horses, colourful tableaux and a final death-defying leap. As the ringmaster's narration melts into Lola's own flashbacks, we lose track of the distinction between circus performance and life, poignantly revealing her whole existence as an exotic masquerade leading to an inevitable decline. The overbearing CinemaScope frame and vibrant colours are breathtaking, while the sadomasochistic overtones lend a dark twist: the sadistic image of the ringmaster cracking his whip to incite the faltering Lola to continue her tale aligns us uncomfortably with the salivating circus audience, for we cannot deny that we too are enjoying the spectacle of her descent.

Unbridled Desire

There is something irresistibly erotic about uncovering shameful secrets. The virtuous ice-maiden suspected of harbouring a wild and disruptive desire beneath the cool surface has been a powerful fantasy since well before Freud – think of the jaded Valmont tormented by lust for pious, prudish Mme de Tourvel. Coldness and detachment leave a void that cries out to be filled with fantasy. Hence the wicked appeal of Catherine Deneuve, a more decadent star than Monroe or Bardot precisely because of her butter-wouldn't-melt appearance. In films from Polanski's *Repulsion* (1965) where she plays an uptight young lady driven to murderous deed by repressed desire to François Ozon's kitsch musical *8 Femmes* (*8 Women*, 2002), where a catfight with Fanny Ardant turns into one of cinema's sexiest kisses, Deneuve embodies the well-groomed blonde with a tempestuous inner life. The most iconic example is Luis Buñuel's *Belle de Jour* (1967), in which Deneuve plays Severine, a reserved married woman obsessed with masochistic fantasies, who takes up daytime prostitution to satisfy her cravings and curiosity. Buñuel wisely uses pared-down luxury rather than excess in his mise-en-scène, recognising that fantasy scenes in which Severine is brutally horsewhipped or pelted with mud are all the more pleasurable for their violation of a restrained and orderly world.

Like other surrealists, Buñuel realised that letting repressed desire burst forth on screen made for exciting art, as in the infamous scene where a woman sucks a giant statue's toe in *L'Age d'Or* (*The Golden Age*, Buñuel and Dalí, 1930). But shocking surreality is not the only way for cinema to lead us into uncharted sexual territories. The documentary-style cinema of Monika Treut takes us into the backrooms and bars that other cameras ignore, delighting in the widest possible panoply of sexual proclivities. In *Die Jungfrauenmaschine* (*Virgin Machine*, 1988), a young journalist sets out to research an article on romantic love. Reaching a dead end in Hamburg, she moves to San Francisco where she discovers a thriving queer scene and undreamt of erotic pleasures. Once again it is a performance that provides the most absorbing moment of the film. We watch Dorothee (Ina Blum) watching the mesmerising Ramona perform a strip-tease in drag, mimicking a dirty machismo that culminates in an unforgettable masturbation mime with a beer bottle. Of course following a character's sexual awakening will always be ripe with potential for decadent pleasures (see also Anaïs Nin's sensual journey of discovery in *Henry and June*, Kaufman, 1990), but a supplementary gratification in *Die Jungfrauenmaschine* is a purely cinematic one: the delight of watching the ghosts of

Greta Garbo and Marlene Dietrich reappear in Blum's languidly expressive face, rendered in dreamily luxurious monochrome by cinematographer Elfi Mikesch.

A Dark Room, a Big Screen

Something many decadent films share is a fascination with cinema itself. Yet as we move towards the end of the first decade of the twenty-first century, cinema has become something relatively marginal and displaced, as increasingly we watch films on dvds and mobile phones. This only serves to confirm cinema as the one truly decadent mode of movie viewing – with all the delicious and dangerous ambivalence the word decadence contains, flicking as it does between toxic decline and life-affirming hedonism. On the one hand multiplexes surround their ever-shrinking screens with multiple layers of franchised and packaged consumerism, while town centre cinemas are transformed into bingo halls and sex clubs. On the other hand, the cinema theatre still persists, albeit often derelict and struggling, poised perilously on the edge of contemporary corporate-dominated experience. As we lurch between wild selfishness and spending sprees and puritanical self-abnegation, cinemas remain the finest place to indulge – and share – in the magnificently dubious spectacle of decadence.

The Child

Nicholas Royle

The light was just beginning to fade when I found the shop.

I'd been wandering around the 'Northern Quarter' for much of the afternoon. When I last lived in Manchester, in the 1970s, the Northern Quarter didn't exist. It was a grey area between Shude Hill and Ancoats then. A post-industrial hinterland of broken windows and empty warehouses. Tib Street was full of pet shops; it smelled like a hamster's cage. There was the odd record shop, perhaps, but nothing much going on. I left for London in 1982 and didn't start coming back until the 90s. I had no reason to visit Oldham Street or anywhere else in the Northern Quarter, as the area started to become known towards the end of that decade. Businesses opened in refurbished buildings, the odd café or bar. Crafts places, wholefood. By the middle of the so-called noughties, when I moved back, the area had changed a fair bit.

I was trying to reconnect, find places I recognised. It was either that or get on with decorating the spare room, as I had friends coming at the weekend.

The smells of straw and pet food had drifted away from Tib Street. The new boutiques that had sprung up were filled either with urban streetwear that didn't seem quite me, or with stuff I'd owned in the 1970s: sheepskin-lined denim jackets, plastic Adidas kit bags, parkas with fake-fur trim. The bookshops on Shude Hill didn't have the allure they'd once possessed. The guys behind the counter were probably the same blokes from twenty-five years earlier. They were certainly wearing the same clothes, and didn't look like they'd washed them.

I was about to head back to my flat in Whalley Range

when I spotted a window deep in shade on the wrong side of Lever Street. A line of videos, couple of DVDs. *The Texas Chain Saw Massacre*. Hitchcock's *Frenzy*. *Emmanuelle*. A naked bulb could be seen burning inside. Low wattage. I tried the door, descended a flight of steps. My nostrils flared at the damp and something else, an animal smell. Out of the gloom came a flash of white teeth, a glistening tongue. I leapt backwards.

'Baz, sit!' said a voice from somewhere.

The Alsatian sat back on its haunches, meek as anything.

Dogs scare the crap out of me.

'Sorry, mate.'

The speaker was a tall dark-haired man in his early twenties. He unfolded his insectile body from the stool where he'd been sitting behind an antediluvian cash register and stood, albeit with a pronounced stoop on account of the low ceiling.

'Stay, Baz,' he said to the dog, then looked at me. 'Are you looking for anything in particular?'

His polite manner was a surprise. I stared blankly at a shelf of exploitation films, only half familiar with the titles.

'Just browsing,' I said.

'Let me know if I can help,' he offered, returning to his stool and picking up a smouldering cigarette.

I looked around. He had an interesting if limited selection. There was an attempt at categorisation but it was no more rigid than his shelving system and certain titles had ended up in the wrong place. Different formats – VHS, DVD – were mixed in together. Apart from a torn *Pink Flamingos* poster, the walls were bare and cracked. Even with my enthusiasm for some of the stock, I found the place depressing.

'There's more stuff through there,' the young man said behind me.

I turned. He was pointing to a plastic-strip curtain hanging in a doorway.

'Your adult section?' I guessed.

'Kind of.' He stubbed out his cigarette and stood up again.

Close to, he really was remarkably tall. I wanted to tell him to stay sitting: it would be kinder to his back. But he was already pushing aside the rainbow-coloured plastic strips. I followed him through. The smell back here was more pungent. The damp was eating away at the plaster, which was crumbling behind flaking paintwork. The decay felt like it might be contagious.

The back room did contain adult material, but not of the usual kind. Instead of videos labelled Playboy or Electric Blue, this guy had stacks of Russ Meyer films and quasi-innocent 70s softcore of the type once screened constantly on Channel 5. Lesbian vampire flicks. *Confessions* movies. Dropped in among the dross were mainstream films with notable erotic content: *Bad Timing, Daughters of Darkness, The Draughtsman's Contract*. I flicked through the Russ Meyer titles. These were the kind of films I'd had to leave Manchester to find. Sex scenes I'd seen on TV as a boy had been witnessed in arse-clenching embarrassment as my mother fiddled with the pleats of her skirt and my father tutted loudly enough to be heard over the soundtrack. I rarely got to see films on my own, but when I did, by sneaking downstairs after my mother had gone to bed and my father was on a night shift, and I was lucky enough to catch something worthwhile, it meant all the more. I stored up fleeting glimpses of nudity. The naked rear view of the headmaster's wife disappearing down a long corridor in *If . . .* the white globes of her bottom ghostly in the moonlight. Cybil Shepherd's shy disrobing, watched by awestruck admirers, in *The Last Picture Show*. Neither scene had actually aroused me, so much as awakened in me a sense of wonder coupled with an equally potent sense of guilt. After staying up late to watch *The Vampire Lovers*, I checked the hamster's cage as part of my routine before sneaking back up to bed. The hamster was lying very still in the wrong part of the cage. I took it out and it felt different in my hand, cold and heavy. I put it back and the following day had to pretend that I hadn't known. Overcompensating, I insisted on burying the remains in the garden. At the back of one of the flower beds, past the remains of my father's latest bonfire, I knelt down and dug a little hole with the trowel, then pressed the body of the hamster as deep into the soil as it would go. For some time I felt uncomfortably guilty about having knowingly left the hamster lying dead in its cage overnight.

My illicit late-night screenings were undoubtedly what led to my becoming a film journalist. I went to London to go to university, then narrowly avoided getting thrown off the course for never showing up. When I wasn't in a Wardour Street preview theatre or catching up on lost sleep after an all-nighter at the Scala in King's Cross, I was ensconced in the college newspaper office in the union building writing up film reviews on a golfball typewriter.

'Some of this stuff's pretty rare,' the young guy said. He had taken a few videos off a shelf and was blowing the dust off them. The title of one of them caught my eye and it was like spotting the twinkle of gold in a prospector's pan.

Thundercrack!

I'd seen it only once, at the Scala, as part of a double bill. The other half of the programme had been wiped from my memory. That was the effect of *Thundercrack!*, the most outrageous and depraved film I'd ever seen. It was also funny, weird and breathtakingly erotic. It turned me on like no other film I'd ever seen. I knew people who swore by the love scene in *Don't Look Now*. Others who got off on *Ai No Corrida*. I even had a friend who said he sat through Cronenberg's *Crash* with a 90-minute boner. The only film that did it for me was *Thundercrack!*

'I didn't know this was available,' I said.

'It's not,' said the tall guy, with a little smile. 'Have you ever seen it?'

I told him about the Scala. 'You're too young probably even to have heard about it,' I added.

'My dad used to screen *Thundercrack!* in Manchester in the 80s,' he said. 'My name's Joe, by the way. Joe Hoffman.'

We shook hands. I told him my name.

'Your dad wasn't . . .' I began.

'Anthony Hoffman, yeah.'

Anthony Hoffman had been a face on the Manchester scene in the 80s. He'd known people at Granada TV and Factory Records and Savoy Books and so on, and was often seen at the same parties as Tony Wilson or David Britton.

'How's he doing these days?' I asked.

'Not so good.'

Unsure what to say, I looked at the photocopied notes on the back of the video box.

'So he used to screen this?' I said, eventually.

'Yeah, he'd hire a 16mm print and book a little back room somewhere. Word would get out and the place would be rammed. He even rented the Apollo once or twice.'

'I had no idea,' I said.

The Apollo had been where I'd gone to gigs. I tried to imagine this guy's father hiring it for a film screening. *Thundercrack!* was directed in 1975 by Curt McDowell and written by McDowell in collaboration with underground filmmaker George Kuchar. A group of characters are forced to spend the night in a big old house where they have sex with each other in a variety of different ways and permutations. Copulation, masturbation, ejaculation – it's all in there and pretty much non-stop. As Kim Newman writes in *Nightmare Movies*, 'The film is too doom haunted to appeal to a gay or straight porno audience, and yet its two hours plus of penetrations, perversions and come-shots make it all but unbearable for anybody else.'

Obviously, I disagree with him.

'The number of times his screenings were raided by the police,' Joe said. 'Ironic, really.'

'Why ironic?' I asked, a bit too quickly.

His only response was to light another cigarette.

'The 80s were James Anderton's heyday,' I remarked.

'Yeah. I don't know how many prints of *Thundercrack!* his lot must have ended up with. My dad told me he never got them back.'

'Maybe they burned them?' I suggested, remembering the frequent bonfires my father lit in our back garden.

'Yeah, maybe.' Joe prodded a patch of loose plaster on the wall with one of his Converse baseball boots. It fell off and a large spider scuttled away. 'I think he was deliberately trying to wind the police up – and succeeding.'

'Wouldn't have been difficult,' I said. Not with the chief constable being a self-declared born-again Christian. Although I'd been living in London at the time, I'd been aware of Anderton's increasingly bizarre pronouncements. It was hard not to be, given what my father did for a living. The mid-80s were strange times. On the one hand you had Nicolas Roeg, co-director of the splendidly amoral *Performance*, making TV ads warning of the danger of AIDS, and on the other there was James Anderton, God's copper, suggesting that people with AIDS were 'swirling around in a human cesspit of their own making'.

'I gather he lives in Sale with his wife now,' Joe said. 'Does a lot of charity work. I imagine he's doing better than my dad anyway, who lives in a nursing home in Old Trafford. Sits there staring out of the window. On one side of the building you've got a park full of dogshit, pissheads and other assorted miserable cunts, and on the other you've got Old Trafford. Pretty much the same view, considering my dad's a lifelong Blue.'

He stared at me with anger in his eyes. I held his gaze for a moment, thinking of my own father.

'How much is this?' I asked him.

'Ten quid, mate.'

As we left the back room I noticed another open doorway on the other side of the shop.

'This place goes on for ever,' I said.

'I've got more space than I can fill, and more than I can afford, more to the point. I'm looking to sublet that side. Dead cheap. Fifty quid a week. Sixty tops. If you know anyone . . .'

'It's tempting,' I said, before I could stop myself.

'Really? What would you sell?'

'Nothing. I'm thinking of starting up a little magazine. A film magazine. Something small, subsidised.'

'Cool.'

'I don't suppose I'll do it,' I said, waving my hands as if I could waft the idea away. 'I wrote some pieces for *8020*, which promptly folded. I approached *City Life*, about doing some film stuff for them, the week before the *Guardian* closed them down.'

'Do you write for anyone else?'

'I write for the nationals and *Sight & Sound*, but I wanted to do something locally. I grew up here and now I've moved back. I want to fit in. I want to belong again. Do you know what I mean?'

'Yeah, yeah,' he nodded, reaching for another fag.

I handed him a tenner for the video and he started hunting around for a bag.

'It's all right,' I said.

As he passed me the video he said, 'Think about the space. I could let you have it for fifty.'

I smiled. 'Nice talking to you,' I said, and moved towards the steps up to the door.

'Wait,' he said, rummaging around in a drawer.

He came over to me with a DVD in an unmarked case.

'Have a look at that,' he said, pressing it into my hands.

I asked him what it was.

'Something my dad shot. I think you'll find it interesting.'

'OK,' I said. 'How much do you want for it?'

'Nothing. Borrow it. Watch it and bob back with it at some

point. There's no hurry.' He smiled uncertainly. 'Keep it to yourself, though.'

I promised that I would, then turned my back on him and climbed the stairs to the street. I looked back through the window and saw him bending down to give the dog a stroke or a pat or whatever it is you do with dogs if you don't want them to bite your face off.

I headed back to the multistorey where I'd parked the car. Leave the ground in Manchester and you can see the hills. I unlocked the car, but instead of getting in I wandered over to the concrete balustrade and looked out over east Manchester at the mountains in the distance, only ten or fifteen miles away. The snow that had fallen a week earlier glowed in the twilight.

My father had often taken me walking in the Peaks at weekends, when he wasn't working.

He did shift work.

He was a copper, my dad. His time on the Greater Manchester force coincided with Anderton's reign as Chief Constable.

When I got back to the flat, I had a bite to eat, then installed myself in front of the TV with a beer, and slipped *Thundercrack!* into the VCR. I was only ten minutes into it when the phone went.

The machine answered and as soon as I heard Simone's voice, I hurriedly picked up the remote and switched off the TV. Simone was history, but the sound of her voice still managed to make me feel guilty about watching something like *Thundercrack!* Without even being in the room. Without even being in the *same city*. Simone was one of the reasons why I left London. And why I would probably never go back. Not until I knew she was either safely attached to someone else or living in another country.

There was nothing much to her message. Could I call her when I got a chance? But I knew that if I picked up the phone

I'd get an earful. The same old questions. The same distortion of the truth.

I stopped the tape. I couldn't watch it now, not with Simone's voice in my head. I picked up the unmarked DVD-R that Joe Hoffman had lent me. I put it in the machine but it wouldn't play. Nothing doing, no menu screen or anything. I tried it in my laptop with the same result. Frustrated, I went to bed, thinking that I would take it back the next day. The fact that it wouldn't play naturally made me even more interested in finding out what was meant to be on it.

In the morning, however, I realised that finishing the spare bedroom had to take priority. Otherwise my guests wouldn't be able to move for wet paint. While I worked I daydreamed about the magazine I wanted to start up. As the hours went by and the walls got whiter, my plans acquired more depth and detail, but at the same time departed further and further from practical reality until I reached a point at which I acknowledged it simply wasn't going to happen. There would be no magazine and I wouldn't be renting Joe Hoffman's spare office space. But I still needed to go back to his shop to query the DVD. When I finished painting, however, it was too late and the next day my friends arrived from London. We had a good weekend; a lot of food and drink was consumed. These were my closest friends and it was good to see them again. I was gratified that they had come up so soon to see me in Manchester. It was the next week before I could get back to the shop on Lever Street, and when I did, I found the window bare and the door locked.

I pushed and pulled at the handle and knocked on the glass. I even got down on my hands and knees and called Joe's name through the letter box, but the shop was empty. No stock, no dog, no Joe. As I stepped back into the road and craned my neck to look at the upper storeys of the building, a police car cruised by. The driver slowed down; he and his colleague stared at me until I turned and walked away.

When the cop car had gone I turned back. The shop had never had a name or a board outside and there weren't any other signs of life in the immediate vicinity. I walked round the block and tried in a couple of CD shops, but neither Joe's name nor my description of his shop rang any bells. I asked in Vinyl Exchange, where they sold videos and DVDs in the basement. Nice folk but no joy. I couldn't think where else to try. Shops like Joe's came and went and these days the trend was definitely towards closing down rather than opening up, even in the Northern Quarter.

I drove back through Hulme, which had changed more radically than the Northern Quarter in the years I'd been away. Gone were the concrete crescents and the Aaben Cinema, where I'd seen what I'd thought was the most outré cinema Manchester had had to offer in the early 80s. Fassbinder. Waters. Wenders. It was nice to think I'd been wrong, but frustrating not to have any way of finding out what was on that DVD.

I heard the yelp of a siren behind me and instinctively went to pull over to let them pass, but when I looked in the mirror I saw a police car with no intention of overtaking.

Apparently I'd been speeding. I protested that I couldn't have been doing more than 35 and I got the full sarcastic treatment. *Is this your car, sir? Do you know what the speed limit is, sir? Have you been drinking at all, sir?* I thought about mentioning my dad, but I could see from his small, flat, joyless eyes that there was no point. I let him give me a ticket just so he'd fuck off.

When I got back behind the wheel, instead of turning left for Whalley Range, I kept going towards Old Trafford. Somewhere in this Escher diagram of pebble-dash council blocks and blood-redbrick terraced housing was Joe's dad, the legendary Anthony Hoffman, sitting staring into space – or at a shitty park. I drove around for half an hour but succeeded only in making myself question the wisdom of having moved back to Manchester. How did I even know that Joe's description of the nursing home's location was accurate. There'd been something of the performer about him, as if he'd been sitting in his lair waiting for an audience to come along. Maybe he was a fantasist and not even related to Hoffman. Or maybe you had to ease yourself out of the nursing home window on a mechanical platform to glimpse either a patch of grass or the white Meccano exoskeleton of the football ground. Maybe he was as full of shit as a lot of people had said his father had been.

I gave up and drove home. At one point a police car seemed to be following me. Just as I was about to make an unnecessary left turn to make sure, it took a turning off to the right. In my rear-view mirror I saw the passenger's face at the side window. It was impossible to say whether he was looking at me or just watching the traffic.

That night I lay in bed unable to sleep as I tried to work out my next move. I was in the middle of formulating a surprisingly simple plan that I decided was bound to succeed when I fell asleep and in the morning could remember not even the slightest detail. I showered quickly and drove into town, parking close to the Apollo Theatre and walking to St Peter's Square. I'd reasoned that Central Library might be able to provide me with a list of care homes in Old Trafford, but when I got inside the reference section I started by looking up Anthony Hoffman in the newspaper catalogue. There was tons of stuff. The illegal screenings of *Thundercrack!* at the Apollo were mentioned. I flicked through bound copies of the *Evening News* and scanned the nationals on microfilm for more in-depth reports. One story in the *Guardian* listed the gear the police were supposed to have confiscated from Hoffman along with a 16mm copy of *Thundercrack!*, namely two 8mm movie cameras, a professional-standard 16mm Bolex and enough film stock to make a dozen full-length features. The article quoted an *Evening News* journalist, John Cavanagh, who claimed that Hoffman and his colleagues were legitimate filmmakers, who, contrary to the story put out by the police, were embarked on a mission to clean up Manchester.

Intrigued by this, I looked up Cavanagh and found a whole bunch of references to pieces of his in the *Evening News* that suddenly stopped appearing around the time he was quoted in the *Guardian* story.

Cavanagh was easy to track down. He was in the book. There were a few listings under Cavanagh, J, so I went for the one in the most down-at-heel district and got lucky. He agreed to meet me and suggested Spearmint Rhino. I wasn't sure I could handle that, so he named a pub in Harpurhey I'd never heard of. Of course, when I got there, it was a strip joint, so I was vying with three naked girls for Cavanagh's attention. Their bellies were bigger than their boobs, but he didn't seem to mind.

'Call me Cav,' was all I could get out of him for the first ten minutes.

I went to the gents and had a bit of trouble finding it. The first door I tried down the darkened corridor that had been indicated led straight outside. Eventually I found it and stood staring at the cracked tiles wondering what on earth I was doing there. On my way back I got Cav another pint, determined that I would wring some information out of him.

You could tell he'd been a decent-looking young man, but had let himself go quite badly. Pouch-like bags under his eyes, grubby shirt buttoned tightly over a drinker's paunch. The girls left the stage for a minute and I pressed him. He'd not written for the paper, he confirmed, since being quoted in the *Guardian*.

'Someone told me,' he said eventually, 'that Hoffman had other stuff confiscated, stuff that was never reported. Films he'd shot on Super-8 at parties in south Manchester. Powerful types, you know. Councillors, magistrates, justices of the so-called peace.'

'Did he ever show this stuff?' I asked him.

'That's unconfirmed.'

'The police had a particular incentive to keep those films out of circulation, then?'

Cav shrugged, then brightened as the girls reappeared.

'Where's Hoffman now?' I asked.

'Some home near Old Trafford.'

'Name?'

His fingers were splayed on his stained jeans as he watched the routine.

I took a twenty out of my wallet and folded it into his hand.

He told me a name and the very next second there was a commotion from the bar area. I heard someone shout 'Police!' and I leapt from my seat and ran to the darkened corridor, where I pushed open the door to the car park. I didn't look back as I ran.

Driving back into town, I took the DVD-R out of my inside pocket and looked at it. The purple underside reflected a rainbow of colours that reminded me of the curtain in Joe's shop. As I waited for the lights to change at the bottom of Cheetham Hill, I wondered if this simple plastic disc was worth all the trouble I was getting into. Then, as a police car pulled silently alongside and I felt my heart rate quicken, I thought about what might be on the disc and why Joe had given it to me. Perhaps because I'd told him I wrote for the papers. It took all the self-control I had not to turn and check out the uniforms in the next lane. I couldn't be sure which cops were after me and which were not. The lights changed and they veered off to the right. I went the other way.

It turned out the place in Old Trafford where Hoffman was holed up was a lot closer to the park than it was to the football ground. It also turned out that there was a dark blue Cavalier parked outside the front entrance with three burly-looking plainclothes men sitting inside it. Still fifty yards away, I backed up and turned around. Admittedly, performing this manoeuvre was tantamount to winding my window down and shouting 'Come and get me, coppers', but it was marginally less risky than carrying on and driving right past them. As far as I could tell, no one followed me back to Chester Road. At the Chorlton turn-off I thought about going straight on to Sale, but resisted that temptation and turned left, heading for home.

I parked two streets away and approached on foot. There was no car outside, and the door hadn't been forced. I climbed the stairs and everything seemed normal. Surely I was being paranoid. The raid on the strip joint was routine and I'd got a ticket for driving in excess of the speed limit. Simple as that.

I unlocked the door to my flat and saw that it wasn't, in fact, as simple as that.

The place had been turned over. Looking at it with cold detachment, which I found I could do, in a looking-down-from-above sort of way, what they had done was quite impressive. Every movable surface was at a new angle to all others. Upended cupboards, overturned drawers. The mattress had been slit open with a knife, pillows eviscerated. Every book or CD or DVD or video that had been on a shelf was now on the floor creating a restless sea of plastic and paper. I was reminded of the Paul Nash painting of downed German warplanes in a Cowley field, *Totes Meer*.

There was a smell in the flat, too, that reminded me of Joe Hoffman's shop. It wasn't damp. It was the animal smell. They had come with dogs.

The TV, DVD player, VCR and my computer were gone, as if to make me think I'd been burgled, yet they'd left no signs of forced entry. It was this detail that made me realise they were laughing at me, but it was a laugh that bared the sharpest of teeth.

I left the flat without bothering to lock the door and walked the long way around to where I'd parked the car. I felt dissociated from reality as I drove over to Sale. James Anderton

wasn't the only ex-Manchester copper who'd retired there. I
parked across the road from my father's semi, its dimensions
presumably much less generous than those of Anderton's
place, wherever that was, perhaps on The Avenue or somewhere like that. I tried to imagine crossing the road and walking up the path. Knocking on the door. But I knew it wasn't
going to happen. I was curious, though. I wondered if my dad
had a DVD player, or maybe an old projector and a little pile
of film cans. I wondered what went on behind those arti-
ficially leaded windows. I fingered the contents of my inside
pocket and started the car engine. The house grew smaller in
my rear-view mirror and I rejoined Washway Road, then
slipped on to the M60, heading in an anticlockwise direction.
Turning the clock back, I thought. Ha-ha. It was getting
towards rush hour, but the traffic moved smoothly enough. I
got off on to the M67 and was held up in a long queue to join
the road to Glossop. At the Glossop turn-off, I kept going,
through Hollingworth and Tintwistle. The first of the reser-
voirs appeared below me to the right. At Crowden I pulled off
the road and drove in a semi-circle to reach the car park.

The first paths were easy, nothing more than gentle diag-
onals up the side of the hill. I soon left the path and struck out
for the quarry. There are two quarries at Crowden: a small one
at the back of the hill only half way up it, and a much larger
one right at the top. It was the latter I was making for and
once I had negotiated the scree slope I found myself having to
grab handfuls of springy grass to help pull myself up a near
vertical section. I was breathing heavily, but the tension that
had knotted my muscles in the car while still in Manchester
was easing. I could feel my heart beating as fast as a child's.
Suddenly into my mind came the first X films I'd snuck into
at the cinema, a double bill of David Cronenberg's *Shivers* and
Rabid at the only picture house there had been in Altrincham
in the 1970s. The slope above me began to level out, or more
accurately, I could see nothing beyond where it stopped, so I

knew I was near the top. The first film I could remember my parents taking me to was *Kes*. I remembered the contrast between the sense of freedom in the long shots of the kestrel's free flight and the stark finality of the shallow grave.

I pulled myself over the last ridge and dropped down into the scoured basin of the quarry.

My father had brought me here several times and no matter how much tension there was between us, it all fell away in the hush of the quarry. The towering sandstone bluffs like the walls of a ruined cathedral. The enormous, unmoving boulders dotted about. A very particular quality of stillness. As if this was a place in which man and nature had reached some kind of settlement. I climbed up the far side and walked up on to the moor. I turned for a moment and looked to the west, towards Manchester. I felt fully removed from the city and everyone in it. Turning my back, I considered the moor. In the distance was a trig point, beyond that and to the right the radio transmitter at Black Hill, where my father had taken me bog-trotting. I began walking. The going was soft – peat, heather, tussocky grass – but I covered a lot of ground. I walked hard for ten or fifteen minutes. I started to run. I felt free. Slowly the radio transmitter slid around to the left in relation to the trig point. When the two were aligned, I stopped, panting for breath, and knelt down. I took the DVD out of my inside pocket, still inside its clear plastic wallet, and inserted it into the damp, peaty earth, which accepted it as easily and smoothly as if it were a machine designed for that very purpose.

When I looked up I saw a pair of peregrine falcons in the distance, soaring and swooping over the quarry.

Hooked on Classics

Michael Bywater

If music be the food of love, it be also the food of harsh
sex, food of the flying swoon, of the needle and the rich
dream-laden smoke; of languor and anger and road rage and
triumphalism and that most decadent of all false sensibilities:
the feeling of limitless power or even, may god help us, One-
ness With The Universe. Drugs? Sex? Perfumes? *Food?* Lordy
lordy, music is even the food of *food* and there's no plush fig
sucked from the glistening flesh of a (she's drugged, dears;
opium probably; *she* doesn't mind) young duchess gone
awhoring that can half touch what goes on in even the most
innocent, the most uncorrupt (but never incorruptible;
nobody is *that*) mind under the influence of music.

I don't mean that terrible stuff, mind. Not the thud and
whop of music stripped of all that makes music music: complexity, variation, tension, the building and relaxing and building and building and then final – *aaah* – release of energy. No;
that music (nk nk nk-nk-nk, nk nk nk-nk-nk until your head
rots). I mean *music* music.

We need to chop the word 'decadent' here. Do we mean
something fallen into decay,something gone irredeemably
wrong – a city crumbling with weeds growing through, a
civilisation at last gasp, a marriage corrupted beyond all
speech or embrace, a life derailed into an empty siding – or do
we mean an exultation in those indulgences of the flesh
which exist solely to *be* indulged? For the former, we have
little to say. Merely the endless whining of the *old*, the *past it*,
the Golden-Agers who have existed since the Golden Age
itself: grim grey withershins in need of Viagra for the soul,

keening endlessly for imaginary days when everything was better. But for the latter (the decadence of chaises-longues in darkened rooms, virgins to despoil, the luxury of musk and ambergris drifting on the air, everything somehow slippery, or to be made slippery, actions unconfined by consequence or consent) then music is the most decadent art of all, and the most fleshly since it stirs that most fleshly of all our organs, the brain itself.

Music is about *nothing*. It has no redeeming connection with reality. When composers try to describe things – the plight of the Soviet people, storms followed by tweety-bird sunshine, *Fingal's* fucking *Cave* – it's just embarrassing. But when music dissociates from the hard physical edges of reality and becomes itself, then unpredictable decadences infect even the most pedestrian of brains. See that middle-manager, waving his hand surreptitiously to the Brahms? His life is orderly, up-to-date, everything accounted for, but as the last movement slides into its Dionysian 6/8 *he is somewhere else*, out of control, exultant, breathing sulphur, riding something, something that bucks and sweats, something he's *holding down* . . . for as long as it lasts, he is *ecstatic*, and there is nothing more decadent than ecstasy. In ecstasy, we are *out of it* and if the opposite of decadence is the smack of firm government (well *of course* it is) then ecstasy is the Enemy of the State: never mind organic peroxides in Snapple bottles, we should be banning music on aeroplanes, *even in peoples' heads*. iPods? We don' need no steenkin iPods. I once went out with a woman who could come on demand, contact-free. It was like *Deep Throat* except, in her case, it was in her head. Music can live there, too, and when you run the end of *Götterdämmerung* in your *own personal head* neither scanners nor goons, not Tony Blair or George Bush or Osama bin Laden, not any of the hordes of jobsworths and peckerheads who are after your vote, your compliance, your hand-luggage or your mind can get *anywhere near you*. You're going down with the gods in an

incandescent apocalypse, riding into the fire having humped
Brünnhilde (all that pan-Germanic breast and striding thigh,
helmet knocked aside and hair streaming) and possibly her
horse Gräne into the bargain, tastes being what they are and
the music world being what it is.

Never mind the dumb flat-eyed little twazzock plugged
into his earbuds. We don't care about *him*; the stuff *he's* been
sold is pre-marketed as decadence – 'listen to this drivel and
annoy your parents' – and is no more the real thing than Ainsley
Harriott powdered chowder is food. No; look over there at
the little attorney with her pretty hair, listening to Messiaen,
coiling in her chair as she is *had* by the *Joie du Sang des Etoiles*.
Why is she breathing like that? Why are her lips parted like
that? *You* can't do that to her. Nobody can. But music can do
it; does it every day. And does it unpredictably. God knows
what Sebastian Bach had in mind when he set his *Et in
unum Spiritum Sanctum* for two twining sopranos but since he
married one – Anna Magdalena – and got into trouble for
having other ones Up In The Organ Loft, it's fair to say he
knew as much about their bodies and what they could *do* with
them as he did about their voices or indeed the sinuous coil-
ings of purest intellect which summon a Holy Ghost of a
polymorphous perversity that, fully apprehended, would send
a bishop running to the brothel in search of a simulacrum.

No; neither purity nor holiness is a defence against the
absolute vital necessity to have Emma Kirkby naked at
an open window overlooking the Grand Canal singing the
Pulchra es from Monteverdi's *Vespers* . . . despite the sad truth
that no man could do, nor any woman accommodate, the
things that the music makes one *want* to do (while simultaneously weeping for the honey-dripping love of the 'Song
of Songs', which is Solomon's).

Violence? We got violence, man. Let a honking politician
or a strangulated, slogan-mouthing PRO show their neck
anywhere near me in the last movement of Bruckner's 8th

symphony and I will bite it to shreds; here's music to be conducted not with a baton but a length of freshly-ripped-out spine, and a torn artery, maybe a sinew or two, hanging from the blood-smeared mouth. Mahler's for running down the street naked, cackling, slashing wildly with a new Feather 'Artist Club' Japanese steel straight razor; *any* Palestrina is soaked in opiates, just as, somewhere behind Nikhil Banerjee, as he plays Raag Manomanjari, there is a cloud of oud smoke, rich as a woman's musk, and – look! here she comes! a red-headed 6'2" nonparametric statistician, slicked with agar, and you've never seen her before but *this is the moment of reuniting*, the one in all those dreams from which you wake, your eyes wet with tears (and who remembers at moments like this that the *music* is in the hands of a chap who looks a bit like a GP, playing an instrument designed by a madman, an instrument which incorporates, as an essential component, a *pumpkin?*)

Oh, *women*. They fill the music-maddened mind. Organ music. The Gabler organ in Weingarten Abbey: there behind the *vox humana* she's hiding, hot, dusty, whispering, *exhausted*, but we'll find her, yes we will. Your man again: Sebastian: his great c minor Passacaglia: we can manage on our own, but to *really* play it you'd need a woman (naked but for a lynx stole) and syrup of mandragora. But you can't take it beyond Ligeti's *Volumina*: the organ-geek listening to *that* one (specs, rubber-soled brogues, fish paste sandwiches) is, in the reality of his mind where all reality is constructed, enfolded in the Great Platonic Vulva, soft and civety and warm. The vagina dialogues. If the womb is where we all secretly want to return, music is what sends us there, too, rendering us useless to society, useless to the Department of Homeland Security, useless to the Halifax Bank.

Sex and violence, and fantasies going so far beyond any thinkable sex or imaginable violence, or any happiness which may exist or grief which may lie in story: music drips its transcendental signifieds upon us and we fall into desuetude, unable even to apprehend our compulsions and desires under its languorous inflaming powers, let alone to name them. Keep your trivia, your cocaine and your wines, your Havanas and furs and sturgeons' eggs; here is music lies a world of gods and sex and swords, of death and revenge, of amber and diamonds and the icy clarity of mathematics; here the planets whirl and hum and women fall back gratefully among the rocks and velvet and we are heroes and angelic, omnipotent and comforted and the stars proceed, as they must proceed, through the pale frozen canticles of infinite space . . .

Oh yes. We are, do you see, utterly *out of reach* under music's enchantment, and that's most decadent of all, that's when a man is an island: an isle . . .

> full of noises,
> Sounds, and sweet airs, that give delight and hurt not.
> Sometimes a thousand twangling instruments
> Will hum about mine ears; and sometimes voices
> That, if I then had waked after long sleep,
> Will make me sleep again; and then, in dreaming,
> The clouds methought would open, and show riches,
> Ready to drop upon me, that when I waked
> I cried to dream again.

A man who cries to *dream again* is no Good Citizen; is fallen into a sort of Decay, born of Fancy: and the subject not of the State but of conjured art and his sensual imaginings. And so both kinds unite, and so I name *Music* as the queen of decadence.

Bonnington Square

John Moore

I am slightly hazy as to which came first, the drugs or the
music. Like many teenagers, I'd 'experimented' with the usual
array of noxious substances: amphetamine sulphate, diet pills,
household products and cannabis – which I certainly hoped
would lead to stronger things. I left home at nineteen, armed
with a student grant, a ticket to London, and no intention of
doing anything but being in a band. Whether I was fortunate
or talented is debatable, but I was single-minded and reasonably astute. When the opportunity came I seized it. I joined
my favourite band – the Jesus and Mary Chain, and became
famous. Although I was more of a hitchhiker and interpreter
for incomprehensible (to most of the world) Glaswegians,
than a fully paid up member, I had my own little coterie of
admirers; and being the only single gentleman on the stage,
was often treated as an honourary Scotsman.

While the Reid brothers moved onto the property ladder,
I was domiciled at Bonnington Square in Vauxhall. There
is insufficient space here to describe the glories of this place –
it deserves its own book, which I might even write at
some stage. Suffice to say it was a decrepit Victorian square
of four-storey, derelict houses, all squatted, and knocked
into whichever shape its occupants desired. Floors were
ripped out to make a theatre, lateral conversions knocked
through supporting walls. Like the rookeries of Dickensian
London, it was possible to avoid police raids, bailiffs and
council writs by scrambling through secret passageways
and leaving in an orderly fashion several doors away.
Occasionally one of the houses would fall down in disgust.

It was inhabited by mad old vegans, political activists, and slumming musicians.

Having hitched a ride to fame with the most notorious pop group of the day, I found myself in the enviable position of being able to indulge in leisure activities almost unimaginable to those less fortunate.

I was determined to enjoy whatever pleasures my status enabled, and my minor fame ensured that most pleasures were usually available in some shape or form. Acquiring ladies for the purpose of sexual congress was by no means impossible, drawn as they were to my column inches in the musical papers, the chance of sharing my future wealth and bearing me an heir, in return for a life of indolence in Surrey and all the cosmetic surgery that gravity would one day require. Some weren't impressed by my bohemian surroundings, but most were prepared to accept that they must suffer for my art – for a while, at least.

But as all great rock'n'rollers know: Wimmin is fine, but they sure get in the way of good writing, and they split when the hits stop, baby, usually relieving you of your ill-gotten gains. Best to keep them at arm's length if you know what's good for you – and while you've got that arm out, why not take the time to roll up a sleeve, and introduce a little something from the medicine cabinet into it? At worst you'll die on the spot, thus creating a legend or, at the very least, sell fifteen more records than you might have done otherwise. Your mum will be interviewed for documentaries about dead pop stars, and find solace in serving tea to the loners who turn up at the family home hoping to breathe in the essence of your tormented soul. Most likely though, you'll spend many happy hours unravelling the mysteries of the universe, discovering the lost chord, and marvelling at the indomitable spirit of the moth you have been minutely observing for the past seven hours. It certainly helps to pass the time.

I was taken under the wing of X, and became a sort of

Sorcerer's apprentice. He lived across the street in a room filled with furniture liberated from a closed down sanatorium. His bed was cast iron with height adjusters and collapsible sides, and on the threadbare rug in the middle of the floor stood a statue of the Virgin Mary taken from the chapel of rest. She'd lost one of her praying hands as he dragged her up the stairs, and she now looked as though she were about to perform a Kung Fu chop.

X was a violinist of sorts, and played in a ramshackle outfit who were quite popular in certain quarters. Everything about him reeked of decadence. He generally wore ancient Saville row suits with frayed cuffs, doused in sandalwood scent to mask their unlaundered odour, and silk cravats and shirts, which bore tiny traces of blood around the sleeves. His mannered voice ranged from a languid drawl to the clipped hectoring of an SS Commandant, and his hawk-like features and black eyes combined the world-weariness of W H Auden with the cold cruelty of Ian Brady. He had a magnificent gift for unpleasantness, which he revelled in, possessing enough negative energy to suck out all the bonhomie from a room in less than a minute, and replace it with unease and anger. Like most great mischief-makers, he was a complete coward when challenged, but could usually turn the situation to his advantage, even at its critical stages. For some arcane reason – possibly because I'd been on *Top of the Pops* and could pay for his drugs, he took a shine to me.

He had been using heroin since the age of fifteen. Now in his mid-thirties, he showed no immediate signs of pegging out, although it was occasionally necessary to hold a mirror to his mouth during our long rests; but he'd spent so long hovering on the verges of life and death that he had become virtually indestructible.

With the tenderness of a father to a son, he introduced me to the pleasures of heroin, and taught me to respect it – not wanting to deal 'with your mummy when her boy turns up stiff.' Our ritual was very precise. Usually he'd let me go first, unless he was gagging for it, in which case the laws of chivalry were suspended and it was safer to stand aside and let him get on with it.

From a Gladstone bag – heavy with books shoplifted from Foyles –he'd produce the correct instruments and the proceedings would commence. Scalpel, spoon, citric and candle, cigarette filter and syringe. The cooking instructions were extremely simple.

Mix contents on spoon to desired strength, add a little water, hold above naked flame until sizzling *et voilà*. . .the last supper. Draw into syringe, inject into self and hope not to die.

My early attempts at injecting often resulted in painful near misses, so out of benevolence and economy, the good Doctor deigned to 'hit me up' himself. Flicking the barrel with casual expertise, he expelled the air bubbles and tapped the needle into place. The thrill of expectation as it pushed against the skin then overcame its slight resistance to pierce the vein, was akin to that of a child on Christmas morning, approaching the tree with its shiny baubles and twinkling lights: you just knew that many of the wondrous presents beneath its pine scented branches were coming your way.

To watch your blood swirl up into the brownish mixture you are about to be introduce to your body is a glorious negation – Life is not sacred, it is something to be played with, interfered with, by those without medical certificates, altered for amusement and risked for nothing more than selfish pleasure. Days were spent listening to records, thinking about music and how to do it better. Notebooks filled with random thoughts, to be arranged cohesively at a later date.

I do not regret any of my drug experiences, except perhaps the disastrous attempt at making crack in a conventional oven in the days before microwaves, or snorting ecstasy, which felt like a brain haemorrhage. I would find it exceptionally difficult to turn down the opportunity to take more, should it arise – in fact, I look forward to passing my dotage in a cloud of opium smoke, surrounded by children who say: 'Look at Grandpa, he's off in a dream again.' I would not actively seek them out now, or spend days on a lousy mattress in south London, surviving on Bombay mix, imagining myself to be de Quincey at Limehouse; but if a nice, un-baseball capped, non pit bull owning dealer moved into the village, I'd be very pleased to pay him a call occasionally. I might even get round to organizing those notebooks as well.

Dead or Alive in Leeds: Johnny Thunders

Stevie Boyd

'I hear he's pretty bad,
Well he's good bad, but not evil'
– from 'Great Big Kiss' by the Shangrilas

Throughout the Eighties Johnny Thunders is a Rock 'n' Roll gypsy, wherever he lays his fedora is home. He often has a Tonto to his Lone Ranger, usually Jerry Nolan, but sometimes the likes of Tony James in London, or Stevie Vayne in Leeds. A lot of people reckon he is on the run from a New York neighbourhood infested with dealers and hangers on, others point out that Leeds is a good place to connect and London, only two hours away by train, is the home of his good friend the Doctor. Whatever the reason, he spends a lot of his Autumn nights in this Northern city.

'You need an escort to take a piss,
He holds your hand and he shakes your dick,
You're so pretty suburban kiddy.
You think you're gonna change, re-arrange this city'
– Johnny Thunders from 'London Boys'

Visits to Leeds are not without incident. The first as part of the Sex Pistols' Anarchy package is curtailed when councillors catch a whiff of the filth and the fury that surrounds the infamous Bill Grundy TV appearance. The second begins with Johnny's band being held at gunpoint for five hours in a

187

hotel[1] overlooking the City Railway Station. This ordeal necessitates fingerprinting on the first of numerous visits to Millgarth Police Station. These prints are reproduced for the cover of the Heartbreakers' album *LAMF* (*Like A Mother Fucker*).

Johnny Thunders is standing in a doorway in Harehills, late '87. He is wearing a full length leather coat that could have been ripped from the corpse of a Gestapo Officer but his teeth are still doing a tango as he shivers and digs his hands deeper into his pockets, 'It's colder than a witch's tit, I think my balls are going to drop off.' He pulls back the flaps of his coat and gestures to his package, remembering a recent incident . . . He's being driven, in a Roller no less, when the cops pull him over to the side of the road. His tight red leather pants make him look as though he's carrying a pair of over-ripe mangoes in his jockeys, so the officers and the guitar slinger engage in a fifteen-minute dialogue regarding why this should be. Finally, Johnny tires of this and whips it out -thus ending the conversation and shedding a little light on why he is also known as the Italian Stallion.

August 1984 and the Heartbreakers meet the Vaynes[2] for the first time. Walking into their dressing room at the Leeds Warehouse[3] they catch them shooting speed. Wise Uncle

[1] The hotel in question was the Dragonara, which has been renamed as the Leeds Hilton. Morrissey notes that Thunders had partied here with the Dolls in '73.

[2] The Dead Vaynes formed in Leeds in the early 1980s. Their leader Stevie Vayne set out to create a post punk/counter Goth movement known as 'Schlock Rock'. Early recruits included ex-members of the Sisters of Mercy and The Abrasive Wheels, who set out to inject some sonic revolution into the sleazy speedfreak scene of Headingley.

[3] The Warehouse is one of the best venues in Leeds. The exposed brick interior complete with Public telephone kiosk was the site of triumphant gigs by countless alternative artists including most of the local Goth fraternity, REM, Nico, and the Gun Club. Marc Almond was a former cloakroom attendant.

Johnny admonishes the boys sternly for their devil-may-care use of narcotics and their casual disregard for their own health, adding, almost as an afterthought, 'You got any Heroin?'

Towards the end of the decade, Johnny decides to return to Leeds under his own steam. Tiny, a snake-hipped kid who resides in my loft is turning tricks in Leeds City Station when he spots a strange little guy bedecked in soft silks and scarves. The guy is looking lost in the station's shopping square and Tiny is thinking of approaching him when he suddenly breaks into a chant, 'Mick, Mick, Mick!'. Johnny, for it is he, has British Railed into town solo. His only prior request was a welcoming party, but no one has arrived. Leeds ain't that big, maybe if he shouts loud enough his road manager will emerge from the shadows by Menzies. Office workers and travellers shoot the little dandy quizzical glances as he continues his call. These are the days before the mobile phone and Johnny's mantra does not trail off until two leather clad figures come through the sliding doors. Mick Webster drives his charge back to Stevie's.

'John Willmot penned his poetry
riddled with the pox
Nabakov wrote on index cards
At a lectern in his socks
St John of the Cross did his best stuff
Imprisoned in a box
And Johnny Thunders was half alive
when he wrote Chinese Rocks'
– Nick Cave, from 'There She Goes, My Beautiful World'

The days and nights in Stevie's Hyde Park flat are permanent twilight zones, torn curtains closed, screening the parade of local rockers from the outside world. The only light comes from the flicker of a small black and white TV screen. The scene is more than a little surreal as the fashion conscious

New Yorker surveys Yorkshire's own Richard Whiteley on *Countdown* (if the two had ever actually met the combination of stripes and polka dots would have been too much for anyone's vertical hold). Stooges' posters peel from the walls and roach ends smoulder on formica table tops as Johnny indulges in some of his favourite pursuits. This being one of his fallow periods, the proceeds of his last record company advance long gone, he goes into semi-hibernation. When he is having a lucid day he taunts his house buddy, making out that Stevie's dog loves Johnny more than him. These guys need to get out more – they need to perform.

Johnny occasionally sees the light of day as he stumbles to the newsagents. Passing the International Stores the man Nick Kent christened 'Prince of the Streets' nods to sari-clad maidens who try to figure out the origins of this stranger. His thick black mane peeps from beneath a cap that could have been liberated from a Greek fisherman, and that tartan piping must surely indicate the old Sicilian clan Genzale. He requires something to alleviate the boredom. It might be that he has watched *Scarface* one too many times, or perhaps he has decided that he has more in common with Bo Diddley than the two chord trick of 'Pills', but whatever the reason, Johnny Thunders is a gunslinger. He begs Mick to take him to the Shooting Range. Mick and Stevie, fearing a ketchup splattered scene of carnage like the one on the cover of *Live At Mothers*, come up with a scheme. They will drive him to the range but only when it is safely closed for business.

I'm lying in bed with some friends (you need to do something to keep warm in Manor Drive) when 'Subway Train' comes on the radio:

> 'I can't ever understand
> why my life's been cursed, poisoned, condemned
> When I've been trying every night to hold you near me,
> But I'm telling you it ain't easy'

John Peel explains that even though the tuning on Thunders' guitar is wrong it is clearly so right for his oeuvre. Dave and his girlfriend have decided to 'Doll me up' so Kelly, her knees either side of my chest, applies warpaint from the box resting on my pillow. This is the last time I see Dave as some months later he takes a dive from a moving train while being pursued by the cops. Ted wanders into my room and despite the fact that I am wearing more make-up than his Mother and the Pete Murphy wannabe upstairs combined, ignores my painted visage while describing an encounter earlier in the night. Turns out that after his shift pulling pints at the Royal he headed to Nafees[4] and found himself seated at a table next to the Doll's guitarist himself. We reminisce about meals we have shared in this place. Once we sent back a Madras containing metal shards only to have the waiter explain that this often happened as tacks from a board holding the various bills fell into the food. Many jokes about staple diets later we were plied with complimentary drinks and piled into a free taxi home.

> 'Every man has inside himself a parasitic being who is acting not at all to his advantage'
> – William Burroughs

While residing in Leeds 6 Johnny's haunts include the Royal Park and the 'Rock "n" Roll' hotel, the Faversham[5] – a

---

[4] Stevie Vayne describes this famous curry house, now known as the Balti King, as a favourite after hours drinking venue for the Leeds rock fraternity – 'Johnny in a curry house was a funny sight and all the rockers in Leeds used to turn up there late on. The look on their faces to see J.T. in Naffees was hysterical and of course Johnny trying to understand the waiters and order food was funny as hell too'.

[5] The Faversham is an enormous Victorian pub built in a walled site just off the University campus. Most of Leeds' budding rockers from the Magnificent Seven to Young Professionals have propped up the bar here. During the Nineties it became one of the biggest draws on the dance scene, but it is now re-established as a live venue and is the local home for Club NME.

place where we share a pint with Joe Strummer after the Clash's busking appearance on the Leeds University steps (1985). In such joints he expounds his junkie philosophy, professing that he takes smack cuz he likes it, rocking out with or without it and it does not affect his ability to play. Something does though. We follow him for a lost weekend of gigs where he does not touch his guitar once. When we reach the Wakefield Unity Hall the place is buzzing with anticipation (there wasn't a lot of rock action here pre-Cribs). The Slaves are the support band and I bump into the singer in the toilets, asking him if Johnny is likely to show tonight. Stevie explains that he's already here but he's spent some time in the Leeds General Infirmary – he had fallen asleep in a strange position and put his fingers out of action!

Friday night in Leeds General Infirmary casualty department is a madhouse, but Johnny insists he needs his 'trapped nerve' seen to and Mick has to take him there. When they arrive it is clear that the battle of the Tetley Ale houses has already taken its toll. People are wheeled in with their eyes hanging out on threads and with various lacerations to their beer-numbed torsos, but Johnny can't figure why they are receiving preferential treatment. Unfamiliar with the concept of triage, he makes his feelings felt numerous times within the first hour of waiting, but he finally explodes when a bevy of medics hurry by with a guy in a wheelchair who seems to be missing a large part of his scalp. Johnny is so wrapped up in his private world that he cannot see the tragi-comic nature of his cry 'No, take me first, take me!'

'Graceful son of Pan! Under your brow your eyes, precious balls, move. Spotted with dark streaks, your cheeks look hollow. Your fangs glisten.'
          – Arthur Rimbaud, from 'Illuminations'

I see Johnny in the Leeds Astoria, hanging out with the

Quireboys. His Midnight tan is coming on a treat, skin so pale he looks like Nosferatu, but just before he goes onstage, he decides to apply some make-up – panstick! To misquote the poet laughalot John Cooper Clarke he's got cold flesh the colour of potatoes and eyes like the tips of cigarettes. Halfway through the set he tilts his mikestand towards my lips. He requires a chorus of 'Gloria' and I willingly oblige. Just then he sucks in his bottom lip and his cheeks consecutively, like on the Whistle Test clip, and half pirouettes, half runs across the stage as another murderous chord rings out.

> 'Hospitals and jails and whores: these are the universities
> of life. I've got several degrees. Call me Mr.'
> – Charles Bukowski, from 'Confessions of a Man Sane
> Enough To Live With The Beasts'

We're in the University Refectory, where the Who recorded 'Live At Leeds', coming down from the high of seeing Mr Thunders playing with The Black Kats. Most people are here to see Hanoi Rocks because they are in the charts with Creedence cover 'Up Around The Bend', but Ted and I want to shake Johnny's hand for a job well done. Round the back we catch some of the players, it's the last time we'll see Razzle,[6] but Andy McCoy will pass our way again, both in the Cherry Bombz and with Iggy. Somebody says we should go to the Phono[7] as Johnny's meeting someone there. The DJ

---

[6] A month or so after the Leeds gig Hanoi Rocks' drummer was killed in a car crash. The driver, Motley Crue's Vince Neil, was found to be under the influence. He received a short custodial sentence.

[7] For a quarter century Le Phonographique was the place for the alternate rocker to be seen in Leeds. The small basement room in a 1960s shopping centre reverberated to the sounds of Punk/ Goth/ Industrial music as the young, not always so beautiful, admired themselves in its mirrored walls.

is spinning some Cramps when Andy tells us that Johnny has hightailed it to the Hayfield.[8]

> 'He hit me and I knew he loved me
> If he didn't care for me,
> I could never have made him mad
> But he hit me and I was glad'
>   – Carole King and Gerry Goffin from
>   'He Hit Me, It Felt Like A Kiss'

Friday night in the Student's Union, Johnny has barely been on stage for half an hour when he starts to look disgruntled. He stares someone down in the front row, while launching into MIA. Halfway through he breaks off, unstraps his guitar and swings it like a claymore, making contact with . . . well it's hard to tell when you are surrounded by six foot hairstyles, goth girls and punk kids, but we think that was skull cracking. Johnny finishes the song and with scant sign of remorse apologizes, explaining that he doesn't want to hurt anyone but this kid was messing with his stuff. We learn later that the guy was trying to pocket Johnny's comb as a souvenir.

I knew he was in town when I clocked his sax player Jamie in the Fav'. Johnny's holding court, a glass of vodka clasped in his rigid digits. He's looking less Pacino-cool and more Ratso-cold, but he's still keeping it together as he disses a bunch of people and gives a big up to a host of others. Names such as Dee Dee Ramone and Truman Capote are dropped.

---

[8] The Hayfield pub was a notorious den of iniquity in the heart of Leeds red light district. It was Chapletown's main drug dive, and features in numerous murder crime files, including those on the Yorkshire Ripper. Alternate sources suggest that Johnny may have ended up in Foxe's on the night in question. The latter was a suburban nightclub in the infinitely classier Chapel Allerton. Here Bowie and Roxy clones rubbed shoulders, and other body parts, with soul boys, especially in the unisex toilets.

No matter how low he gets he keeps it comic – I hear him refer to a mutual acquaintance, in a voice like Joey Pants, as a 'one-eyed cat' (as in the Elvis song) and he dedicates a song to another friend's girl, puncturing any soppiness by concluding with – 'the one with the big tits'. His arm is fucked and it's not because of all those needle holes, but tonight at the Duchess[9] he has Mick Vayne strumming for him. Mick is great but he takes some verbal and a little physical abuse from the man – 'Take it down – this ain't a fuckin' heavy metal song'. I'm looking at Johnny and thinking of his friend Stiv. The erstwhile leader of the Lords of the New Church had been shot on stage a number of times. More recently Stiv got hit by a car and didn't realise he was dead – 48 hours later he keeled over. Johnny fell down a few months later.

'. . . the shattered bone hath laid him groaning among the happier dead.
It is an easier thing to rejoice in the tents of prosperity:
Thus could I sing and thus rejoice: but it is not so with me'
       – William Blake, from 'The Price Of Experience'

'The vegetable serenity of junk settled in his tissues. His face went slack and peaceful, and his head fell forward'
       – William Burroughs from 'Junky's Christmas'

The last time I see Johnny in Leeds, he's fifteen feet tall on the Hyde Park[10] cinema screen. Lech Kowalski is here to present

[9] The Duchess was an inauspicious little venue on one of Leeds main shopping thoroughfares. Promoter extraordinaire John Keenan turned it into the happening live scene of the era. Thunders played there at least three times.
[10] The Hyde Park Cinema is one of the oldest cinemas in Britain. In Edwardian times it housed the Brudenell Road Social Club, but since before World War 1 it has operated as a film theatre. It remains a beautiful feature of Leeds Student land; an art house showing some of the most interesting films the World has to offer.

his cinematic biography of Mr T, *The Last Outlaw*. Watching the celluloid hero shuffle from gig to fix, I'm reminded of what his old mate Tony Parsons said about him choosing drugs over women – with those Latino good looks he shoulda been winning as many hearts as he was breaking. Lech and I had chatted about this project a few years earlier when he was in town for the Leeds Film Festival. The Director started out producing porn, allegedly on the Mafia's dollar, but he is better known for his brave attempts to document the implosion of Punk (see also D.O.A.). The film will eventually surface as *Born To Lose: The Last Rock "N" Roll Movie* and while I pick holes and stress over the abundant input from Dee Dee, I have to agree with *Filmmaker Magazine*, it is '. . . a remarkably powerful human drama and the nightmare flipside to the rockstar dream life and limousines.' We know, we lived it.

'There's something wrong here where the best ones want
   to go
Parker, Lautreamont, Monroe they held it just to throw
The World away who were its grace before they left
To choose to have a point of view oblivious that leaves the rest
   of us bereft'

        – Richard Hell, from *Don't Die*

The Decadent Set-list

Dickon Edwards

Decadent disco is curated (as opposed to DJ'd) and patrons are encouraged to dress up in their own take on period glamour. Cigarillos, braces, tweeds, beads, silk, scarves, unforgiving teddy bears. Drink, dance, and ponder the nights' tenderness to an eclectic but discerning mix of Sinatra (Frank & Nancy), Strauss waltzes, soundtracks, musicals, El records, Gilbert & Sullivan, Ella Fitzgerald, Dory Previn, Doris Day, Bugsy Malone, Cabaret, Chicago, deviant disco, shadowy soul, parvenu pop and insouciant indie.

Bernice Bobs Her Hair – Divine Comedy

Get Happy – Judy Garland

You've Either Got Or You Haven't Got Style – Frank Sinatra

Nice On The Ice – Vic Godard

Initials BB – Serge Gainsbourg

I Wanna Be Loved By You – Helen Kane (1920s recording)

I Feel The Earth Move – Carole King

Casino Royale – Bacharach (theme from the movie)

Dream A Little Dream Of Me – Mama Cass

Anything Goes – Harpers Bizarre (theme from *The Boys In The Band*)

The Lady Is A Tramp – The Supremes

I'll Keep It With Mine – Nico

How Does That Grab You Darlin'? – Nancy Sinatra

Move Over Darling – Doris Day

The Number One Song In Heaven – Sparks

Mrs Robinson – James Taylor Quartet

Yada Yada La Scala – Dory Previn (this works fantastically well)

Elizabeth Taylor In London: with John Barry CD, (on El Records, naturally) is arguably the most stylish album ever made. Against a stirring, swooping orchestration by Mr Barry, Ms Taylor recites various texts related to the capital: Wordsworth's 'Westminster Bridge', Queen Victoria's diary entry following her husband's death, Queen Elizabeth's Tilbury speech ('I may have the body of weak and feeble woman . . .') and Churchill's post-Blitz statement comparing the city to a defiant rhinoceros.

Decadent Travel

The Decadent Traveller

Medlar Lucan & Durian Gray

I was at A***n*n in the south of France, and went up with
my luggage to the station which was being rebuilt. A branch
line had been opened the day before, and all was a chaos of
brick, mortar and scaffolding. The water closets were temporarily run up in wood, in a very rough manner. A train had just
brought in many passengers. I was taken with violent belly-
ache, and ran to the closets. They were full. Fearful of shitting
myself I rushed to the women's which were adjoining the
men's. 'Non, non, Monsieur,' screamed out the woman in
charge, 'c'est pour les dames.' I would have gone in spite of
her, but they were also full. Foul myself I must. 'Oh, woman, I
am so ill, – here is a franc, show me somewhere for God's
sake.' 'Come here,' said she, and going round to the back of
the wooden structure, she opened the door of a shed. On the
door was written 'Control, private, you don't enter here.' In I
went rapidly. 'Shut the door quite close,' said she, 'when you
come out.' It had been locked. I saw a half-cupboard, and just
in time to save my trousers made myself easy on a seat with a
hole in it.

It was a long compartment of the wooden shed and running at the back of several privies. No light was provided,
excepting by a few round holes pierced here and there in the
sides; but light came also at places through joints of the
woodwork roughly and temporarily put together. There were
chests, furniture, forms, cabinets, lamps, and shelves and odds
and ends of all sorts in the shed, seemingly placed there till
the new station was finished. The privy seat at which I sat
was one end. The privy enclosure had no door, and looking

about when my belly-ache had subsided, and I could think of something else, I heard on my right, rustlings, and footsteps, as of females moving, and a female voice say, 'Make haste.' Then doors banged and opened, and just beyond my knee I saw a round hole in the woodwork through which a strong light came into my dark shed. Off I got in a trice and kneeling down looked. It was a hole through which I could have put my middle finger, a knot in the wood had fallen or been forced out, in the boarding which formed the back of one of the women's closets, and just above the privy seat. What a sight met my eyes when I looked through it!

A large brown turd descending and as it dropped disclosing a thickly haired cunt stretched out wide between a fat pair of thighs and great round buttocks, of which I could see the whole. A fart followed, and a stream of piddle as thick as my finger splashed down the privy-hole. It was a woman with her feet on the seat after the French fashion, and squatting down over the hole. Her anus opened and contracted two or three times, another fart came, her petticoats dropped a little down in front, she pulled them up, then up she got, and I saw from her heels to above her knees as she stood on the privy-seat, one foot on each side of the hole. Off the seat then she got, pulling her petticoats tightly around her, and holding them so. Then she put one leg onto the seat, and wiped her bum with two or three pieces of paper which she held in one hand, taking them one by one from it with the other, wiping from the anus towards her cunt, and throwing each piece down the hole as she had done with it. Then looking at her petticoats to see if she had smirched them, she let them fall, gave them a shake, and departed.

She was a fine, dark woman of about thirty, well dressed, with clean linen, and everything nice, though not looking like a lady. The closets it must be added, had sky-lights and large openings just above the doors for ventilation, so they were perfectly light. The sun was shining, and I saw plainly her cunt from back to front, her sphincter muscle tightening and opening, just as if she had arranged herself for me to see it. I recollect comparing it in my mind to those of horses, as I have seen many a time, and every other person must have seen, tightening just after the animals have evacuated.

The sight of the cunt, her fine limbs, and plump buttocks made my cock stiff, but my bowels worked again. I resumed my seat, and had no sooner done so than I heard a door bang. Down on my knees I went, with eye to peep-hole. Another woman was fastening the closet door. It was a long compartment. When near the door, I could see the women from head nearly to their ankles; when quite near the seat I could not see their heads, nor their knees which were hidden by the line of the seat; but I saw all between those parts.

It was a peasant-girl seemingly about twenty years old, tall, strong and dark like the other. She took some paper out of her pocket, then pulling her petticoats well up, I saw the front of her thighs and had a momentary glimpse of the motte. She turned round, mounted the seat, and squatted. She then drew up her petticoats behind tighter, and I saw buttocks, turds and piddle. She did not lift up her petticoats quite so much in front, yet so light was it that the gaping cunt and the stream were quite visible. She wiped her bum as she sat, then off she went, leaving me delighted with her cunt, and annoyed at seeing what was behind it.

Then I found from looking around and listening, that there were several women's closets at the back of all of which the shed ran. It was a long building with one roof, and the closets were taken out of it. Through the chinks of the boards of one closet I could see the women enter, and leave, could hear them piss, and what they said in all of them; but in the one only could I see all their operations. I kept moving from one to the other as I heard their movements, their grunts, and their talk, but always to the peep-hole when there was anything to see, – and there was plenty.

I had now missed my train, the two women I expect must have gone off by it, and for quite an hour the closets were all empty. I began to think there was no chance of seeing more unless I stayed longer than an hour when I knew an express train arrived. I resolved to wait for that, wondering if any one would come into my shed for any purpose, but no one came in. I had eased myself, and covered up the seat; but a strong stink pervaded the place, which I bore resolutely, hoping to see more female nakedness.

There had been a market at A★★★n★n that morning. Some of the farm-people had come by the train for the first time, the junction railway only having just been opened. I had heard them say so on the platform before I was taken short. Hearing voices just outside my shed, I cautiously opened the door ajar and peeped. Groups of market people had arrived, and were standing outside the station, mostly women with baskets. The eaves of the shed-roof projecting much, gave a little shade from the sun, and they were standing up against it. That told me there would be another train soon; so I shut the door.

In a few minutes close to my door I heard two female voices, 'I want to do caca,' said one of them (in French of course). 'They charge you a penny,' said the other. 'I won't pay a penny, – we shall be home in twelve minutes when the train starts.' 'I shall piss,' said one in broad French. She was close up against the spot where I stood, a board only between us. I heard a splash, then two splashes together. I opened the door ajar again, and peeped. They were both standing upright, but pissing. Both laughed. 'I must do it somewhere,' said one. 'Go over there then, – they won't see you.' 'No I'll go to the woman, and say I haven't any money when I come out.' The next minute she came into the privy with the peep-hole. On my knees I went, and saw the operation complete. Such a nice little girl. She sat some minutes after she had dropped her wax, pull- ing her petticoats well up from time to time. I had such gloat over her cunt. Once or twice she put her hand under, and felt it.

Spite of my diarrhoea, my prick got so stiff, and I was so randy, that with my eye to the hole and gazing on her round bum and gaping cunt, I frigged myself. My sperm fell on the partition in front of me. I sat looking at it, when I was shitting again. The girl went back to her companion by the shed, and said she had been obliged to pay, and it was a shame. I opened the door, feeling as if I must see the girl's face again. They saw me. 'There's some one in there,' said one, and they moved away.

After that the woman in charge wiped the privy-seat, which I suppose was dirty. Then two or three women came in. Old, and dirty were one or two of them, who sat on it English fashion. I saw their skinny buttocks, and the back-view of their cunts. It sickened me, for they all of them shit, which revolted me. Yet the fascination of the cunt made me look at all of them, – I could not help it. One woman had her courses on, and moved aside a rag to do her needs, – that nearly made me vomit. That woman squatted on the seat.

For a quarter of an hour or so no one came. A trumpet, a railway-bell, and a hubbub, then told me the express train was coming in. Then was hurry, and confusion, a jabber of tongues in many languages. All the closet-doors banged at once, and I heard the voices of my country-women.

Pulling her clothes up to her hips a fine young English woman turned her bum on to the seat. It came out of a pair of drawers, which hid nearly her buttocks. As she sat down her hand eased her drawers away from her cunt. Splash, trump, and all was over. The hair of her cunt was lightish. She was gone. Another came who spoke to her in English, and without a moment's delay pissed, and off she went.

Then a lady entered. As she closed the door I saw a man trying to enter. She pushed him out saying in suppressed voice, 'Oh! for God's sake are you mad? – he can see from the carriage-window.'

'Not there sir,' I heard the woman in charge cry out. The door was shut, and bolted.

The lady, young and handsome, stood quite still, facing the seat, as if overcome with anxiety; then feeling in her pocket, took out some letters, and selecting some, tore them in half, and threw them down the privy. That done she daintily wiped round the seat with a piece of paper, lifted up handsome laced petticoats, and turning her rump towards the seat daintily sat down. She had no drawers on. She must have fancied something, for she rose again directly, and holding her clothes half-way up her thighs looked carefully at the seat. Then she mounted it, but as if she scarcely knew how to do it, stumbled and bungled. She stood upright on it for an instant, and then I could only see half-way up her legs. At length the bum slowly descended, her petticoats up, and adjusted so as to avoid all chance of contamination. I saw the piss descending, but she was sitting too forward, and the piss fell splashing over the edge of the seat. She wriggled back opening her legs wider, and a pretty cunt with dark hair up to her bum-hole showed. My cock stood again. She jumped off the seat, looked down the privy, gave her clothes a tuck between her thighs, and went off.

Then came others, mostly English, pissing in haste, and leaving, and bum after bum I saw. Then came a woman with a little girl. She was not English, she mounted the seat, and cacked. Whilst doing so she told the child to 'pi-pi bébé' on the floor, which she did not. When she had finished she wiped her arse-hole with her finger, – how she cleaned the finger I didn't see. She then took up her child, held her up over the seat with her clothes up to her waist, her cunt towards me, and made her piss. The tiny stream splashed on the seat, and against the hole through which I was looking – a drop hit me on the eye. How funny the hairless little split looked to me. To think that her little split might one day be surrounded with black hair like her mother's, and have seven inches of stiff prick up it. Her mother's hair was black, and she had a moustache.

Again a row. 'Not there Monsieur, – l'autre côté.' 'It's full God damn it – I am not going to shit myself,' said a man in English. 'Vous ne pouvez pas entrer,' – but he would. A big Englishman – a common man – pushed the woman in charge aside, and bolted the door muttering. 'Damned fool, – does she think I'm going to shit myself!' He tore down his trowsers, and I moved away, but heard him let fly before he had sat on the seat (he had the squitters), and muttering to himself, he buttoned up and left. I heard him wrangling with the woman in charge.

Instantly two young ladies entered, sisters seemingly, and English, – nice fresh-looking girls, both quite fair. One pulled up her clothes. 'Oh! I can't sit down, – what a beastly place, – what beasts those French are,' said she, 'dirty beasts, – call the woman, Emily.' Emily looked outside. 'I can't see her, – make haste, or the train will be leaving.' 'I can't sit down.' 'Get on the seat as those dirty French do, and I'll hold your petticoats up. Take care now, – take care.'

'I shall get my feet in it,' said she. 'No you won't.' She stood fronting me, and pulling up her petticoats till they looked as if tied round her waist in a bundle, showing every part from her motte, to her knees, (my eye just at the level of her bum), and saying, 'Don't look and laugh' – but laughing herself, she got on the seat. A prettily-made creature, not stout, nor thin, with a cunt covered with light-brown hair. She squatted. I saw the bum-hole moving. 'I can't do it like this,' she cried, 'with all this nastiness about me, – are my clothes falling down?' 'No, – make haste, – you won't have another opportunity for two hours.' Out and in went the anus again, the pretty fair-haired quim was gaping, the piddle began to fall. She wanted to piddle badly enough. I said aloud in my excitement at seeing her beauty, 'Cunt, cunt.'

The girl got upright, I could now only see half her legs.

'Hish! Did you hear?' said she. Both were silent. 'It must be the woman in the next place.' 'It sounded like a man.' Then she spoke in a whisper. 'No it can't be.' She squatted again laughing. 'It's no one.' Her evacuations dropped and off she got. 'You go, Mary,' said the other. 'I only want to pee, and I'll do it on the floor.' 'The dirty creatures, why don't they keep the place clean?' Squatting I watched her face. It was all I could see then, and suppose she pissed. I only saw her hitch up her clothes, but nothing more.

Then the closet-woman came, and wiped the seat grumbling, women opened the door whilst she was doing so, then others came in, and for half an hour or so, I saw a succession of buttocks, fat and thin, clean and dirty, and cunts of all colours. I have told of all worth noting. The train went off, and all was quiet. I had again diarrhoea, and what with evacuating, the belly-ache, and frigging excitement, felt so fatigued that I was going away. As I opened the door the woman was just putting the key in. She started back as she saw me.

'Are you ill?' she said. 'Yes.' 'What a time you have staid, – why did you not go?' Then all at once, as if suspecting something, she began looking at the backs of the women's closets, and found the hole, and looking half smiling, half angry, 'You made that,' said she. 'No.' 'Yes you did.' I declared I had not. 'Ah! Méchant, méchant,' said she (looking through the hole), and something about the chef de la gare. 'You have been peeping through.' 'Certainly.' I was so excited, so full of the adventure, that I had been bursting to tell some one, and talk the incident over. So in discreet words I told her about the man, and the woman, and her letters, and other incidents, till she was amused, and laughed. Then spite of my illness my lust got strong as I looked at her, for she had a cunt. She was a coarse sun-tanned, but fine stout sort of tall peasant woman about thirty-five years old. So I told her of the pretty little splits, and nice bums I had seen, all in select language. And I so longed, Madame. 'Oh! if I had had them in here.' 'Ah! no doubt.' 'Or if you had been here, for I wished for you.' 'For me? – ah! ah!' – and she slapped both her thighs and laughed. 'Mais je suis mariée, moi, – ah! méchant, méchant.' 'Here is another five francs, but I must have a kiss.' She gave it seemingly much flattered. I said I should come the next day. 'Ah! non!' she must tell the Chef, it was her duty, – it would be useless if I came for that hole.

We talked on. She was the wife of a workman who it seems travelled up and down the line almost continually with officers of the railway, and only came home about once a week, or ten days. She had no children. Whilst talking my diarrhoea came on. My paper was gone, she produced some from her pocket, and simply turned her back whilst I eased myself (the enclosure had no door), as if it was the most natural thing in the world. Finally after saying that she would not dare to let me in the next day, yet on a promise of ten francs she said she would, and volunteered the information, that by an early train many farmers' wives would probably arrive for the market, that many would come by the line just opened She must report the hole to the Chef, – it might cost her her place if she did not, and it would be stopped. I kissed her again, and whispered in her ear, 'I wish I had seen you sitting, and that you had come in here afterwards.' 'Ah! mon Dieu que vous êtes méchant,' she replied laughing, and looking lewdly in my eyes – and I went off. I had been there hours.

I took my luggage back to the hotel, eat, got refreshed, went early to bed, awakened quite light and well, and got early to the station. She was awaiting me and directly I approached, took no notice of me, but opened the door, looked in, closed it and walked away. I guessed what the game was, loitered about till no one was on that side, then slipped into the shed, the door of which she had left ajar. Soon after in she came, and gave me the key. 'No one is likely to come,' said she. 'It's only the Chef and Sous-Chef whom the seat was made for, and now they have new closets on the other side of the railway;

but if they should, say that you saw the door open and wanting the cabinet used it.' Then off she went, but not till I had
kissed her, and asked her to go and sit on the women's seat. I
found the peep-hole plugged up, and could not push the plug
out. I hesitated, fearing to make a noise; but hearing a woman
there, my desire to see cunt overcame all scruples. With my
penknife I pointed a piece of wood, applied it to the plug, and
taking off my boot to lessen the noise, hit it hard with the heel,
and at length out tumbled the plug. I expect it fell down the
seat-hole.

Two well-to-do French peasants came in. One got on to
the seat and to my annoyance shit and farted loudly, both
talking whilst stercoratious business was going on, as if they
had been eating their dinner together. She had huge flappers
to her cunt, – an ugly sight. The next pissed only, and I was
rewarded by a sight of a full-fledged one, and a handsome
backside. One had a basket of something for the market
which they discussed. One said they must give the caretaker a
halfpenny, and they evidently thought that a great grievance.
What had they been in the habit of doing in such necessities
previously I wonder. One said she would take care not to pay
it again. The closet accommodation at railways in France was
at that time of a very rough primitive kind, seats had not long
been introduced.

For half an hour all the women were of that class, many
quite middle-aged. More women came into that privy, than
into the others I could hear. (I had given the keeper the ten
francs.) They were mostly full-grown, and had thickly dark-
haired cunts. Almost all the women mounted the seats, some
pissed over the seat as they squatted. I was tired of seeing full-
grown cunts, disliked seeing the coarser droppings, and left
the peep-hole weary, but the cunts took me back there.

Two sweet-looking peasant girls came in together, they
must have been about fourteen or fifteen years old, only, and
both had slight dark hair on their cunts. When they had eased

themselves they stood and talked. One pulled her petticoats up to her navel, the other stooped and looked at her cunt, and seemed to open it, then the other did similarly. They spoke in such low tone, and in patois, that I did not understand a word they said. Both girls wore silk handkerchiefs on their heads, had dark blue stockings and white chemises. They were beautifully formed little wenches, and I longed for them with intense randiness, but restrained myself from frigging, determining to find a woman somewhere to fuck, and I felt again an overwhelming desire to tell some woman of the sights I was witnessing.

I missed a good deal of the talk when women were together, owing at times to noise in the station; yet the women who came by express trains talked very loudly, nearly always. They seemed in a scuffle of excitement, ran in, eased themselves, and ran out quickly; and if two together, spoke as if they had not the slightest suspicion of being overheard.

No one had yet noticed the peep-hole, though so large. The women seemed mostly in a hurry, pulled up their petticoats, and turned their rumps to the seat directly they had shut the door. At length a splendid, big, middle-aged woman came in, and was most careful in bolting the door, then turning round towards the seat, she lifted her clothes right up, and began feeling round her waist. I wondered what she was at. She was unloosing her drawers. She was dressed in silk, had silk stockings on, and lace-edged drawers [drawers were only then just beginning to be worn by ladies]. Peeping from between the drawers every now and then was the flesh, but nothing more suggesting what was behind.

Apparently unable to undo them, she broke the fastening with both hands, and the drawers fell down to her knees. What a pair of lovely thighs she had, but I only saw even those for a second, for her petticoats fell. She disengaged her limbs from the drawers, pulling the legs one by one over her boots, rolled up the drawers tightly, and put them into her pocket. Then pulling up her petticoats as she stood sideways I had a glimpse for a second of a splendid bum, and the edge of the hairy darkness. Then she dropped them, stood still and looked. I felt sure she was looking at the hole, and drew back. When I looked again the hole was plugged with paper. I did not move it till I heard she had gone.

Although now growing tired of seeing backsides, and cunts gaping in the attitude in which cunts look the least attractive; yet I felt annoyed at missing the sight of this lady's privates, and could scarcely restrain myself from pushing the paper through. I thought she told the closet-woman, for I saw that woman look in directly she had left.

For a full hour I then saw nothing. I had not heard a train, and looked at my watch. It had stopped. I peeped out of the shed-door, saw no one, went out, put my head round the corner, and saw the care-taker knitting in the shade. She saw and followed me at my beckoning. The train had not arrived, it was one hour behind time.

She came into the shed. 'Talk low,' said she, 'for some one may be there and hear.' I told her of the lady and her drawers. She said the lady had told her of the hole. We both laughed, she called me, 'Sale, – méchant,' but did not stop my kissing her. I got more free, and from hinting got to plain descriptions. She took no offence. I told her of the two girls looking at each other's cunts, that I longed to be kissing one of them; that the sight of their pretty slits made me long to have one of them (I used chaste words). 'Or both,' said she. 'I'd sooner have you, for I like plenty of hair.' In the half-light I saw her eyes look-ing full into mine. She laughed heartily, but stifled the noise, and I was sure that she felt lewd. I kissed her, and pinched her. 'What fine breasts you have.' Then her bum. 'Laissez-moi donc.' Then my hands went lower. 'My God let me feel your cunt.' 'Hish! talk low,' said she. The next minute I was feeling her cunt. 'What hair, – delicious, – ah! foutre, – faisons

THE DECADENT TRAVELLER

l'amour.' But she coquetted. 'Now don't, – if any one should come, – I won't,' – whilst gently I edged her up against the side of the shed, one hand full on her cunt all the while. 'You must not, – mais non.' Then out came my prick, and she felt it. Another minute's dalliance. 'Let me put the key in the door,' said she, 'and then no one can let himself in.' She did, and in another minute standing up against the shed, we were fucking energetically. Didn't she enjoy it!

We had just finished when we heard the train-signals, and off she went. 'Come back.' 'Yes, yes presently.' Down to the peep-hole I dropped, holding my prick in my hand; there already was a cunt pissing in front of me. English I guessed, for she was half sitting on the seat. Then for half an hour was a succession of backsides and quims, mainly English and Americans (a first-class train only). I knew them by face and dress, and nice linen, and because they nearly all sat or half-sat on the seat, whilst others mounted it. I wished my country-women had mounted also, to enable me to see their privates better. They nearly all piddled only. There was a restoration at the station. Nearly every woman of other nationalities shitted, they wanted I guessed, full value for their ten centimes.

Another woman plugged the hole with paper, a knowing one who did it the moment she entered the privy. I pushed it away directly she had left, she grunted much, and was a long time there.

Then I saw the cunts of an English mother and four daughters, just as the train was ready to go. They had from what they said been eating and only just came in time. The girls looked from fourteen to twenty years of age, the mother not forty.

Luckily some one before must have fouled the seat. The mother entered first with the youngest. 'Stop dear,' said she in a nice quiet voice, 'the seat is filthy.' She opened the door, put her head out, and I expect called the woman. Returning, 'Get on to the seat, dear.' 'How Mamma?' 'I'll show you,' and she got up, but daintily hid her limbs from her child. 'Look the other way dear.' The girl turned her back, and then she pulled up her clothes, and I saw the maternal quim and piddle. Then she helped the girl up. 'I'll tell Clara what to do,' said the mother, 'take care of your clothes dear,' and she left the privy. The girl did take care, and showed her nice little bum and unfledged cunt charmingly. Piss only again thank God.

The other girls entered afterwards. Each smiled as she mounted. Would they have smiled, had they known my eye was so near their bum-holes? Piddle only. Then the fourth followed and piddled. The train moved off, directly they had left.

The care-taker soon came round to the shed. I told her all, talked baudy, soon at her I went, we fucked, and after our privates had separated we talked. There would not be another train for some hours, she usually went home to dinner, any one could go to the closets then without paying. I wanted to go home with her, but she refused it. She would be there at *** o'clock, an hour before the *** p.m. train. Yes on her honour. I gave her a louis. 'How good you are,' said she. She was surprised. I had promised her nothing for fucking her. We both wanted that, and therefore did it, – that is all.

I went to my hotel, eat and drank, and before the time, let myself into the shed with a key she had given me. She came back early, and dropped her eyes. She was a stout woman with large waist and haunches, a sturdy, plump, well-fed peasant with good eyes, and bronzed cheeks, a good bit of flesh for a fuck. I wonder how I had cheek to attack her for all that. Now however I had felt her hard buttocks, and in my randiness her cunt had seemed divine. I had whilst waiting, pulled down a dusty, long, cushioned seat from the miscellaneous heap of things, and we sat down on it. I began feeling her. 'Let me see your cunt.' 'Haven't you seen enough women's?' 'No I must see yours.' 'Tell me about the two girls again, – I think I know them,' she said. On being asked I told her, and a lot more. 'Que vous êtes méchant, you men, – do you so like looking at women when they are doing caca?' 'No I did not, – I could not bear it, but their thighs, their lovely round bums, their cunts, anything to see those parts, – I will see yours,' I got her to stand up; and then with the modesty like that of a newly-married woman permitting her husband, she let me see. It was not a bit in the manner of a harlot. I looked at her wet quim in the dim light, and soon we fucked again.

Then we questioned each other. What she had to say was soon told. Her husband had for many years held his post, he was here, there, and everywhere, and came home once a week if lucky, but generally once in ten days, and then had an entire day to himself. She had the post of privy-opener given her, because of her husband, and made more money than he did though only in pennies. It would be a good deal more now, if they let her have it all, for there would be more trains, but they would divide it, for there were to be closets on both sides. 'Then you only get fucked (not mincing words now), once in ten days.' 'That's about it,' said she laughing. 'You long for him to come home?' 'That's true.' Just then we heard some one in the privy. I looked, she would not, and went off with a moistened quim to attend to the people. A train was coming in.

Back came she afterwards, and we talked for two hours. My cock was ready. I laid her on the form, and straddling across the seat, and holding her legs up across my arms, entered her quim. But she nearly fell off the seat, it was so narrow; so again up against the wood-work, we copulated. She was well grown, so it was not difficult. She took to the fucking, as if I had a right to it, and she liked it, but I always disliked uprighters.

Again we sat down and talked. 'You won't want your husband now.' 'He comes home to-morrow,' and she showed me a little scrap of dirty writing-paper with, 'On Tuesday' written on it, and a mark at the bottom with a date. 'That's his mark,' said she, 'he can't write. I've been frightened to-day, for sometimes he comes without writing, – I'm here to meet him.' We then kissed each other. 'You are very handsome,' she said. 'You are beautiful,' said I. 'Am I really?' 'Yes, and fuck divinely.' 'Do I really?' said she in a most flattered manner.

'Directly he comes he fucks you here?' 'He's never been in here in his life, but he makes love directly he gets into our rooms,' she replied in a quiet tone, as if she'd been telling a doctor her ailments. Still we sat and talked. The shed had been only built for storing things quite temporarily, the privy was for the Chef, but it had not been used by any one for some time. The hole in the wood could not have been there long. How made, she knew not. She must have noticed it, had it been there long, for she washed the seats continually. Holes were often made by men in the sides next to the women's closets, they bored holes to look at the women, she wondered 'pourquoi mon Dieu,' why they wanted to see when they were doing their nastiness?

Again through the peep-hole I saw such a nasty, dirty, frowsy, beshitten backside, and the chemise of an oldish-rab-bit-arsed female, that a disgust which had been gradually intensifying, made me indifferent to seeing any more, and females came and went without my even looking. I now sat on the cushioned though dirty form comfortably (before I could only sit on the privy-seat), waiting for the privy-woman to come back. But curiosity still got the better of me. An express train came in with English and Americans, and I looked. People who come by train are always in a hurry, sometimes they have wanted to ease themselves an hour or more, and then let fly before almost they get their breeches down, or their petticoats up, very often indeed they let fly at random over the seat. Then those following them finding the seat dirty, mount it to avoid fouling their clothes.

'It's beastly,' I heard in a high pitched American tone. Two nice, young, shortish girls, were there. 'Let's go to the next one.' 'There is some one there, – there is not time, – get on the seat.' Up got the girl with her face towards me. 'Not so Fanny, – turn round stupid.' 'I can't, – this will do,' said

Fanny, and pissed out of a dear little cunt covered with light-ish brown hair, set in delicious buttocks. I put my eye close to the hole, and the piddle spashed into it, for she peed on to the back of the seat, and how she wanted it! 'Make haste Fanny.' 'Oh! I did want so, – I've not done it all day. Then up got the other in other fashion, close to my peep-hole, and watered! In shape of bum, thigh, and cunt the two were as like as two pins, pretty, fleshy little bums, round little thighs, plump as a partridge. I was so lewd I could scarcely resist a desire to call out to them, and say I had seen their charms. The last one turned round when she had done, and got down. 'Oh!' said she, 'there is a hole in the wall.' 'Oh! if –' said the other. That was all I heard, for they quitted the privy like lightning, putting their heads together, and lowering their voices to a mumble, and talking earnestly. Afterwards when the train had left, back came the keeper to me, and said the young ladies had told her of the hole.

She begged me not to go there the next day, for her husband might arrive by any train; but I did, and had her. I dined at the hotel, and at night having nothing better to do, strolled towards the station smoking a cigar. – The attraction of cunt I suppose did it. She had said that she left directly after a particular train, and some other woman took her place for night-work. There she was, – no her husband could not arrive now till next morning. Let me go home with her, on no account would she. Between the station and the town were some woods being made into public gardens. Walking there against her will and in the dark, I talked lewdness to my heart's content, and at length had her with her back up against a tree. 'Lay down, – it's quite dry,' said I, and on some coarse sort of dryish herbage, – I could not see what – I fucked for the last time and on the top of her. We got up whispering adieu, when we saw dimly a man and woman who began the game. She was scared 'Let me go, and you stay,' said she. Just then their vigorous love-making made a great noise. Off she went,

I in a second or two followed and overtook her. 'C'est une sale putain,' said she, 'she has commenced coming here of a night to meet men going to the station – it is disgraceful, – I shall inform the Chef to-morrow.' Then the closet-keeper kissed me, and went off with her cunt wet, and a Napoleon which I insisted on her accepting.

The next morning I left A★★★, but could not keep my promise, and went to her at the station. The blood rushed into her face, she looked scared, and shook her head seemingly in a funk, and I departed by the next train.

I have often wondered at the affair, and at that woman. Had she been a whore? Did she in her husband's absence usually have a bit of illicit cock? My impression is that she was steady and honest; that I caught her just when she was hot-blooded, that my doings were so baudy, that her lust was roused, and so she was helpless at my first attempt, and then having slipped, thought she might as well have all the pleasure she could. She had no children. French women don't see so much harm in an outside fuck or so. I had promised her no money, had offered no inducement whatever but my prick. It was lust which stirred lust, and we gratified each other. What more natural?

The adventure left me in an unpleasant state of mind, for I could not bear at that time anything connected with the bum-hole. With women, if I thought of that orifice, it destroyed voluptuous associations. Now I could not look at the prettiest woman without thinking of her shitting and farting. The anus came into my mind when dancing, dining, or talking and whether randy or not; and when the tingling in my prick made me look, and long for a woman, thinking what a leg she had, what thighs and quim perhaps, my mind went to her bum-hole spite of myself. I was punished heavily for my peeping. It was a year or two before my mind recovered its balance, and I was able to think of their sexual organ and its beauty and convenience without reference to its unpleasant neighbour!

Fast-Food and Fellatio
The Quest for Houellebecq

Christopher Moore

Decadence in Paris, eh? Should be a breeze. But I'm scuppered. The dictionary reckons decadence is 'refined aestheticism, artifice, and the quest for new sensations.' In my Anglo-Saxon mind, twenty minutes in the Louvre followed by ciggies over a literary journal covers 66.6% of that. 100% if the coffee's any good. My idea of decadence is, I suspect, the same as that of many of my compatriots: a loose coalition of sex, drugs and rock 'n' roll, of the kind unavailable in London. I've stumbled upon crones bearing time-mottled thigh at Strasbourg St Denis. I've bought aspirin and dried basil looking for pills and weed on Grands Boulevards. But for a tourist, even one who lives here, my Paris, *côté débauche*, might as well be Pontefract.

There's no shame in resorting to a guide book. Especially when its genital humour and deconstructionist observations had me laughing like a loony on the Victoria Line. Well the former anyway, the latter hit outside the intellectual ballpark of a mere *rosbif* brought up on Tesco and Jeremy Paxman. So, Michel Houellebecq, I dedicate this tour of the French capital to you. Or more specifically, to following in the footsteps of Michel and Bruno, the half-brothers in your book *Atomised*. I point out that I use *Atomised*, the *J'ai lu* (think Borders bargain-bin) edition to be precise, purely for location. And, of course, to seek out Bruno, a hard-drinking libertine whose life follows the classical model: man seeks world class fellatio, man finds world class fellatio, man falls in love with she who provided, provider dies following bizarre coital accident at swingers' haunt *Chris et Manu*, man sees out days in mental asylum. But first I head to the 15th arrondissement in search of Michel. Before detailing the ideal way to clone the human race, then topping himself in rural Ireland, Bruno's straight-laced alter ego lived in Rue Frémicourt.

On this unremarkable street, a *Club Med* sign hovers over a billboard offering 'relaxation . . . Chinese and African,' (€30). Inside, writhing flesh in lycra gets sweaty to techno. A good start, depending on your reading. Alas, it's a gym full of off-duty management consultants treading mill. One of these identikit neo-humans, in a T-shirt bearing the words *team success*, sneers out disapprovingly as I sneer in. If rue Frémicourt was ever decadent, it's now grown up and works a 50-hour-week – the leave accrued over the 35-hour standard affording bi-annual visits to the beaches of Tunisia. It probably doesn't buy dog vids, go to swingers bars or expose itself in public toilets.

On to Monoprix – where Michel was a loyal customer. According to MH: '*after a few years of work, sexual desire disappears . . . people turn their attention to food and drink.*' But there's no lost libido at the rue de Grenelle branch. If you're into easy anti-capitalism, the stars of this well-heeled *quartier* are getting jiggy at a natives and colonialists swingers night. I loiter at the fruit bar, where uniformed black people serve the produce of fifteen nations to panting white people. Much of it seems to come from UN-designated problem zones – they've even shipped pineapples from the Ivory Coast. The British contribute a tin of corned beef (€1.69). Moving silently among the heaving flesh, I spot a fifty-something Catherine Deneuve-a-like in the *desserts gourmands* section. She coaxes a porno nail up and down a '*pot de crème*' (€2.29). If that's not mutated desire, I don't know what is. Elsewhere a middle-aged gent groans into his camel coat as he fingers a shrink-wrapped salmon *steak haché* (price unmarked). He's a dead-ringer for Poirot (David Suchet, thankfully, not Peter Ustinov – but relief is always relative). A kind punter clocks that I'm a bit nervous on my first visit and points out the booze. I buy a four-pack of *Vieux Papes* (€5.99) – France's premier wine cum paint-stripper. I've often made the case that drinking '*The Pape*,' is decadent, it has never been upheld. To stop myself feeling dirty, I throw in some UNICEF fruit juice before buttoning-up and hitting the street.

Time now, for the unpromising task of Bruno's bulimia-ridden youth. Fast-food and faster regurgitation in the fifth arrondissement don't appeal, but it's in the script. A hot dog gobbled on rue Gay Lussac, I head to the Tunisian patisserie on rue de la Harpe. Here I learn that Czech tourists can eat more baklava than I can. It's just a pre-cursor to the leg's highlight, though: McDonald's on Boulevard St Germain, surely a veritable repository of Houellebecqian theatre. No. The clientele is standard issue: monkeys in Nike, Japanese tourists, serial killers. There are a couple of breaks from the norm. Some bored-looking Sorbonne parents feed their spotty offspring. In the corner, a man of indeterminate age and nationality, dressed entirely in tennis casual, ploughs intently through five cheeseburgers and a bottle of Perrier. I start to worry, it took Bruno most of his adult life to get from fast-food to fellatio, I've got about six hours. 'It's OK,' I tell myself, this bit of the trip was always just a mood thing. Nevertheless, I decide to get going on the *The Pape*, which is bearable heavily iced and through a straw. Tennis man finishes his cow and heads for the gents, *The Pape* takes me in his wake.

Standing next to tennis man I obey the rules: no talking, no peeking, get the job done. It seems the rules don't wash here. He starts to blather. But this isn't French. In fact it's no recognisable European language. Before I know it, he's done the job but is showing no signs of putting it away. He's still blathering and, by now, starting to grin inanely. He moves towards me and I'm now in no doubt he wants me to see his tool. I mutter something about Ivan Lendl and head for daylight. I'm unsettled but buoyed. I could have seriously lost my way after that shoddy consumerism as care-free sex analogy in Monoprix. But now somebody has shown me his cock in McDonald's.

Apologies are due to big M.H. here. I couldn't find the adult cinema of Bruno's youth, *Le Latin*. That aspect of my trip will lead inevitably to Pigalle, but for now there's an opportunity to catch-up with some true decadents on the way north. They drink copiously, sleep around, go to underground parties, expose themselves in public and still turn up to work seven days a week. Nowhere does tramps like Paris. There's none of the money-for-glue sleaze of London, none of the juggler-ethos of Barcelona. These guys are trousers-held-up-with rope, ruddy-faced, bulbous-nosed alcoholics. And this evening I am among them, for their tipple of choice is *The Pape*.

Night falls as I arrive *chez Bruno*, rue Rodier in the 9th arrondissement. The view hones onto Paris's only skyscraper at Montparnasse. There are plenty of those ubiquitous shops where you can sate all your scatter cushion needs, but are fucked if you want a pint of milk and a sack of spuds. You get the impression that, when rue de Rodier was young, it probably didn't buy dog vids, go to swingers bars or expose itself in public. But it probably had friends who did. It's starting to rain and a little dog plays in a puddle. I've always hated little dogs. I find it amazing that well-to-do Parisians, otherwise adept at hiding their job in asset management behind an artily-draped scarf, should choose as the ultimate accessory a squawking, shitting rat on a rope.

It's a question I'm pondering as I reach Boulevard de Rochechouart: 'a rotten area,' according to bourgeois Parisians. A multicultural one in Anglo parlance. And a haven of whoring right on Bruno's doorstep. I dive into my next destination where it becomes Boulevard de Clichy. The assistant, a porno Catherine Deneuve, runs a cracked nail down her

Danone *crème chocolat* (€1.99 for four in the Monoprix next door). She's in a gold spandex miniskirt and probably past sixty. With a little dog and an artily-draped scarf she could pass for fifty-eight. *Porno shop* certainly does what it says on the tin, on VHS and DVD. A few titles stand out: *I fist my aunt* (€19.99), *She's got a boner* (€14.99). One leaps out: *It's not just my dog* (€24.99). And from the footage captured on the cover of this challenging work, it certainly isn't. I look at the spandex, then back at the DVD. I feel sick. It could just be the *The Pape*, a second bottle is volatile sherpa.

DVD's & Sex Ciné is just over the road, and again I'm pleased for the clarity of the sign-posting. I hate it when the hoarding says *B&Q* and you end up at a dwarf orgy. The clientele is overwhelmingly middle of the road: Civil service lifers, Monoprix middle-management, a few pissed scousers. A man resembling David Suchet fingers a shrink-wrapped '*fully functioning*' rubber vagina (price unmarked). It's called *The Clone*. The joint backs out into a number of dingy stairways and corridors. A large black guy guards one of them. I scan the tariff, 'relaxation . . . Chinese and African (30€). He tells me there's a special deal this week that offers a free 35 hours in the *salle royale* for those who knock-up 50 hours' attendance. A punter wanders out. He's just like the rest: thirty-something, Monoprix bag, *team success* T-shirt.

Tentative inquiry suggests I am unable to afford *The Clone* and besides *The Pape* is starting to preach. Time for my final port of call in the fourth arrondissement. Judging by the queue, it's celeb night at *Chris et Manu* on rue St Bon – and Catherine Deneuve and David Suchet are in front of me. I think of cross-channel stereotypes. Namely that *rosbif* wears his 'decadence' on the outside. Hence the vomiting, fisticuffs and occasional street-shagging witnessed on a night out in Albion. He's also prone to bursts of moral outrage anchored in the sands where Tesco and Paxman meet the protestant tradition. *Froggy*, meanwhile, acknowledges that, while debauchery occupies the mind, you've got a better chance of actually practising it if you keep up the respectable veneer. Hence it being OK for your colleagues to ask if wife is getting on well with your girlfriend.

'M'sieur, no seengle guys 'ere.'

I can't believe it, the snobbery. As I protest, a bottle of *The Pape* works itself loose and shatters comprehensively on the floor.

'And you cannot breeng your own booze.'

The game's up. I slide past the waiting management consultants and head for bed.

I bump into a friend the next day (nice French girl, consultant at the Ministry of Employment, Jack Russell). Relating my heroic trip, I tell her decadence is in the mind and is all about context anyway. She tells me I am a trenchant loser and that only the English think M.H is cool. And that she had a cracking night at *Chris et Manu*. I look shocked. There's one bottle of *The Pape* left.

Dickon Edwards with Anne Pigalle. Photo: David Bird.

El Hombre Indelible
Shane MacGowan and his New Romantic Butler in Tangier

Dickon Edwards

Ireland Online, 8th Dec 2005:
'Pogues frontman Shane MacGowan infuriated band members by taking an impromptu holiday to Morocco when he should have been rehearsing with them.'

The Independent (UK), 16 Dec 2005:
Pogues accordionist James Fearnley's diary:
'The first rehearsal for the Christmas tour. We don't expect to be seeing Shane MacGowan. He's in Morocco, or on his way back from Morocco. It's a mystery how he gets there without help, since his manager had not accompanied him. It's a further mystery how he gets back.'

★ ★ ★

It's a contender for one of the most Decadent phone calls one can receive.

'It's Shane. Do you want to go to Tangier with me for a week? I'll pay.'

And so a few days later, the singer is teaching me how to eat oysters, while we wait at Heathrow for one of the few direct flights to Tangier.

'How's this for an alternative *Brideshead Revisited*!' And he giggles that trademark white noise giggle. The first time I heard his laugh I was, quite frankly, frightened. But by this time, after months of being in his company, the sound is charming and infectious.

My introduction to Shane MacGowan came when he played a secret gig at The Boogaloo, the nearest bar to my bedsit. It was the owner Mr O'Boyle who approached me in the corner shop next door and invited me into the pub.

Strangers often feel the need to tell me what better-known person I look like, unbidden. The common comparison I get is Andy Warhol, or if they're of a certain 80s pop vintage, David Sylvian trying to be Andy Warhol. Shane MacGowan said I reminded him of Paul Bowles. This immediately endeared him to me, both flattering my appearance and revealing he knew all about lesser-known Decadent heroes. In London, more people have heard of Shane MacGowan than Paul Bowles. In Tangier, the reverse is true. Celebrity is relative.

He's often bracketed next to George Best and Ozzy Osbourne, as if all legendary over-indulgers are alike. I doubt those other two notably dissipated names are as literary-inclined as someone whose collected lyrics were published by Faber & Faber. While it's undeniable the decades of Deca-dence have damaged parts of his brain, it's only the parts for walking and speaking that have paid the price. Put him in a hotel room for a week without alcohol, and he'd still come out convincing the uninitiated he was drunk beyond belief. His intelligence, talent and memory remain impressively intact.

Over the subsequent months, I spent many a late-night drinking session at the Boogaloo with him. He'd frequently amaze me with an in-depth knowledge on a wide field of literature, music and cinema, and not just the Irish side of things. His travel bag was dominated with books: works by Joyce, Plato, Burroughs, Kerouac, Dorothy Parker, and the entire James Ellroy *LA Confidential* trilogy. He re-reads *Finnegan's Wake* every day. Shane MacGowan is the most

well-read man I've ever met. There is decadence, and then
there is Decadence.

When he saw I had time on my hands and not too much
money, he kindly employed me on a few sporadic errands
during his Highgate-based period. I would occasionally do his
shopping, house-sitting, even help him find his socks. Regulars at the Boogaloo would unkindly refer to me as his 'New
Romantic Butler'. Though this was a tag he didn't care for, I
was happy to let it stick. If a good joke fits, wear it.

We'd talk about Tangier, the city that connects Bowles and
Burroughs. I mentioned that I'd love to go there sometime.
And so here we were, just the two of us, in Tangier, Morocco,
early December 2005. A nervous fake-blond younger Englishman in a white suit and make-up, with an older man with
black hair in a big black coat, getting annoyed when hearing
himself referred to as English or American ('I'm Irish! Irish!').
English and Irish; White Suit and Black Coat; Innocence and
Experience.

Tangier is another planet. People in scarfs, cowls and hoods
mingling with the modern, ululating howls from exotic
temples, streets with varying names on different maps, streets
which are really one-person corridors in buildings, desert and
ocean vistas around the corner, drugs and street hustlers, the
bizarre and the bazaars; indecipherable but beautiful alphabets,
indecipherable but beautiful everything. William Burroughs
was dubbed 'El Hombre Invisible' while he wrote *The Naked
Lunch*, due to his skulking in Tangier's shadows. Shane
MacGowan must be 'El Hombre Indelible'. He seems impossible to erase.

We booked into the Hotel Continental in the Medina,
Mr MacGowan aptly taking Room 101. It's a beautiful old
place, as seen in Mr Bertolucci's *Sheltering Sky* movie. Rather
amusingly, it's also alcohol-free, so I was dispatched to the
Ville Nouveau to stock up on gin and tonic. He may no
longer be a heroin addict, but he's still a gin and tonic and

cigarettes junkie. To stop those, he said, would kill him. For much of our week-long stay, Mr MacGowan was happy to remain in the hotel room, reading, drinking, relaxing, clearing his head of London before having to rehearse with the reunited Pogues ('reformed' sounds misleading) for a high-profile Christmas tour.

'I didn't come here to wake up.' he snarled after two days without eating or leaving his room. I had no answer to that. Although I dismissed the hotel staff's suggestion of a doctor, it was difficult to tell what was entirely normal and what was a cause for concern. So I was relieved when Mr O'Boyle flew in to join us for the middle of the week.

I'd brought Michelle Green's biography about Tangier's literary renegades, *The Dream at the End of the World*. One passage recounts Jack Kerouac not leaving *his* hotel room for days, trying to sleep with the noises of Mr Burroughs's pederasty going in the next room. I read this passage aloud to Mr MacG and he replied: 'I've heard worse things coming from a room next door.' And he giggled that white noise giggle.

Though I happily shopped for him, my blood pressure drew the line at majoun and kif, the local narcotics. He grumbled slightly, but acquiesced.

'I wouldn't expect my sister to buy drugs for me, so I guess I shouldn't expect it of you.'

As it turns out, he managed to find a supply of kif without me, which kept him happy while I did my tourist bit: Scott's Bar with its curious paintings of beautiful Arab boys in Scottish regimental costume, the ex-pat Pet Cemetery on the mountain with its 1940s cat graves, the cliffside café where you can sip mint tea and gaze out across the Mediterranean to see Spain on one side, Africa on the other. I sat in all the bars and cafés connected with those dead literary hooligans. Tangier (only fools spell it Tangiers) is the original Decadent Destination. Fifty years after the Interzone closed down, the city isn't what it was, but it's also not what it could be. I feel the flame must be kept burning somehow, and I hope to go back.

Our return trip on this occasion was the only fraught side of the holiday. Just before we boarded our connection to Casablanca, the Tangier airport staff refused to let Mr MacGowan on the plane. 'You can go, but not your friend. He is clearly too drunk.'

'He's always like that! It's a permanent condition.'

'Listen, my friend. I know when someone is drunk.'

'I'm not going without him,' I barked nobly, feeling my halo ascend. Though any attempt at heroic selflessness was rather compromised by the thought of what the other Pogues and their fans would do to me, should I return to London Shane-less.

I tried to explain that I could vouch for him, that he'd be in my care, that he was a famous musician with concerts booked, that it was vital we got on the plane. But the airline man was having none of it. 'Come back tomorrow.'

After a few minutes of utter panic, I calmed down and phoned The Boogaloo from the airport. Mr O'Boyle mused that to try flying tomorrow was pointless: Mr MacGowan would be the same, the airport staff would be the same. Instead, he said we should take the scenic route. Get the ferry from Tangier to Algeciras, take a taxi up the Spanish coast to Malaga, then hop on a plane to Stansted. And if in doubt, put Mr MacGowan in a wheelchair at the airport. No one ever questions a wheelchair.

This impromptu excursion went surprisingly swimmingly. Not only did the passenger ferry staff accept Mr MacGowan, they were happy to point him to the bar on the top deck. It was just like being back at The Boogaloo, but with a view of the sun-drenched Mediterranean passing pleasingly by. We made it back to Stansted with no hitches, and drove straight to the Boogaloo to continue where we left off.

Part of the Process

Karina Mellinger

Mary and Tony are going for a weekend to Venice to revive their flagging marriage. Even now, squirming in their leather seats in the First Class Lounge at Heathrow, sipping from flutes of chilled vintage Krug, they both know this trip is a bad idea.

It reminds Mary of the first night of their honeymoon when they stood side by side on the balcony of their suite at The Georges V and watched the fireworks which spelt out their names spilling down over the Seine. She knew marriage to Tony had been a bad idea then.

And it reminds Tony of their first date when Mary arrived at the Royal Opera House wearing an orange trouser suit, almost as hideous as the emerald silk dress she has on now. That's when he first knew a relationship with Mary was going to be a bad idea.

But, bad or not, life goes on and their marriage guidance counsellor, Diana, has told them that going on a holiday may sound like a cliché but it really can make a huge difference.

Diana says she has cancelled her other plans and she will be at their complete disposition the entire weekend of their stay. They can ring her whenever they want. That's how much she wants their marriage to work. So they're off to Venice to give things one last try. They're doing it for Diana. More than anything Mary and Tony really don't want to let her down.

★

When they land at Marco Polo Airport Mary immediately disappears to the ladies lavatory so she can ring Diana and tell her about the flight, how it had been a nightmare, how her langoustine had had a metallic taste to it, how the novel she was reading had ended implausibly and how for the entire journey Tony had rustled his copy of *The Telegraph* like a man possessed.

Diana suggests to Mary that her reaction to the newspaper noise may be related to their previous discussions about Mary's feelings of sexual inadequacy. Will Mary reflect on that? Mary says she will. Diana says she'll ring her soon to see whether she's come to any conclusion – would Mary like that? Mary says she would.

Diana tells Mary that to calm herself down she should do the Body Contact exercise they have been practising together, the one where Mary rests her hand gently on her thyroid, heart, liver and pubic bone for three seconds and says to each of them in turn, 'I accept you.'

Mary looks at herself in the mirror above the long line of handbasins.

She touches herself. She says, 'I accept you. I accept you. I accept you. I accept you.'

Two women are standing next to her washing their hands. One of them says to her friend, 'Questa qui è matta.'

The other woman shrugs. 'Cosa vuoi – è inglese.'

Mary feels better already.

*

Mary and Tony walk out of the airport into the hot sunshine. Tony flinches. Warmth he likes but this kind of heat he finds oppressive, excessive. They have booked a small, exclusive hotel on the Venice Lido. That way they can absorb the aesthetic energy of the city without actually having to plod round it. They walk down the pier to their waiting speedboat. Tony notices that the driver has a slight squint. Tony is frustrated. You don't come to the most beautiful city on the face of the Earth to be ferried around by someone who looks like that.

They set off across the lagoon. The water is flat and soft and giving like a turquoise cashmere carpet. Then, of his own volition, without even bothering to ask if this is something Mary and Tony would like, the driver does a detour up the Grand Canal instead of going straight to the hotel. This is annoying as Tony wanted to get to the hotel sooner rather than later to check the latest Nasdaq prices. The motorboat splices past Piazza San Marco, Santa Maria della Salute, Palazzo Dario, Palazzo Loredan, Santa Maria della Carità. Mary scrabbles in her handbag to find her favourite lipstick which she thinks she must have left on the bloody plane.

Tony looks at the buildings filing past. The driver turns to Tony and gestures towards them with a squinty-eyed look of pleasure and pride.

'Una meraviglia!' the driver cries.

'Yes. Very nice,' Tony says.

Tony feels the lagoon water spray onto his face and a mild sensation of sea sickness at the pit of his stomach. He is with a woman with poor dress sense and a man with a squint. He wants to be happy but how can he?

He texts Diana, 'Life is so imperfect!'

She texts back, 'This awareness is part of your process, Tony. Cherish it.'

So he does. Thank God for Diana.

★

When they arrive they find that Diana has arranged for flowers – white roses, tuberoses, calla lilies and gingers – in the bedroom suite. The room is swooning with their fragrance. Tony has them removed before they set off his hayfever. There is a hand-written note from Diana: it says 'I'm so proud of you both.' Tony feels tears well in his eyes. They ring her to say thank you, taking it in turns on the phone. She asks how they feel going down to dinner. They both say it's going to be tough. Diana says she is there for them. Tony and Mary both wish she were.

When the time comes, however, Tony and Mary feel they cannot face the hotel dining room so they arrange instead for room service. As they cannot decide what they want to eat they order a buffet. The hotel sets up a table outside on their private terrace, a wide platform of ornate terracotta, engorged with jasmine and bougainvillia, edged with steps down to a small lawned garden which leads to the hotel's private beach.

The sun is setting. The sky has settled to a rich russet streaked with lemon and red.

Mary and Tony decide they would rather have supper in their room so they can watch the evening news on TV while they eat. They have the table brought in from the terrace.

The waiter fills their glasses with a 2001 Chardonnay delle Venezie. He presents them with ripe melon and peaches and figs and with Mozzarella Bufala Campana, Carpaccio and Prosciutto Veneto Berico-Euganeo. Tony doesn't care for starters on principle. Mary has never liked raw meat, for Christ's sake. She nibbles at a bread roll.

Mary and Tony leave their mobiles out on the dining table, just in case Diana rings.

Mary knows she should make small talk with Tony but doesn't know where to start. She texts Diana, 'Nothing to say!'

Diana texts back, 'Relax. Silence is rich with possibility.' Mary sighs with relief. The waiter removes their empty plates. Mary notices that he is very handsome with high, taut buttocks. Of course. Italian men are so predictable.

The waiter returns with a large tray laden with dishes. He sets the tray down. He says, slowly, 'C'è Vitello in Salsa di Cacciagione al Tartufo, Fritto Misto di Mare, Moleche Frite, Cozze all'Aglio e Prezzemolo, Sardine in Saor, Bigoli co'l'Arna.' He looks intently at Mary and waits.

Mary looks at the dishes paraded before her. She sniffs. 'Ugh. Garlic,' she grimaces. She puts up her hand to indicate revulsion and refusal. Tony accepts some of the veal but nothing else. He's not sure what any of the rest of it is and, anyway, he never has much of an appetite after a flight.

A pianist from the Accademia di San Rocco arrives and sits at the Fazioli grand piano in the salone just off the terrace. She plays the last movement of Schubert's Sonata in D Major. The music seeps in through the open doors of the room. The waiter bows his head in reverence. Tony gets up and closes the doors. He can't concentrate on the bloody news with that noise going on.

Mary and Tony sit wordlessly. Tony chews; Mary picks at the crust of her roll.

Finally, when the news is over, Tony puts the TV on mute and announces that he thinks this is getting silly and that they should ring Diana.

'Fine,' says Mary eagerly.

They dial Diana's number. 'Hi Diana,' says Tony. 'Look, Diana,' he says, 'this isn't going very well. Could I just put my mobile on speaker phone and you just stay on line for a bit?'

'OK, of course, I'm here for you.'

Mary and Tony both sigh with relief.

Tony returns to his supper.

'How is it?' Mary asks politely.

'How's what?' Tony asks desperately. Jesus, not another analysis of his existential state, he prays, please God no.

'The food.'

'So so. Aren't you going to have anything?'

'I'm finishing this cigarette first.'

'Yes, I noticed that.'

'What's that supposed to mean? Is this the prelude to another lecture about smoking? Because I don't think I could handle that right now, I really don't!' Mary shrieks.

'You see, Diana – even the most trivial comment is misinterpreted.'

'Let her express herself, Tony,' Diana advises calmly over the airwaves.

'Is this part of her process?' Tony asks in a thin, tired voice.

'Yes, Tony, it is,' says Diana.

'OK,' he whispers meekly.

'The fact is,' Mary continues loudly, 'I can't stop thinking about the langoustine I had on the plane. It was definitely off, I could taste it, I could smell it, and I think that it may have been a metaphor for my marriage. That too is off, over.'

'OK, Mary, this is good,' Diana says reassuringly. 'You're getting in touch with your anger. That's good.'

'No, it's not! You know I can't do anger without you here, Diana,' Mary trembles.

'I know that,' says Diana.

There is a knock at the door. When the waiter opens it there is Diana.

'Diana!!' Mary and Tony both cry as they rush over to embrace her, their bodies colliding spontaneously against each other for the first time in years.

'I thought I'd better come to support you in case things got really tough so – here I am.'

'Marvellous!' Tony beams. 'Waiter!' he instructs, 'bring another place setting!'

'No,' says Diana firmly, 'no, I won't actually sit with you, I'll just sit near you, so you know that I'm here, so you've got the confidence to really be yourselves.' Diana goes over to a low armchair at the edge of the room.

'Oh. OK,' Mary and Tony both mumble in disappointment. Dejectedly, they walk back to their seats.

The waiter brings a bottle of Vin Santo and cheeses and desserts. Quartirolo Lombardo, Robiola di Roccaverano, Provolone Val Padana. Zabaione, Tiramisu, Panna Cotta, Amaretti,

Cioccolatini con Aceto Balsamico di Modena. Tony takes one of the biscuits but it's terribly dry, nothing like Digestives. Mary pings her finger against her cut-crystal glass. Eventually the handsome waiter clears the plates of uneaten food away. 'Non è piaciuto?' he asks them both.

'What did he say?' Mary asks.

'God knows,' says Tony. Why should he care what the waiter has said?

★

It's time for bed. Tony and Mary undress and put on their pyjamas. Diana sits quietly on the chair at the foot of the bed.

'Thank you for being here,' says Tony humbly.

'No problem,' says Diana. 'Use me as you need me.'

'Fine,' says Mary gratefully.

Mary and Tony get into bed. Tony reads *The Financial Times*, *The Investors Chronicle*, *The Wall Street Journal* and *Money Week*. Mary watches *Casablanca* on TV and orders a new Fendi handbag from the internet on her laptop. There is a reproduction in oil of Lorenzo Lotto's 'St Catherine' on the wall. The saint is holding her head at an irritating angle. Mary gets up and takes the painting down.

Eventually Tony feels sleepy and turns out the light. Mary nods off at the bit where things get emotional in the film.

★

Diana takes off all her clothes and walks out onto the terrace. She feels the terracotta stone still warm with the heat of the day. She feels it glowing, vibrating under her feet. The waiter comes and takes her in his arms and kisses her. He massages Vin Santo into her breasts; he wipes Zabaione down the length of her back and licks it off. He crams Carpaccio into her mouth and eats it out of her. He wipes ripe figs across her

238

thighs, and smears Panna Cotta up between her legs then devours it all.

★

The next morning Mary and Tony wake up. Diana is there, awake, in her chair. Tony has an erection. He says to Diana, 'I had an amazing dream in the night.'

'Dreams are good,' Diana says.

He turns to Mary. 'Shall we take a boat to the islands today? There's the cathedral of Santa Maria Assunta on Torcello which is a thousand years old.'

'Jesus, Tony,' says Mary, 'I don't think I can be bothered, not in this heat.'

'Yes. Maybe you're right,' he says. He reaches for the phone to order breakfast and then to ring the office in London.

Diana smiles.

Decadent Sex

Forbidden Fruit

Elizabeth Speller

The defining moment of my life was when Jeremy Naismith-Green's father put his tongue in my mouth. Never mind that he was egged on by Jeremy, his nasty little brother Tom and my cousin timing us with a stop-watch (in those days he timed everything: the length it took him to pee, to bicycle to the post box or finish a gobstopper; it stood him well in the long run: now he works as a city lawyer, his day fragmented into six minute intervals charged exorbitantly to his diaspora of clients). Never mind the mistletoe – in fact, God bless the mistletoe – which I had been hovering under for an hour in the chilly, liminal area between the stairs and the front door, with only Tom showing any interest in kissing me and, from the chewing I'd observed earlier, only to pass his slimy gobbet of chewing gum into my mouth.

But then, suddenly, he was there. Owner of the area's largest leather factory. Three children, a big house with a high hedge, a wife who played bridge and whose hair never moved, a Rover car and a sports coat. Indisputably a grown up.

'Kiss her kiss her!', the boys yelled with the same excitement they usually showed for egging each other on to something really repulsive, like letting a slug crawl up your arm or pouring boiling water on ants.

And then he kissed me.

Laughingly at first; a brush of his slightly scratchy lips on mine, but they didn't leave. They pressed a little harder and the hand that had rested, light as a feather, on my hip became two and moved from a matter of balance to control, holding me, almost imperceptibly, against him. Meanwhile under the

243

increased pressure of his lips, mine opened a little and inside the scratchiness, his too were soft. My cousin had been counting backwards from ten but, having arrived at nought to find things at no kind of conclusion, began again at sixty. Vile Tom was jumping about on the third step of the stairs in an attempt to be at eye view.

Mr. Naismith-Green's head turned a little so that we were a better fit and the hand round my waist became fingers; I could feel each one against my flesh. My open cardigan fell back and the tips of his thumb on the other side rested on my viyella shirt, just on the lowest curve of my bra, while the rest of his hard cupped my rib cage. 'Thirty-siiiiiix, thirty-fiiiiivvve.' My cousin slowed his counting to funereal pace.

And then, our mouths were wet and the tip of his tongue parted them further and I could smell soap on his face and, where my shirt had come untucked, because I was on tip-toes, his cuffs rubbed against me. His tongue went further in, or perhaps my mouth just opened wider, and our teeth clashed for a second and either the boys fell silent or I shut my eyes and it all died away, but as he steadied me from losing my balance, I could feel something – him – against my thighs. And then Jeremy said 'Dad . . .' plaintively, and my cousin said, 'three, two, one, Blast off!', with a certain lack of conviction and Tom jumped off the stairs and tried to pull the mistletoe off the hall light and suddenly Mr Naismith-Green was himself again; jolly, adult and in charge. But I was never *myself* because it had, thus far, been the single most exciting experience of my life.

The Cow Shed

André Pieyre de Mandiargues

'Are you an aficionado of the brothel?' he asked me.

'It's a good deal more interesting than solitaire or *jeu des graces*. But is there one, in this town of Protestants, with their frigid pricks and black feet?'

'Not officially, but if you'll allow me, this evening I'll take you to a certain establishment which I frequent. It's a place not entirely devoid of a certain charm.'

So Sir Horatio took me on an expedition to one of the lower class districts on the other side of the river Aar. We went down a stinking alley and stopped in front of a dark doorway. Here, he rapped out a long and complicated pattern of beats on the door with the ferrule of his walking stick. This was done so that I'd be able to remember the pattern in the future. The door was opened, the English diplomat was recognised and we were ushered into one of those 'lucky cowsheds'. These are to be found in great numbers in some of the more backward cantons of German-speaking Switzerland where none of the girls are particularly keen to make their cunt or arse available to all-comers.

Under a roof of large beams was a vast room with a white wooden floor. Around the walls of the room, I recall, were a series of square stalls each one of which contained a pedigree Emmenthal cow. The animal was provided with a thick bed of straw, but dirtier than might have been expected given its role. In the middle there were tables where the customers, of which there were a fair few that night, sat and drank beer from huge tankards. As soon as these were empty, they were refilled by serving girls who were perfect representatives of the Berne type. By that I mean they were round-bellied, with heavy pendulous breasts, fat arses and shapely legs – rather exciting, for all that they exuded an air of monumental stupidity.

'Try your luck. An ecu a go,' announced the owner, as he paraded from one table to the next an object which struck me as repulsive. It was the belly of an old doll which had been hollowed out like a piggy bank, its cunt edged with rabbit fur. Into this cunt, exactly the same size as a coin stamped with the head of William Tell, the revellers stuffed their cash.

Most of the time, absolutely nothing happened. (The owner of the cowshed did good business). However, now and again, after the insertion of a coin, a Swiss national flag would pop up from the navel. In this case, all the barmaids quickly gathered around the winner allowing him to choose one of them. Curiously, to my way of thinking, they stood with their backs to the winner. Although from the front they displayed the utmost modesty, buttoned up to the neck, at the back their dresses were lifted to reveal their buttocks, unimpeded by any underwear. Apparently, in German Switzerland the only thing a woman is judged by is her arse.

Having chosen his prize, the winner led her to a cowstall. Some closed the stall doors, which meant that during their 'private moment' all we could see were the upper parts of the cow. The majority, on the other hand, left the door wide open to besport themselves in front of their friends who were still at the table. They got undressed publicly, often hanging their trousers and shirt on the horns of the cow, then stripped the scrubber and fucked her underneath the belly of the bovine in full view of everybody. The cows remained placid enough. They were well and truly used to all this.

Sir Horatio and I tried our luck on a number of occasions, and I was the first to succeed in running the cross of Geneva up the flagpole. I plumped for the least buxom of the females, a choice which was loudly mocked by the drinkers. She was a real beauty, at least as far as her shape was concerned. But she shared with her peers such a thick hide that it felt more like running my hand over rind than over a woman's skin.

When the two of us were naked, I didn't shut the doors. I thought that in a gesture of gratitude for having brought me to such a delightful dive, Sir Horatio might like to watch me fucking.

It's a strange sensation to be lying totally naked, albeit with a really beautiful woman, stretched out on a bed of straw soiled with cow pats and urine, between the legs of a cow which could crush you or seriously injure you with one blow from its hoofs.

My companion (she told me her name was Litzi) made me lie with my face more or less directly under the animal's arse. While Mlle Litzi, who was positioned on top of me, energetically rubbed the rear end of the animal, I was fondling the swollen udder of this huge animal and amused myself by pulling on the teats and squirting warm, creamy liquid over the two of us.

Later on, Sir Horatio's flag went up, but he shut himself in very carefully and nobody could see how he took his pleasure with the young fat girl he had chosen. Some of the regulars, however, were heard to say that the cow had never been so upset. The diplomat emerged from the cowstall at the end of three quarters of an hour.

'I will let you see my prick another time . . .' he said to me. '. . . and when it's erect, which is a rare occurrence. I only did it today for a little amusement.'

The girl was dripping with cow piss. She was twisting her long, sponge-coloured hair to try and dry it out a little. But in vain. She was looking very put out, which was delightful to see, and it occurred to me that I'd been rather stupid with mine to find nothing better to do than ride the lazy bitch and shower us with milk. Sir Horatio was as buttoned up as ever, more like he'd just stepped out of a lavatory rather than a stable of whores.

Pony Girls

Tom Holland

'Be ye not like to horse and mule,' the *Prayer Book* instructs us, 'whose mouths must be held with bit and bridle, lest they fall upon thee.' Decadence, which is the transmutation of baseness into beauty, feeds naturally upon injunctions such as this. Perhaps it is not surprising, then, that on the outer fringes of the decadent imagination, where fabulous creatures lurk, one of the most exotic of all should be a human–pony hybrid: a man or woman literally treated as a horse. Like the centaurs supposed to haunt the wilds of ancient Greece, such a figure might seem almost too fantastical to be true – and yet the pony-slave, though elusive, is not altogether a myth. The bitting, the restricting, the reining in of animal passions: the very language of the moralist can be refined, imagination willing, into the most exquisite depravity.

Ironically, the earliest known person to be associated with such a symptom of decadence was also the first zoologist to argue that different species could never mix: the philosopher Aristotle. A celebrated Renaissance woodcut shows the Stagyrite bitted and bridled, with his mistress Phyllis in the saddle on his back. In a foreshadowing of almost every such subsequent illustration of the theme, the rider lashes the rump of her human steed with a whip. The inspiration for this portrait, however, was not classical but drawn from a medieval poem, in which 'Aristote chevauché' was offered as a warning against the capacity of lust to overwhelm reason. But as is so often the way with such fables, the lesson titillates more than it instructs. The very extent of the philosopher's fall, his debasement from the heights of logic to a bestial status lower than a slave, becomes, to those predisposed to see it so, delicious in itself.

When Christopher Marlowe, a man whose sadism was evident in almost everything he wrote, came to pen that other Renaissance masterpiece of pony play, *Tamburlaine the Great*, the thrill of humiliation was openly acknowledged. 'Holla, ye pampered Jades of Asia': with this celebrated, and much parodied, line, Tamburlaine lashes the backs of two kings he has defeated in battle and harnessed to his chariot. Other kings follow tethered behind him, and Tamburlaine loses no opportunity to revel in their transformation. They will sleep in stables; they will drink from pails; they will 'die like beasts.'

What gives added piquancy to this role reversal is that Tamburlaine had originally been a shepherd, very much lower-class, and a foreigner to boot. The vertiginious drop which separates human and beast is widened yet further by class, for it is a curious feature that in almost all the classics of pony-slave erotica, the victims are exquisitely well-bred. In Anne Rice's *Beauty* trilogy, for instance, the princes and princesses who are sent to the village suffer a humiliatingly utilitarian slavery, in which their iron-shod boots and horse-tailed dildoes, their harnesses and bits, have no function save to make their wearers more efficient as workhorses. And all this is taught them by rude-handed grooms, strutting around the stables, 'scrubbing down their charges or rubbing them with oil,their attitude one of casualness and busyness.'

This could only seem utilitarian in a fairy-tale setting, of course. Even scenarios in ostensibly contemporary settings are invariably located in remote fantasy fiefdoms, whether in the deserts of Arabia or amidst the jungles of South America. Yet while this hardly serves to make them any the more realistic, it does enable one further tooth to be added to the ratchet of equine humiliation. For the victims of your typical ponygirlrearing Sheik or hacienda-owner are very pointedly not only aristocratic; they are also very white.

Or to be specific, Anglo-Saxon. This perhaps comes as no surprise when one realises that the earliest and most influential examples of ponygirl literature – and the emphasis is very much on ponygirl – were French. In a succession of anonymous novels published on the theme in Paris during the twenties and thirties, diabolical humiliations were practised by assorted subject peoples upon the Miladies of the British Empire. 'In the Rajah's Stable', reads one typical chapter heading; 'Race Day at the Wadi', another. One sequence of illustrations in particular does more to highlight French attitudes towards their imperial rivals than a whole series of historians' tracts. In the first illustration, a Duchess poses snootily at a Viceregal soirée, in the second she cowers in a stable before the pawings of two Sikhs, while in the third she has recaptured the hauteur which she wore in the first. But gone is her gown and glittering tiara, and in their place are all the appurtenances of the fetishist's art: harness, bit and bridle, blinkers and nodding feathers, rings through the nipples with tinkling bells. A Rajah looks on at her proudly, a curling whip in his hand, and it is evident that he is preparing to take his new pony for a ride: for haughty though the Duchess may appear, yet she is fastened by elegant chains to the shafts of a cart.

The implausibility inherent in this image is precisely what makes it so gloriously decadent. No one wanting to go for a spin would rely on a delicate former duchess to last the course. But it is both the glory and the agony of those who surrender to their own depravity that the imagination is never quite sufficient. So it is that human ponies are not confined to novels and fantastical illustrations; as with every decadent fantasy, there are those who seek to make it true. Dildoes with horsetails can certainly be found; so too boots in the form of hooves; so too farms with stables fitted for humans. Yet if anything illustrates the power of the erotic as opposed to the pornographic, it is to compare a photograph of a human pony, however handsome and muscular, however beautiful and slim, with a line illustration of a similar sight, or a paragraph describing such a scene. The appeal of *equus eroticus* exists not despite but because of it being a contradiction in terms. Sometimes the decadent becomes more powerful for being an exploration, not of the possible, but of what can never be.

The Story of B

Belle de Jour

My decline into decadence started early, but by no means finished then. While at the age of sixteen I imagined that I had thought of all there was to do with sex, tried it all and found it all wanting, by seventeen I knew that there were entire planetary systems – if not universes – still to be explored.

When I met W, I was no virgin. Sex in public, role-playing, costumes and BDSM. Cross-dressing boyfriends who liked the taste of the crop were a particular favourite. I knew that something was very different about him from the way he kissed me (biting my lower lip until I tasted blood). We drove round London and he told me about Ian Fleming's bit on the side, an aristocratic lady who liked it rough. Very rough. As in bruises, and then some.

'Bring it on,' I said, and he smiled. After all, everyone has to have an ill-advised affair that they later regret.

One night he came by my place. I'd requested that he bring whatever toys he thought suitable, but the only thing in his hands was a bottle of Bailey's. No wicked spiked nipple clamps, no dildos, no blindfolds? No kinky kit? He said whatever he needed, I already had. Fair enough then. We sat at the kitchen table listening to the Smiths and drinking and laughing.

Upstairs the mood changed. He walked into my bedroom like he knew it already. Opened the wardrobe and threw my things onto the floor. Kicked a black PVC vest and micro-mini in my direction. 'Wear that,' he said. He found my whips, including the rubber multi-tailed cat, which could deal blows that ranged from silkily teasing to vicious – depending on the user. At least I assumed it had vicious potential. I'd never known a lover who actively endorsed drawing blood.

'Top on, bra off,' he said. As I stood, arms behind my back, he whipped my breasts. Hard. The angled tips of the rubber tails felt like they were on fire. And this was with clothing on. 'Strip,' he said. I was surprised to see there were already weals across my breasts, raised double lines like tram tracks. He pulled himself out of his trousers and went, as they say, to town. His free hand alternated between squeezing his thick cock and smacking my face with a jaw-popping force. I'm not averse to pain. There is something about the shock of cold, of a sharp smack, that clears the head. In the instant the whip licks your body there literally is no room for anything else in your mind but that sensation. It's too strong. And in a world where people spend the larger parts of their free time and salaries pursuing any experience that will take them out of themselves, I can say with certainty this does it. I didn't notice the blood until he told me to go to the shower.

And then the reason for the Bailey's became apparent. We waited until his tumescence faded slightly and let his bladder go all over me. The salty streams felt like acid on my wounds. I opened my mouth and caught the spray. When I leaned over to chase the dregs to the drain, he took me in the arse. There was no need for foreplay. I was, in more ways than one, already wet.

If you're going to regret an affair, regret it for all the right reasons. Not because you grew tired of each other after several years of cohabitation until the day you found an empty condom wrapper in his briefcase. Not because you chose stability over excitement. Regret it because you may never feel that way again. Because when you tell it to others, they won't understand. Me, I don't regret a thing.

Househusband

Brock Norman Brock

*Step out from the woods and onto the heath. London below fills
the valley, a sea of sparkling lights. A million lights, a million
lives . . . a million . . .*

. . . Other Men's Wives

Rain.

But the cold has gone. Suddenly everything's muggy. And
in the air, something's sweet. The apple trees are in blossom.
Or perhaps it's cherry trees. Suddenly, as if by magic, flowers
are everywhere – in the trees, on the ground, you can't turn
your head without seeing them waving their exotic little
sexual organs at you, like a new crop of Thai table dancers just
hitting puberty. 'Hey, Mister, look-see, look-see . . .' the tiny
cherry blossoms tease.

You're standing in the rain outside of your child's school,
idly fingering a little downy pistil or stamen when you realise
that you are hard. You look up to see if anyone has noticed.
The white mothers sit in their red Volvo estates, double-
parked, windows all steamed up from mugs of tea and gossip-
ing. They're talking about you. You can't see their faces
behind the fogged windscreens, but you can feel their eyes on
you. The Bengali mothers, too, huddled around the school
gates, under dark umbrellas, veiled, yashmacked. They're looking at you, too. You shift your weight from one foot to the
other to ease off some of the pressure on your erection and
there's a little ripple of reaction from the women, like a herd
or a flock, as if they might panic and take flight if you were to
make any sudden movements.

Wolf in sheep's clothing.

Cock in the hen house.

Househusband.

The rain comes down harder. One of the red Volvo estates flashes its lights at you. Passenger door opens. 'Get in, get out of the rain,' she says. You do, and say, 'Some Spring.' She nods yes and smiles. You can't remember her name but know that her little girl is called Lily or Rose or Buddleia and has bright red hair. You believe that she is a gardener, or possibly a florist.

You'd taken yours round to hers once, a children's tea party. The children disappear upstairs, leaving you to make small talk with the other mothers there, but it's women's small talk, all schools and gardens and childhood diseases, and you find your eye wandering over the domestic details of the house. You notice that she uses black rubber gloves to do the washing up, where your own wife prefers yellow.

Later, there was a bump or a crash, then crying. The children had been bouncing on the marital bed. Someone had knocked over a lamp. The children are sent downstairs for their tea but you stay behind to help her to put the bedclothes back together. Under a pillow is her nightie, surprisingly feminine. It is flesh-coloured and silk. One shoulder strap is missing its hook, and has been tied back on with a make-shift loop.

She sees that you are holding it. 'Old thing. . .' she is beginning to explain and then stops.

From downstairs now you can hear the other mothers gathering their children to go. 'It'll take them at least ten minutes to get their coats and shoes back on,' she says. 'Don't stop.' She's under you and your hips are grinding together in a slow, hard, bone-to-bone semi-circle. Above her head, her hands are splayed out like fruit trees with gnarly fingers. Her legs are unshaved and prickle like nettles.

At the end of the party, her husband had arrived, pleased with himself for having been able to get away from the office early and not a little uncomfortable with the fact that another man had been in his house in the middle of the afternoon. He is annoyed that the other children and guests are leaving just as he's got there. He corners you and makes aggressive, men's small talk, all office politics and sport and public transport. He puts his hand on his daughter's head, petting her hair proprietarily as if it were his wife's red cunt.

Outside, the rain comes down now in sheets. You can't see a thing through the steamed up windows except the dark shadows of the Bengali women around the school gates. Inside the car, the air is even heavier and more humid, like a greenhouse. The back is loaded full of cuttings and bulbs, bits of trellis and bags of potting soil, one of which has been ripped open, giving everything a dark and peaty smell.

She reaches across and brushes your collar. 'Pollen,' she says. Her fingernails are dirty with soil. She laughs a little, awkwardly, when the pollen falls onto your lap but doesn't break eye contact and continues brushing, then grabs onto your cock. 'Like a root,' you cannot help but think.

The bell has gone. You can hear the engines of the other Volvos start around you. Sylheti voices pass nearby. Children's laughter. As she goes down on you, her head accidentally hits the lever and turns on the windscreen wipers. For a moment you are exposed to the outside before you reach across her and switch them off and the rain obscures you once more.

The car gently rocks.

Spring has sprung.

The Art of Roman Decadence

William Napier

To truly achieve Roman levels of decadence you will need a great deal of money and no scruples. You will also want a menagerie of wild animals, some obedient slaves with no appreciation of their human rights, and amorous inclinations towards at least one other member of your immediate family.

The Romans had a number of ways of capturing their wild animals. Libyan lions, for instance, could be caught in the wilds of North Africa by having a scented and oiled-up slave get down on all fours and offer the animal his or her anus. When the lion was fully mounted and dreamily engaged, a gang of more pro-active slaves would leap out from the undergrowth, wrestle it to the ground, and sedate it with large draughts of Armenian brandy. The poor beast, having already suffered the indignity of involuntary coitus interruptus, would then be securely bound and shipped back to Rome for slaughter. Quite why they couldn't have caught it with a goat and a net is a mystery. Presumably it was just more fun this way. Animals were more often to be found in the dining room than the bedroom, for all the Romans' decadence, although there is one charming image of very mild bestiality from the life of the Empress Theodora. In her days as an actress, before she married Justinian, she used to perform a tableau of Leda and the Swan, covering her naked body with grains of barley and having a swan softly nibble them from her body whilst she squirmed and arched her back with every appearance of orgasmic delight. In her girlhood Theodora used to perform oral sex on passers-by in exchange for a copper or two (at that age too young to accommodate them any other way) and even after becoming Empress, when her husband's back was turned, she liked to organise some quite spectacular orgies for herself – if her venomous biographer Procopius is to be believed. She would take on three men at once, only complaining that 'nature had not given her a fourth or a fifth orifice' so that she could take on more, and she frequently exhausted as many as thirty lusty young slaveboys in a single night. Procopius also tells us that she caused earthquakes by black magic, and during the course of her reign murdered, 'I suggest, a million people.' So perhaps his evidence, like that of so many Roman historians, is not always entirely reliable.

The Emperor Tiberius enjoyed relaxing in the warm rock pools of that notorious sexual theme-park which was his villa on Capri, his penis covered in breadcrumbs so that mullet would come and nibble at it. He liked to have little boys swim along underwater and nibble at him as well, whom he called his minnows, while obliging groups of three or more beautiful boys and girls had sex in various positions in the nooks and grottoes of the surrounding gardens. The walls of his villa were covered in pornographic murals, and he set up an official government department 'for the originating of unfamiliar carnal pleasures.' Suetonius tells us that as a dirty old man Tiberius even went so far as to do unmentionable things involving milk, honey and unweaned babies.

Nero isn't known to have had sex with a swan or a mullet, but he did like to dress up in animal skins, however. He would then arrange for men and women who had particularly offended him to be tied naked to stakes, whilst he attacked their genitals as if he were a wild beast. He also managed the rare feat of raping one of the Vestal Virgins, Rubria by name, and murdering his aunt with a lethal dose of laxatives. But if he hated his aunt, at least he loved his mother. Rather too much. It was clear that his mother, Agrippina, had no problems with this attachment herself, however, even encouraging him by coming to his private quarters after lunch, when he was sleepy and half-sozzled, alluringly dressed to stimulate his attentions.

But it was Caligula who really set the benchmark for incest, along with other decadent staples such as wanton gluttony, over-dressing, spending money that he didn't have, and taking a passionate interest in theatricals. He also liked dressing up as a girl in a blonde wig and a long robe. The object of his incestuous affections was his sister Drusilla. It was their granny, Antonia, who first caught them in bed together, in the very act of defloration. But it didn't stop the relationship flourishing, evidently. Caligula was so proud of his inamorata that he had a little amphitheatre built specially, where for a denarius or two, the unwashed multitude could come and gawp at their Divine Emperor buggering his sister on stage. He also liked to have another partner involved, ideally the North African gladiator Superbus, who would bugger him at the same time as he was violating his cherished sibling. Incest, homosexuality, exhibitionism, group sex and even a kind of prostitution all in one. Quite a feat of the decadent imagination.

Caligula had his other sisters, Agrippina and Livia, gang-raped for twenty-four hours as a punishment for plotting against him, but Drusilla remained a firm favourite until her tragically early death at the age of 23 from, as the doctors said, 'a surfeit of buggery.' She had just finished a lengthy session with her brother and seven extra studs recently shipped in from Caesariensis, in modern-day Algeria. With much weeping and lamentation, Caligula affectionately sodomised her corpse one last time, by way of fond farewell, then had her declared a goddess. After her cremation he masturbated onto her ashes. Greater love hath no man. Caligula should also be remembered for having both created and choreographed the world's first (and surely last) authentic 'snuff' ballet, Laureolus, which included ritual slaughter for real, the victims being played by criminals condemned to die anyway. By the end of the performance there were only three dancers left alive, on a stage strewn with dead dancers' body parts and awash with blood.

It is with some relief that one turns to the pretty boy Heliogabalus, who for all his faults was comparatively free of cruelty and sadism. Where Heliogabalus excelled was in hedonism and poor financial management. He was the first Roman to wear pure silk (strictly linen and wool up till then), and his preferred dishes at banquets included camels' heels and the combs of living cockerels. If the essence of decadent cuisine is to eat the smallest, most superficial part of the largest or rarest animal and then throw the rest away, Heliogabalus had it down to a fine art. He ate flamingoes' brains and the heads of parakeets, fed his dogs on foie gras and his lions on parrots and peacocks. He served dishes of mixed salads such as peas and gold coins, lentils and onyx, or rice with pearls. He kept a private brothel for himself and his friends, and never slept with the same woman or wore the same pair of shoes twice. (Some Freudian connection, surely.) The quintessential decadent moment came at a dinner party; he let down such a huge cascade of violet and rose petals from the ceiling onto the heads of his diners that several of them suffocated to death. Like his Imperial predecessors, he too loved sex in public and dressing up as a girl. He had himself carried around Rome in a litter drawn by naked women, whose buttocks he would whip as they processed. Before he stepped down into the street, gold dust would be sprinkled before his feet. The Romans' taste for sex, violence and spectacle all came together at the games where whores proliferated to such an extent that, for a change, it wasn't just the Emperor who benefited. It was considered all part of a good afternoon's entertainment to get some passing hooker to bring you off just at the climactic moment during the slaughter down in the sand; or failing that, you could pass the time by trying to ejaculate onto the people below. 'The bald pates of senators were favoured targets,' one authority tells us. The equivalent nowadays would be to take your seat in the public gallery of the House of Commons along with wife or girlfriend, mistress or whore, and get her to masturbate you while you aimed your erection straight at the burgeoning bald spot of Tony Blair or David Cameron. A delightful way for us to revive the noble values of Ancient Rome, but alas, probably not one that would be permitted in our dour and puritanical times.

Film tie-in edition of *Prayer-Cushions of the Flesh*.
Cover design by David Bird.

Prayer-Cushions of the Flesh

Robert Irwin

'Are you one of the concubines of the Harem?' he asked doubtfully.

She let out a laugh that was half delighted, half scornful,

'Ha! I could not bear to have anything to do with the Harem women. No, I am one of the animal girls who work in the Imperial Zoo. I would much rather serve animals than the ninnies of the Harem.'

'There is an Imperial Zoo? Where is it?'

She gave him a curious look,

'It is here. You are in it. Why else should you be talking to an animal girl and standing in front of a cage containing a panther? This is Babur's cage.' And she pointed to a brass plaque attached to the bars at the top of the cage. The inscription in swirls of decorative calligraphy announced that THIS IS THE PANTHER, MARVELLOUS IN HIS BEAUTY, WHOSE BREATH IS SWEET AS THE SPICES OF JAVA.

'But last night there was no panther,' said Orkhan who was wondering if he was going mad. 'Last night I saw a woman who said she was called Mihrimah stand behind those bars and start to undress herself in front of me.'

'Ah! So it was Mihrimah? That girl thinks that the sun shines out of her arse, that moonlight issues from her cunt and she believes that she is the mother of cosmic mysteries, that her body is an orchard, a sea, a desert, a fountain, a mirror, a mystic robe and, at the end of it all, a bloody Prayer-Cushion for man to kneel on as he prays before the Holy of Holies. She's mad, quite mad . . . She also thinks that she can walk into the Zoo and do what she likes, take over its cages, turn out the animals, give orders to the staff. The insolence of those courtesans and dancing girls takes my breath away. The reality is that Mihrimah and the rest of the concubines are good for nothing, except fucking – and doing embroidery. But they lie about in the Harem and thoughts of sex rot away their soft insides and eat up their little brains. All that Prayer-Cushion rubbish that they preach . . . it's only the product of not enough proper sex. Cooped up in their cramped dormitories, they pleasure one another and fantasise about men, but all they ever see is eunuchs.' She paused to calm herself and get her breath back, before continuing, 'But we are all prisoners here, women, eunuchs and animals. Of course, the main zoo is over at the Hippodrome. This is only a little zoo within the Harem for the pleasure of the Sultan's concubines. We have wild boars, gazelles, porcupines, a buffalo, a small herd of giraffes . . . Two of the giraffes are homosexual and they use their necks to court one another.'

She placed her gloved hand in his. Her eyes sparkled.

'Come and see the homosexual giraffes.'

She led him up out of the pit and down a roofed and cobbled street that twisted between cages and storerooms. They came to a low doorway over which was written, THESE ARE THE SULTAN'S HUNTERS WHO SIT ON THE GLOVES OF LADIES AND WAIT TO BRING DEATH FROM THE SKIES. Roxelana ducked in and Orkhan followed her through the imperial mews. Hawks in plumed leather helmets stirred restlessly on their perches. Roxelana explained that this was a short cut. Then they emerged out through another low door into the high-roofed and airy giraffe stable. HERE ARE THE HAPPY OFF-SPRING OF THE MATING OF CAMELS AND LEOP-ARDS WHO ARE CALLED GIRAFFES

'Everywhere in the Harem is so cramped,' said Roxelana. 'Apart from the hammam, I think this is the biggest building there is.'

A giraffe lazily sought to entwine his neck round that of his neighbour. Hands on hips, Roxelana stood gazing up at the animals in rapt delight. Orkhan followed her gaze. The creatures did not resemble the giraffes in the bestiary which he used to study in the Cage. They were strange, but then everything was so strange to him, and surely Roxelana was the strangest creature in her zoo. She slapped the flank of one of the languid giraffes, seeking to urge it on in its seduction, then turned to Orkhan and smiled. He was certain that he had never seen such strong white teeth or such brilliant eyes before. Suddenly he realised that he was desperate for her – desperate to feed off her energy and drink from her overflowing life.

'Aren't they wonderful?' she said, pointing at the animals who had begun to nuzzle one another.

'Never mind the giraffes,' he said. 'What about me?'

He yanked at her arm and pulled her down on to a heap of straw. She pulled up her skirt, ready for him.

'Now, quickly. If you want me, it must be now, before the jinns come.'

Those were the last words that it was possible to make sense of, as she started to moan noisily. She gestured to him to make haste as he struggled out of his robe. Even in the dung-scented air of the giraffe stable, he could smell Roxelana. Her skin, caked as it was with dried sweat and saliva, stank. Also, it seemed that she had used rancid butter to give her helmet of red hair more of a sheen. The insides of her thighs were moist and smelt of cat. Like Anadil, she was clean-shaven between the legs. Driven by the cravings of the viper, he tried to thrust his head down there, but she was impatient.

'Not like that. I want something bigger than your tongue inside me.' She wrestled under him and pulled him up and grabbed at his cock. She reminded Orkhan of his brother princes with whom he used to wrestle. Powerfully aroused, he entered her masterfully. However, the sensation of mastery hardly lasted more than a moment, for she so fiercely bucked and thrashed under him. Her eyes rolled and her teeth were gritted. Finally, she made such a great heave that he was unable to stay inside her. He withdrew and lay beside her and waited for her frenzy to abate.

'I am accursed!' she wailed. 'Forgive me, master, yet it is not my fault.' Now she was weeping. 'It is the fault of the jinns. Whenever I even think about sex, the jinns enter my body and possess it. It is the jinns who make me do such frightful things.'

She buried her head in the straw and continued to weep. Then, as her sobbing subsided, she raised her tear-stained face to Orkhan and said,

'I need to be purified. You can purify me. You can whip the jinns out of me. Please, I need to have the jinns driven out of me. They cannot bear the pain, but I, Roxelana, can bear anything. If you flog me, O Sultan, I promise you that you will then be able to enjoy my body as is your right.'

Now she was in a new fever of impatience. She stepped out of her black skirt and with trembling hands set to unlacing her bodice. The bodice fell to the ground and, as she turned away from him, Orkhan saw that her broad shoulders were already covered with a light tracery of scars. Then she turned to him again and presented him with the whip.

'Flog me now,' she implored. 'I am begging you for it. I need it.' And she turned away and bent to present her back for chastisement.

Orkhan struck at her a couple of times, but she was not satisfied.

'Harder. It must be harder. You have to draw my blood, for the jinns are in my blood. You have to let them out.'

Her broad bottom seemed made for whipping and he struck at it again and again. Ugly red weals began to break up its milky smoothness. For the first time since his release from the Cage, Orkhan felt himself to be truly a sultan and, as he continued to lash out at Roxelana, he began to fantasise about how he would deal with Anadil and the other ladies of the Harem. He worked a little way up her back before pausing for breath.

Then she said,

'You must be able to do better than this. Harem girls have whipped me harder than you have. Come on, I really want to feel it – your touch of mastery.'

Her words had the effect she desired. Orkhan struck out at her in a frenzy. Now she was crying and calling out to him, but his rage was such that it was some time before he could hear that she was begging him to desist. He stopped and she turned to kneel in front of him and kiss the whip.

'Thank you, master. Now you may do with me what you wish,' and she lay back once more on the straw. This time it was different. The devils having departed, she docilely lay back and allowed herself to be penetrated. She embraced him tenderly as he moved inside her.

She sighed as he came within her,

'Thank you master,' she said again and kissed him hungrily. 'It has always been hard for me, for the jinns that come into my body will not allow me to acknowledge the supremacy of a man. Now at last I am at peace.'

And Orkhan observed that her eyes were dulled, sated. Yet, it now occurred to him that, with her back such a bloody mess, she must have been moving on a bed of agony as she gave herself to him.

'Did I hurt you?' he asked foolishly.

'Of course you did – a little, but women are used to pain. They are better capable of bearing it than men,' and she smiled patronisingly at him.

'I do not believe that. Everyone knows that men are stronger, tougher and better able to bear pain.'

'With respect, O master, perhaps men think they know that, but I do not. Women are born equipped to face far more pain than men, for nature has prepared them in advance to suffer the travails of childbirth. And every month I experience such pain that you cannot imagine. Your whipping was a little nothing by comparison.' The brightness was back in her eyes again and she looked at him mischievously. 'You could never stand such a whipping as the one I received from your hands.'

'You are being absurd, Roxelana. I should certainly be much better able to endure it than you were.'

'Then let us try it, shall we?'

Orkhan hesitated. Why, after all, should he submit to being whipped by one of his animal girls?

Seeing him hesitate, she urged him on,

'Come on my lord! It is only a game, like my game with the panther. Such sports make us feel more alive, for, though we may walk through life as if we walked in a dream, the flick of the whip can wake us up. Turn and turn about,' she insisted. 'You will enjoy it. Trust me.' And she gave him a brilliant smile.

Tempted by the challenge, seduced by her smile, he agreed. Then she led him to a corner of the stables, and pointed to a pair of manacles which were attached by chains to the wall.

'Put these on,' she said.

Once again, he balked. Now she was angry and stamped her foot.

'You have to wear these. Otherwise it is not fair. It will not be a real challenge, if you can cry off at any moment, or turn round and snatch the whip from me and start beating me again. You have to trust me. You have to trust me, as I trusted you. Believe me, you will find that half your delight comes from trusting the lady with the whip. Trust me, it will only be a gentle whipping – like a series of butterfly kisses on your body.'

Orkhan offered his wrists to the manacles.

'We sometimes put an unruly monkey in these,' she explained, as she snapped them shut.

'Now its my turn!' she cried and the whip sang in the air.

Orkhan was unable to stop his body wincing as the thong made its first incision in his flesh. She was more skilled with the whip than he had been and the blows fell fast and accurately.

He heard her cry out,

'Oh my beloved, I swear to you that I am only marking your body because I desire it. My whip is making a map to guide my loving kisses.'

Then suddenly the blows increased yet further in ferocity and she seemed to be talking to herself in a foreign language, in which guttural words mingled with groans and hisses. It was not long before Orkhan, half swooning, slumped against the floor. Then she was upon him, pressing herself against his back and licking his blood.

'You are mad,' he groaned.

'So I am,' she replied. 'My jinns have come back and they want your blood. Oh my beloved master, forgive me, but I cannot hold back from this.' And she resumed kissing and licking at his wounds.

At last she raised her face from his body and gave a deep sigh. When she next spoke, her voice was calm and gentle,

'Now the kiss of the whip has taught you a little about the strange delight of suffering. Even so, you still have no idea about the pain of being a woman. In order to really make love to a woman, you will have to learn what it feels like to be one and to be made love to as a woman.' She ran a hand over his hair.

'Don't go away, will you?'

And she was gone, leaving Orkhan chained on the floor of the giraffe stable.

When she returned, she nudged him with her foot and used it to turn him as far over as his chains would allow. Looking up at Roxelana, he first noticed that her mouth was rimmed with blood. Then he saw a large, greased and gleaming red thing attached by an intricate array of straps to the lower part of her belly and he moaned in dread.

'This dildo,' she said, pointing to the thing 'consists of a unicorn's horn sheathed in red Cordovan leather. It is only used for the deflowering of virgins.'

Then she briefly caressed his mouth with her foot, before kicking and turning him again, so that he was lying face down on the straw. She prodded him again with her foot.

'I want you kneeling.'

'When I am free you will pay for this.'

But, she struck at him with the butt of the whip and he did as he was told.

'How will I pay for it?' Roxelana demanded sarcastically. 'Have me flogged, will you?'

As she spoke, she knelt over his bottom and spat on her hands before using the spittle to moisten the passage of her instrument in advance. Then she mounted him and rammed the dildo in, or rather, she attempted to, but Orkhan was very tight.

So she began to whisper hotly in his ear, begging him to relax and calling him her 'handsome darling' and her 'play-thing'. But all the while she continued to thrust with the horn between her legs. It felt like a great fist which, in beating its way upwards, was seeking to cleave Orkhan from bottom to top. It was as if he was being impaled on the shaft of the animal girl. It was as if he was carrying the woman inside him. It was as if he was being possessed by a dark demon who would not be denied entrance.

There was a final shudder as she at last succeeded in driving the horn into him. Pleasure and pain, exquisitely compounded, surged within him, overwhelming his will, so that he suffered orgasm.

Roxelana stroked his head. He could feel her breasts pressing against his back. He was in agony, and yet he longed for nothing more than to be able to turn to embrace his violator.

'Now, my Sultan, a door has been opened for the Holy Rapture,' she whispered, and giving the dildo a final twist, she continued 'It is possible that you are now ready to yield to the total extinction which is perfect love.'

She might have said more, but at that moment they heard the sound of women's voices outside the stables. Roxelana thereupon swiftly unstrapped herself from the dildo's harness and slipped away. Orkhan briefly fainted.

When he came to, he saw that Perizade was kneeling beside him and drawing gently on the harness of the dildo to extract it.

Lobster

Guillaume Lecasble

Lobster comes to his senses. He can't understand it. His shell is red, which must mean they've killed him – but he's alive. Yet the bay leaf smell coming out of him is definitely a death smell. The same smell that accompanied the death of all his kinsfolk. It's how his father smelled, and his mother, when they went by in front of him with their shells red, plopped onto their backs with their claws folded rearwards.

Images start coming back to him – the simmering stock, the way his eyes were scalded by the steam, and of course that smell of bay leaves. After that it all goes black, right until his awakening in this cold salty seawater. Alive! He's got to accept that he's alive, despite his shell having the smell and colour of death.

Right in front of him, Angelina is bent over, her hands purple from the cold, trying to break Maurice's fingers. She's not getting anywhere. Sudden death and freezing water have paralysed his sinews and fused his bones together. In one fluid movement she stands up, flicks back her tousled hair and pins it up with a brooch from her dress. Lobster recognises her, thinks 'she's the one who ate my dad'. Unknown feelings brew in him. Vengeance and desire make his flesh tingle in a way he's never felt before. He's attracted to this woman. He, a lobster, attracted to a woman. He comes closer, the better to see. The better to clarify this shocking situation. Angelina's beauty is enough to bring on fevers, and Lobster feels one mounting in him. His body heats up, but it doesn't stop his craving for vengeance. He doesn't know what to do – for the first time he is being forced to use his reason, rather than his instinct.

Angelina was so nervous, so frozen and exasperated by the stiffness of the corpse clutching at her life that she didn't notice Lobster's feelers brushing against her ankles. Although he was murmuring 'she ate my dad,' his gaze was already climbing the length of her legs, right up to the satin of her panties. The fabric was billowing around her cold-tensed buttocks. Pale downy hair stood up over goose bumps. 'She ate my dad,' he told himself again, 'she ate my dad.' It didn't stop these shimmering hints of fabric causing his whole body to flood with desire. He was bowled over by human flesh. Lobster was experiencing lust for a woman. 'Has that scalding made me see the world from a human perspective?' he wondered. But who cared – this lust was a fact and he was starting to enjoy it. He was feeling desire for a shell-less body. A supple, soft, silky body. A body with no hard edges. He was feeling desire for flesh, for skin. This feeling overwhelmed him, decided him: he opened his pincers and snap! cut through the wrist that had been imprisoning Angelina. Maurice's body floated away, taken by the current. Angelina thought she saw a little devil in the bloody water. She couldn't understand the hand still attached to her ankle. She crossed the dining room against the current, icy water up to her thighs, blood in her wake. She, who wanted to die. She just needed to lie down. But that hand was stopping her from escaping into death; it was pushing her towards life. She shivered. The cold had entered her body and her mind; she didn't know what to think of this severed hand. Had her will to live cut it off? Or was it a product of the madness rising in her with the cold?

She reached the staircase and climbed the first step but the cold was numbing her mind. She fainted, upright and motionless with seawater up to her belly. Lobster swam to her purple feet. Cut off the bloodless hand with his pincers, and climbed up the inside of the leg as far as the clenched knees. He was amazed at the pleasure he felt from being held in this way. His pincers slipped between the thighs, prising them gently apart.

His feelers were just able to reach the satin of the panties. They fluttered, made the labia quiver. Under the shimmering material a hint of life was returning. Angelina's thighs relaxed. Lobster pulled back his feelers. Tensed and released his tail. His strokes were fast and powerful. He was making headway. He sank himself into her warming muscles; his tail did not falter. He moved forward, a centimetre at a time. Yes! Suddenly he could see the fabric clearly, glistening, pearl-like. He brought his pincers forward. Caught hold of the lace border. Pulled back the slippery satin and snipped right through it. The panties opened, the two separate pieces floating soft as seaweed in the swirl. The hair round the vulva was undulating. Lobster put his pincer in and closed it on the clitoris with the dexterity of a practised lover. What he did to Angelina next so warmed her insides that she returned to life, arching her back. Lobster was thrown into the air, stiffening his tail as he slapped back against the water in time with Angelina's rhythm. And so their wedding dance began: Angelina and Lobster at the foot of the elegant dining room staircase. Her creamy woman's body, convulsed with pleasure, trailing a bright red crustacean with one pincer secured in her hairs and the other working her clitoris, as they moved between air and water, water and air; the exuberance of these two bodies as the water spurted between her buttocks and surged around her thighs.

The bay leaf aroma embedded in Lobster's shell invigorated Angelina, returning her to consciousness. Her heat was triumphing over the cold water. Her thighs kept parting and closing. Lobster was dripping with vaginal juices. Angelina thrust more quickly, coming down rhythmically against the water. The foam around them was a glory to their union. Angelina arched her back, buttocks surging out of the water. Lobster, intimately attached to her, was shaken by staccato vibrations. Angelina reached orgasm for the first time in her life. Pleasure quivered under her nails and shook her jaw. Her toes felt connected to her throat. Unfamiliar sap was running right through her. Gently, her body relaxed and re-entered the water now warm from the fever of their union; Lobster floated motionless on his back with his pincers splayed.

Happily afloat on the swirl of the sinking ship, Angelina slipped a hand between her legs, picked up Lobster and put his head inside her mouth. She rolled her tongue around his eyes and mandibles. As Lobster was rinsed in saliva he dreamt of his new life – a pleasure to be re-lived again and again.

The sirens that had been wailing for an hour brought Angelina back to the reality of the shipwreck. She slipped Lobster between her breasts.

Carrion

Jeremy Bourdon

Remember my soul, that thing we saw that lovely summer
day?
On a pile of stones where the path turned off, the hideous
carrion . . .

Baudelaire

Pain ripped through my groin as I reached to the top shelf for
Marmite. For a fortnight now Marmite is all I have been able
to eat. Only this acerbic yeast paste has relieved the tension
between my legs. These past weeks have further crushed my
frail character, but I have always felt aged beyond my years, a
dead man given a young body but no more youth. Still, only a
sickened being can capture that deepest sadness which is the
most touching aspect of the human condition.

Disease is the auger point of a pain. That poisoned pinprick
strikes out from my spleen. It has produced hard pustules on the
perimeter of my lowest chakra. These chancres are savage. They
have surrounded my yoni, come to wreck my once proud
member. For days the only cloth soft enough to touch my skin
has been my organic cotton yoga suit. It was the palest colour
of fresh Devonshire cream, now it has turned a putrid yellow.

Though I have never been of the soundest constitution, I
shy from doctors. I feel as though their modern cures cannot
help me. Their microscopes could never magnify enough to
view the depth of my sickness. But now it has made itself
known to all who might be unfortunate enough to witness me
unclad. More welts appeared every day. I could not go further
alone. I had to reach someone to attend my particular issues.

I came across the advertisement on the horoscope page of a popular press publication:

Cures long forgotten
Save them so besotten.
020 8473 1494

I went to him, on the eastern artery. At night Mile End Road crawls with tainted women, a thoroughfare of debauchery. As the jaundiced child of a homeless whore it was not unfamiliar territory. The imposing brick terrace had the presence of a singular building. Gargoyle birds, one either side of the entrance guarded the building. I pressed the buzzer's white button with a chalky slide. No one spoke, only a signal from the speaker and a click in the crested gate. I walked carefully beneath the gaze of the twin falcons, not just because my inflamed groin had caused me to move in a tight buttocked prance for weeks, but because these birds seemed ready to leap from their granite perches, caught mid screech by Medusa herself. When I emerged from beneath the front garden's canopy I looked up a small yet imposing flight of stone stairs. I found myself drawn to one room by an urge stronger than just the promise of natural light. I was not disappointed. The medical man was sitting in his office well lit by the room's southern exposure. The glare left his body obscured by shadow as he faced me.

'You see,' he said. 'You were beckoned here by forces of which you are not completely aware. I did not call for you.'

I agreed that it was, in fact, me that had rung him two days ago, as a result of his advertisement. He, in turn, assured me that it was not he who had placed the ad, rather that occasionally his patients find themselves inclined to advertise on his behalf. He closed the blinds. As he did his shadow crept across the room so I couldn't register much aside from his enormous desk backed by many austere volumes bound in leather, and an ornate screen of early 18th century Oriental origin.

'My name is Doctor Jean Keyser, you may address me as 'fellow.' He said as he directed me to remove my foul garments behind the screen.

Some days earlier I was so low not even the beauty of Baudelaire's prose poems could shed light on my hermitage of pain. Shrouded in darkness I saw only one solution. I designated several indurate buboes for deflation. I heated a sewing needle and stabbed while the needle was still burning red. It was no doubt these particular six creatures: one old, one new, two big, two small, that turned my fellow's face.

After a brief visual observation my fellow unwrapped a pair of sterilized white cotton gloves. He requested me to lie back. I lowered myself across the unsavoury leather bed. He waited a moment before holding his hands to a variety of points on my abdomen. Throughout this experience I was calmed, as though I was slowly being adjusted from the state of nervous excitement, which had defined my last two weeks, and towards a place where my lack of control was inconsequential. I have always considered myself a man from another time, and with this treatment from a previous century the out of sorts feeling which has always determined my life slipped away.

'Mmmm, I would like to perform a test.' Said the fellow. 'First you must understand the relative nature of science. Treatments and tests come and go, not unlike ladies' fashions. However, just because one is no longer in style does not mean it isn't suitable. For the most comprehensive treatment, a fellow with extensive historical knowledge best serves a patient.

'Doctor August Paul von Wassermann perfected his test in 1906. It involves machines and calculations which are not easily discovered one hundred years in the future. You will be pleased to know that it is with the utmost competence I can carry out this test, so as to ascertain whether or not you have Syphilis.'

'Syphilis?' I said. 'The dreaded pox?'

'Indeed' my fellow continued. 'Qui Ha. All the signs are there, toxic heat invades your lung and spleen.' I had known the source all along.

'Your breathing is shallow, your liver is damp and hot, Yang Mei Yi Ji San.' I had drowned my sorrows in so many mulled wines.

'You say you haven't been so very hungry? Look at your genitals.' Christ. Look at my genitals. Look at them. I had done nothing but stare and sweat for the past two weeks.

'Soon, Long Dan Xie Gan Tang, the toxic heat will be all through your blood.' No escape.

'What's to be done?' I asked with a tremor.

On the shelf next to us, my fellow opened a silver case with a click. From it he produced a syringe obviously stolen from a vet of the previous century. He held it through one of its steel finger loops and gathered several syringes, from the look of them also designed primarily for horses.

'The equipment must sterilise. You will follow me.' My fellow led me through a door I hadn't seen before.

He left me, alone and naked, in a square room, a small book room. There were no windows. The electricity glowed dimly through barley brown lampshades. The lights were uncanny six foot gas lamp conversions. I covered the diagonal of the room in three fast paces. There were no other doors. I stopped and turned on my heel. I considered the incongruence of the furniture. I circled the perimeter of my cubicle. The carpet, though handmade, had been chosen for a room of a different colour. The chair's arms were flat and angular, almost modern, but their cushions' fabric weaved around moulded foam. Unable to sit for fear the battered furniture might carry some virus; I had little else ahead of me but to face my predicament.

I felt the sores; the biggest one I hadn't seared increased its pressure. The room's air was warm and dry, the rug and chairs horded dust, yet the air was pure. Nothing but the atmosphere of this perverse ensemble took account of its books, some old and cracked, some with gold letters still gleaming, all bound in deep red leather. Standing, nude and singular I was calm and well, healthy for a brief moment.

Returning to my reality, I hurt. To continue in my current course is to walk straight under the bridge of death. No fellow of this age, nor one long gone, will manage my complaints. I must change the course of my present incarnation. All coolness has deserted me, and I have begun to sweat again. To divert my mind from this timeless cell, I move quickly to a bookshelf. All the books are titled the same, some barely legible, but all the same words through different eras.

When I turned round from the shelves I was startled to see the door opened. My fellow stood on the threshold.

'You are ready now.' He said.

I returned to the office. It was blazing with light. It could've been a new day. I had no idea how long I had been confined. Everything in the office was draped with impenetrable white sheets. I could feel my aura heating as my blood moved faster and my heart beat erratically.

'Settle yourself on this bed', as he pointed to a plinth in the middle of the room. On the bed my fellow again moved his hands just millimetres from my bare skin, occasionally he applied pressure to specific points, repeating a chant I could not recognise:

'Muh em ep in am om. Oorug yah-ah, troom laaka, maan tas laaka aaham, laaka aaham, laaka eeris, laaka eeris, eeris tas. Muh em ep in am om.'

My consciousness began to dim. I saw my fellow lift the polished syringe. It was filled with glowing bile. The glistening needle hit my deep femoral artery in the bottom of my groin. I tried to scream but could not.

I was paralysed as I heard my fellow's words. He hoarsely whispered 'Carrion.' It was the title of the books.

Confessions of a Flesh-Eater

David Madsen

The remaining hours of that night, a night pregnant with the intoxicating realisation of opportunity, I reserved for myself and my beloved alone. I selected a juicy, pungent flank from the cold-store – one that seemed to have been waiting for my coming, aching for my embrace, soundlessly crying out for the worship I alone could give! – and carrying it on my shoulders like a bride across the threshold, I bore it aloft to my little attic room.

I stood for some moments absorbed in contemplation of the huge crimson-deep, fat-speckled expanse of flesh; it lay on the bed like an expectant lover, its silence a high eloquence, its motionless passivity an initiation of seduction rather than a response to it – both paradoxes of passion. Its entire presence was a metaphysical contradiction: it was dead yet shockingly alive, moving perpetually in its own stillness; it was dumb, but the nexus of emotions it aroused in me constituted a lyrical epiphany in honour of stupendous obsession. Oh Christ, what wonders were to unfold? I trembled all over, as with a fine fremitus.

I undressed myself slowly and clumsily, with all the shy *gaucherie* of a virgin lover: I hopped from one foot to the other as I pulled off my trousers, catching my sock on the buckle of my belt; a shirt-button snapped and split; my keys slipped out of my pocket. When at last I had finished, standing there erect beneath my underpants, sweating and shaking, I understood with poignant clarity how patient and how courteous my beloved had been; it gleamed richly in the amber-gold light of the shaded lamp, waiting only to satisfy my hunger, to satiate, to plunge me into ecstasy.

I placed my body carefully across it, tucking my arms underneath it, so that we were locked in an embrace; I lay my cheek against its lightly corrugated surface and, inhaling deeply, was at once inebriated with the sour-sweet odour of chill clotted blood, of heady amino-acids, of a hundred other numinous ichors exposed, expelled and inspissated – this, surely, was the intoxicating perfume that quickened the nostrils of Yahweh as he stirred his forefinger into the chaotic primal slime which was to become Adam!

With much deliberation I drew my underpants down over my buttocks, so that the revelation of my final nakedness came gently to my beloved, with subtlety and finesse – a last love-offering, a final token of foreplay before the great consummation; they slipped to my ankles and I kicked them to the floor. The impress of damp, ripe flesh, the solid interstratification of flesh and fat against my exposed genitals, was sensational. Then I spread my thighs as widely as I could, curling my legs around each side, pulling myself up and over the great meaty bulk. I kissed its fibres lingeringly, I licked it, gnawed at it with exquisite tenderness, as a young husband might lick and gnaw the stiffening nipples of his new bride. Under the heat of my body it was becoming warmer and slightly greasy, so that when I began the first slow, tentative thrusts, I found myself slipping and sliding in an exquisitely arousing manner, and I knew for certain that at this moment, my beloved was answering the urgent call of my increasing passion.

I could no longer see the room or its contents, nor do I think I was actually aware of them; I swam, like a foetus in amniotic fluid, in an infinite ocean of blood-red flesh. I was conscious of my movements but not their immediate intention; hence, I knew precisely what I was doing when I rolled onto my back, opened my legs, and pulled the great carcass on top of me, but not quite *why*. I was reduced to a pure and simple empiricism: everything was sensation, nothing was reason. We moved together like a horse and rider, my beloved and I; when I arched and bucked, so too did the carcass; when I lifted myself and sank back again, it did likewise; when I parted my arms and thighs to embrace, the contours of the resulting concavities were instantly sealed by dead-weight, wine-rich, blood-red flesh.

Moaning, moaning and shuddering, I clung to my beloved in a sexual systalsis as I released my seed – helplessly, copiously, repeatedly – naked flesh to naked flesh, meat to meat, perfectly and completely made one in a true and mysterious conjunction.

I heard a voice, which was my own and yet entirely unfamiliar, whisper:

'Oh, I love . . . love you!'

Then:

'What the hell are you *doing,* for Christ's sake?'

Master Egbert stood in the rectangle of harsh yellow light that was the doorway: huge, shocking, like an unpredicted eclipse.

'Fucking a side of beef?'

It was then that I lost consciousness.

In the Gallery

Hélène Lavelle

My lord, the Comte, drove us to the art gallery, set at the end of the long parkland drive. The number of cars indicated a light sprinkling of visitors inside – enough, but not too many. While my lord opened the bottle of claret I adjusted my make-up. Outside the car, we breathed in the autumn air, and drank a little wine as we looked around the park, taking no heed of the attention we were attracting from other people getting in or out of their cars. We were on a promenade, and a hunt, and dressed for it.

The Comte: a young mid-forties, good-looking with a trimmed tawny beard and bright, piercing blue eyes; a strong, confident demeanour, comfortably masterful without a hint of the boorish self-importance that some so-called 'masters' need to affect. Dressed in a long raincoat, long black leather riding boots (and the spurs that make women go weak), white duelling shirt, chamois waistcoat with watch and chain, and broad brimmed Italian hat, he held an ivory topped cane and cut an easy, aristocratic figure, good-natured, but most certainly not to be trifled with.

Beside him I, the Lady: forty or so, a trim figure and a fine featured face (some, including my lord, consider her beautiful, but I will be appropriately modest . . .), wearing a black fitted jacket, red knee-length skirt, white blouse, and slightly extravagant accessories – a black riding hat with a short veil, a white lace *jabot* at her throat, black lace gloves, a large display of white lace from the breast pocket of her jacket, and high heeled ankle boots furnished with buckles and chains that hinted at somewhat unorthodox erotic leanings.

The other visitors would then have seen the Comte say something to the Lady and kiss her on the lips, then see the Lady hand her empty glass to the Comte, step back, incline her head to him as though acknowledging a command, turn, and walk across the gravel and up the stone steps into the gallery. The Comte, at a leisurely pace, put the wine and glasses into the boot of the car, lock up, and, a few minutes after the Lady, followed her into the gallery.

The gallery has a long main hall, two storeys high, lit through large windows in the roof, overlooked by balconies on the second story, and a maze of interconnected rooms, leading off the main hall north, south, east and west. Small groups, couples and single visitors meandered through the hushed atmosphere, admiring the fine collections of 18th century art, sculpture, furniture and porcelain, and the display cabinets of art and curios from India and points further East.

The Lady made her way unhurriedly, enjoying the echoing click of her heels that drew the glances, and sometimes the stares, of other visitors. Men's eyes filled with desire as they saw her, their wives sometimes thin-lipped with jealousy and disapproval, or on occasion as enchanted as their husbands by the vision the Lady presented. Sweet scruffy art students sketching before classic Gericaults gawping openly, until the Lady inclined her head in greeting to them, prompting one or two to smile awkwardly, others to duck their heads down to concentrate a little too hard on their work, and one girl to blush crimson as she tried to tear her eyes away from the Lady, who smiled to herself as she imagined the flood of untamed thoughts and fantasies that would cascade through that girl's dreams and imaginings that night.

The Comte also draws looks, especially from women who catch a glimpse of the boots, the spurs, and the handle of the riding crop protruding from his boot. I have seen them go faint on occasion.

That is the point of promenading. Not only is it pleasing for us to dress up and draw the public gaze, it is a kind of performance art – an awakening for those who see it, sometimes arousing them, sometimes alarming them – and, more even than that, it is a statement by those of erotic proclivity, that we are proud of what we are and what we delight in.

This day was not merely a promenade, it was a hunt.

Somewhere in the gallery, Charmian, our handmaiden, would be perusing the art. The rules of the game are simple. Whichever of us – the Comte or myself – finds Charmian first, takes her as personal slave for that day (although, in reality, it makes little difference, since she always ends up serving us both). In the meantime, should the Comte and I encounter, we do not greet one another in any way that passers-by would recognise. What any observer would see is the Lady dropping her glove and bending the knee to retrieve it, effectively curtseying to the Comte, although he does not acknowledge her gesture.

After a delicious half an hour tinged with anticipation, I saw Charmian first, in the main hall, standing before a splendid Delacroix. A pretty girl in her mid-twenties with long straight black hair, she is a little shorter than me, with a rounded figure. But she was not dressed as I had instructed. I had told her to wear her long white dress and black velvet waistcoat, yet here she was in her 'sexy secretary' clothes – fitted grey suit jacket with a fine stripe, cream blouse with a floppy bow at the throat, an ostentatious display of pale yellow silk flowering in her breast pocket, one corner reaching up almost to her shoulder, the rest cascading almost to her waist, and a matching silk tied in a large bow in her hair behind the crown. She even had her half-rimmed glasses on! However, instead of the matching suit skirt, she wore a long skirt of black taffeta reaching to her ankles, raised just enough to show off her shiny pointed fetish ankle boots.

As my heels clicked across the floor towards her (although I looked at the paintings as I went, so it was not obvious where I was heading), I could see out of the corner of my eye that Charmian had been attracting her own fair share of attention. This amused me. When she first offered herself to us, she had been as shy as a mouse – now she dressed extravagantly, even outrageously.

As I approached her, she turned to look at me, and waited. Only when I was two paces away, did I look at her. She gave one of her slightly impish smiles, and without a word, placed her hands in the pit of her stomach, and bowed extremely deeply, her long black hair and silk at her breast pocket all but sweeping the ground before her.

I looked down at her, savouring the gasps – half shocked, half enchanted – from those in the gallery. Few things are as exquisite as the sight of a young woman bowing herself down like this. How inept of the western world never to have really understood the delights of female obeisance – both to see, and to do. And what a perfect way to startle the innocent. I commanded her to rise, and I reached out to touch the smooth milky skin of her cheek, the cool silkiness of her hair, and allowed her gentle moist lips to kiss my fingers, which she did so sweetly, with utter submission, spiced with just a hint of girlish eagerness.

'My Lady.' she murmured.

'You are mine today.' I told her.

'Yes, Mistress.' she replied. One or two of the nearer visitors were straining to overhear the conversation. I did not mind.

'You want to please me, don't you?' I asked.

'Oh, yes!' she exclaimed.

'Whereas I want to hurt you.' I said. She stiffened slightly.

'Yes, Mistress.' she said, very humbly.

'You have disobeyed me, dressing like this.' I went on.

'Yes, Mistress.' she whispered.

'Why did you disobey?' I demanded. There was a pause.

'To make you want to hurt me more.' she answered with a slight catch in her voice.

I smiled, then slapped her across the face, making her cheek redden prettily. She whimpered, and kissed my hand with renewed passion and gratitude.

'Thank you, Mistress!' she whispered.

I am very fond of Charmian. There is one simple thing about her, she loves to be humiliated and punished, and she loves those who humiliate and punish her.

I let her take my arm, and we promenade across the floor, our heels clicking and echoing. At the foot of the staircase that leads to the upstairs balcony, the Comte awaits us. He had watched it all from the balcony. So he had seen Charmian first, but had wanted me to find her. Charmian and I stopped before him. I lowered my head, while the girl made another of her beautiful bows to him. The onlookers saw the Comte kiss both the women on the cheek, and offer the Lady his arm to promenade out with her, followed meekly by the girl.

We walked out to the car, retrieved the glasses and the bottle of claret and sauntered in a leisurely manner into the park. Charmian serving us wine, my lord and I rewarding her with wine from our lips. We reached a secluded grove among the trees. There I told my lord how Charmian had disobeyed me in the manner of her dress.

My lord decided she must be punished, and ordered her to bend, which she did, docile and obedient as ever. Taking the riding crop from his boot he surveyed her.

'Raise her skirt,' he commanded me. I obeyed, lifting the girl's skirt over her back to reveal her buttocks, so smooth, so tender, so white. My lord swished the crop through the air and brought it down hard, making her whimper and leaving a scarlet mark across her flesh. He inspected the effect of the blow, then struck her again, and again, each time raising a perfect red weal across her buttocks.

The sight of a girl suffering always has the same effect on

me, arousal, pity and a burning desire to see more. I bit my lip and felt myself moisten. My lord looked at me. He always knows.

He touched the girl between the legs. She sighed with pleasure.

'She is soaking,' he observed.

'She is dressed extravagantly,' I pointed out, 'She has been bowing down. She has been kissed. Now she is whipped.'

'She is soaking,' he repeated. 'Without permission.'

He handed me the crop.

'Punish her,' he said.

I took the crop, as was always the case, I could not help but beat her very cruelly until the poor damsel was sobbing and begging.

'Have you had enough?' I enquired, with no intention of stopping.

'No, mistress!' she exclaimed. I went on flogging her, my lord gave her permission to masturbate, and we let her climax noisily, again and again as she was thrashed and humiliated. I stopped whipping her and let her subside slowly to the ground, moaning her thanks to me.

Decadent Gastronomy

The Decadent Sausage

Medlar Lucan & Durian Gray

Take pigs' throats and cut out the fat, but keep the clean, smooth glands. Slice the loins finely; also the ears (well scoured), and the snouts; peel the tongues and wash them thoroughly in hot water; bone, scrub and singe the trotters; clean the testicles. Lay the ears, snouts and trotters on the bottom of a good clean pot and cover with coarse salt. On top put the tongues, then the throats, loins and testicles sprinkled with fine salt. Let the pot stand for three days then swill out with red wine. Soak the lot with red wine for another day. Drain, rinse several times to get rid of the salt, and dry with clean white cloths. Pack the ingredients tight into a sausage skin. Use at once or store.

This recipe comes from a cookbook by Christoforo di Messisbugo, chef to the Duke of Este in Parma in the 16th century. They don't make sausages like that any more – in Parma or anywhere else. But if size is what you're after you can still, in Italy, get a massive thing called a *bondola*. It's a kind of *mortadella* – with the weight and dimensions of a 12-inch naval cannon – fatty, pink and rather slimy on the tongue. Sometimes it has emerald pistachios set into its spam-like bulk. It's rough peasant fare, as the cliché goes, and you eat it (when you're extremely hungry) sliced very thick on bread.

Elizabeth David said you could get good *mortadella* in Bologna. (A good one means pure pork, not 'a mixture of pork, veal, tripe, pig's head, donkey meat, potato or soya flour, and colouring essence'.) This was in 1954, but it's probably still true. Italy, just as much as Germany, is good sausage country, and conservative in its cooking habits.

Lucania, in southern Italy, was the place for sausages in

ancient times. Apicius, the Roman gastronome, says the ingredients were pork or beef, nuts, parsley, cumin, laurel berries and rue. They were cased in long narrow pieces of intestine and hung in the chimney to smoke. *Lucanicae* was the Latin name, which lives on in Italian *luganeghe* (still long and thin, but unsmoked now) and Greek *loukanika*.

You can make sausages out of practically anything, which may be why there are six hundred different kinds listed in that great sausage-hunter's bible – Antony and Araminta Hippisley Coxe's *Book of Sausages*. The Roman Emperor Heliogabalus is supposed to have invented the shrimp, crab, oyster, prawn and lobster sausage. Apicius gives a recipe that includes calf's brains and almonds. Eskimos fill sausages with seals' blood and offal. In Arles they use donkey or horse meat, in Madrid a mixture of veal and sardines, in Westphalia the brains of pigs. Traditional recipes boast delicacies such as black bear (Germany), porpoise (England), reindeer (Norway), rabbit (England again), and armadillo (Texas). Postmodernists may like to try another English recipe: Christmas pudding sausages, fried in egg and breadcrumbs and served with brandy butter.

Sausage names can be very poetic. *Larousse Gastronomique* mentions the *Gendarme* – 'very dry and heavily smoked' – which suggests a philosophical detective out of the 1940s. Then there's the *Saucisson Princesse*, made of diced ox-tongue, the *Jagdwurst* (or hunter's sausage), the *Punkersdorker*, 'a strong, juicy German salami', the *Puddenskins*, the *Felino*, the *Black Hog's Pudding*, the *Alpiniste* . . .

Sausages are also medicinal, which is why great thinkers like Rabelais have always taken them seriously. They operate like wine, tobacco, jokes, sunshine, sex, anchovies, rock'n'roll, etc, according to their own arcane laws, which have nothing to do with the beliefs of men with stethoscopes and white coats. Someone who truly understood the healing power of sausages was that fabulous old queen Madame de Maintenon, wife of Louis XIV. When she and *le roi soleil* were both very antiquated and sinking fast she recorded this touching little digestive swansong:

'I seldom breakfast, and then only on bread and butter. I take neither chocolate, nor coffee, nor tea, being unable to endure these foreign drugs. I am German in all my habits. I eat no soup but such as I can take with milk, wine, or beer. I cannot bear broth – it makes me sick, and gives me the colic. When I take broth alone I vomit even to blood, and nothing can restore the tone of my stomach but ham and sausages.'

Decadents, like clapped-out French monarchs, are always on the look-out for elixirs to restore their rogered constitutions. They should never overlook the sausage. In the words of the writer Francis Amunatégui, founder of the A.A.A.A.A. (*Association Amicale des Amateurs d'Authentiques Andouillettes*), 'The appearance of a hot sausage with its salad of potatoes in oil can leave nobody indifferent. . . . It is pure, it precludes all sentimentality, it is the Truth.'

Brekadence

Malcolm Eggs

The height of brekadence is not showing up mid-afternoon at a Primrose Hill gastropub and ordering a full English with, say, an extra sausage. It is not two plates of bacon and eggs, cooked at home and eaten in bed with a newly incumbent member of the opposite sex. The tasty orthodoxy of pork and eggs, widely regarded as the spiritual epicentre of today's leisurely English breakfast, hogs more than its fair ration of the limelight. Measured against some of the extravagances of breakfasting history (the wild boars of ancient Egypt, the cacao and capsicum of Montezuma), these stalwarts of the full English can be a somewhat unadventurous snack. And if we are to find the perfect decadent breakfast, it won't be achieved by staying in bed, affecting nonchalance – for that is to mistake the meaning of the search. For the determinedly decadent, breakfast is an event. It does not fuel a journey, as is the case with the Underground croissant: it is a destination. In a society that expects us, upon waking, to hasten to work without further ado, the act of breakfasting is itself an act of decadence – and the more serious our commitment to this least fashionable of meals, the closer we are to achieving a state of purest subversive opulence.

Contemporary inspiration can be found at Norma's in Le Parker Meridien Hotel, New York, with their 'Zillion Dollar Frittata'. Launched in the spring of 2004 with a price tag of $1000, it's possibly the only omelette that has ever made the international headlines. It serves one and consists of six eggs, a tablespoon of chives, some butter, five tablespoons of heavy cream, a lobster and 10 ounces of caviar, Also of interest are the lavish country household offerings of late 19th century England. Writing in his masterful 'Breakfasts, Luncheons and Ball Suppers', Major L . . . prescribes: 'fish, poultry, or game, if in season; sausages, and one meat of some sort, such as mutton cutlets, or fillets of beef; omelettes, and eggs served in a variety of ways; bread of both kinds, white and brown, and fancy bread of as many kinds as can conveniently be served; two or three kinds of jam, orange marmalade, and fruits when in season; and on the side table, cold meats such as ham, tongue, cold game, or game pie, galantines, and in winter a round of spiced beef of Mr Degue of Derby.'

Now we don't all have time for such a spread every day; and sadly none of us will now ever have the opportunity to taste the spiced beef of Mr Degue. But here is a grander vision of breakfast than that exemplified by the humble fry-up. Here is the breakfast as social crescendo – and the sleep of the night before as but a rest to prepare for breakfast-time. One suspects the mysteriously named Major L . . . would rather face the firing range than have to cram in a cereal bar at a bus stop on his way to a job flogging handsets from a call centre.

So the perfect decadent breakfast can be eaten out or at home: as long as you give yourself up to it, utterly. Spare no expense and take your time. If you eat it out, decide on the venue weeks in advance and be sure to choose one that has the good taste and culinary gusto to include fish on their breakfast menu, as per Thomas Love Peacock's wise assertion that 'the breakfast is the prosopon of the great work of the day. Chocolate, coffee, tea, cream, eggs, ham, tongue, cold fowl – all these are good and bespeak good knowledge in him who sets them forth: but the touchstone is fish.' Prepare your invite list with care – an uncomplimentary mix of people will be a pain during that time before you eat (one sensible modern convention is that breakfast is not just limited to the morn-ing). Splash out on bottled water: tap water rarely arrives.

If it will be cooked at home and you want to opt for

something simple and traditional like bacon, eggs, sausage, beans, mushrooms, tomato, toast, black pudding and bubble and squeak, then be sure to ignore the supermarkets. Go to farmers' markets, fruit & veg stalls and independent butchers: even a premium supermarket sausage bears no resemblance to the real thing. Time it well, serve it hot, and don't let the beans take over. When choosing the number of guests, bear firmly in mind the demands each guest makes on the cooking process. When choosing the social mix, consider who will make it easiest to navigate the inevitable labyrinth of compliments and silences. You will arrive at the most decadent of all conclusions: the finest breakfast you have ever eaten, prepared for one.

Eats

Andrew Crumey

Dining with friends in a Paris restaurant, I was overcome by an uncharacteristic urge to experience a frisson of gastronomic danger. Tete de veau; the face of a calf whose head has been boiled, brains and all, in a pot; seemed as close to the edge as I was likely to get, and having placed my order with the terminally harassed and engagingly insolent garçon, I sat back and relished the prospect of feasting on exquisitely tender meat of a kind banned in Britain, not because of the cruelty inflicted on the living calf, but because of fears that its cooked cranium might be a bouillon of BSE.

My companions were unimpressed. 'In Japan . . .' said one, going on to tell us about the venomous puffer fish he had tasted in a restaurant there, a fabled delicacy that as a source of farcical death among corpulent businessmen is second only to auto-erotic asphyxiation. 'In Indonesia . . .' said another, explaining how he had feasted on raw otter, and telling us it was predictably vile before handing the conversational baton to Vera, the quietest and most unassuming of our group, who had nevertheless, it turned out, during her former career as a lab technician, imbibed alcoholic chemicals from the top shelf that ought to have left her blind, mad or dead, but had instead merely given her a hangover.

All, it seemed, had at one time or another savoured condemned meat, yoghurts so far past their sell-by date they were on the point of running out the door, or even, in one case, tinned cat food, the dismal foie-gras of lonely geriatrics, tasted however not out of impoverishment or confusion, but instead out of nothing more than jaded curiosity, the most insatiable appetite of all.

And then there was Alex. In the realm of dangerous food, Alex took, so to speak, the biscuit. A congenital victim of nut allergy, he had diced with death in dinner halls and restaurants throughout his short but hectic life, aware at every moment that his next bowl of breakfast cereal might be his last. As a child, he declared, he'd played Russian roulette with a packet of Revels. We drank his health, suitably humbled.

Portrait of an Englishman in his Chateau

André Pieyre de Mandiargues

The shit was very tasty. I helped myself to as much of it as I had the fish sperm. I would have taken more if the negroes hadn't carried it away. The next dish to arrive was stuffed cow's vulva, so I was informed. From the gastronomic point of view, they were full of the most refined ingredients imaginable. Very white in colour and plump, they floated in a bone marrow sauce like little inflatable boats. To accompany them, we had giant asparagus. These Edmonde served to us one at a time with mock prudishness. Having consumed all that, the black waiters returned from the kitchen with two dishes of seabird brains. At first sight I was rather taken aback by their curious arrangement; for each brain, somewhere in size between a hazelnut and a walnut, had been stuck onto a beak. The idea was to pick up the little skull (which had been thoroughly cleaned), raise it to your lips and pull off the mouthful of brain which was crisp on the outside and a little raw in the middle.

'Go ahead, eat!' said Montcul, surprised by my reluctance. 'They're exceedingly rich in phosphorus, you know'.

I ignored his advice, however. The brains had an after-taste of fish oil which put me off. And then I began thinking, not without a certain unease, about the bloodbath this dish must have entailed – several hundred seagulls killed for just two plates! And yet, why hadn't I considered that it must have required slaughter on a similar scale to provide one dish of vulvas? The reason, no doubt, was because I found the vulvas delicious, whereas the brains were disgusting. This opinion was not shared by the negroes. They polished off both plates of brains avidly.

When the dishes of seabird brains had been removed, Viola stuck her tongue out in such a way that made my balls tingle and informed me that dessert was about to appear. I assumed this meant fruit, gateaux and such like, but when I saw Gracchus and Publicola enter, staggering under the weight of an enormous dish, I wondered if I hadn't become drunk without realising it, or perhaps I was having some sort of mystical hallucination. Their dish was piled high with lobster, langoustine, crab and prawns. At moments it looked as if they were about to drop the lot (if this was just play-acting, we were certainly taken in by it) but finally they succeeded in placing it on the table. Nothing could have provided a more elaborate adornment for the silver table than this monstrous prickly bush made up of claws, humps, antennae and spikes. However, an even greater delight awaited us. The chef had removed the salty meat from these crustaceans and replaced it with confectionery. So, when we tore off a limb or cracked open a shell, we found inside creme bavaroise, citron and rose jam, chestnut puree, walnut, vanilla and chocolate paste, praline or coffee fondant, pistachio marzipan and sugar flowers. The pleasures of the palate were mixed with the delight of unexpected and heedless destruction. After a while (during which time I had consumed the contents of a small lobster, an edible crab, two velvet swimming crabs and a handful of prawns) the serving dish was almost empty. Nobody spoke during this course, except to announce, like in a card game, what we had in our hand. It was a veritable feast – but then, the voice of our host returned us to other matters.

'Edmonde', he stated, 'If I were you I'd be stuffing myself less and thinking more about my arsehole. No matter that you have been put to the test by Caligula's weapon and every other cock that's visited this chateau! I tell you, taking a great prick made of ice in the arse is another matter. It's been known to split a person's guts.'

'Oh please no, anything but that!' she begged. 'Punish me any way you wish, if you think I ought to be punished. Let me be buggered by everyone here, even the women, with those dreadful dildoes of yours. Have me beaten. Bring in the dog. Anything you want, but spare me the ice.'

'You will be spared nothing. Have the great penis brought in immediately.'

While Gracchus went out to the refrigerator, our host turned to me and said:

'My dearest Balthasar, you will carry out this operation. The honour is yours as it's your first evening at Gamehuche. But above all, do not let this whore off lightly. I'll be most put out if you do. I was exaggerating just now when I said she was almost indispensible. There is nobody here who couldn't be replaced from one day to the next, if that's our pleasure.'

It was a most gentlemanly offer, and I'd have liked to thank him in a similar fashion, but Gracchus had already returned with the great prick. My words were interrupted by cries of joy when this object appeared. It was lying in a long vessel lined with seal skin. This vessel in turn had been placed in a dish of crushed ice so there would be no reduction in its size during preparations for its use. Wearing woollen gloves, I took hold of the prick by the balls and felt the weight of it in my hands. It felt like one of those wild west Colts which could shatter an alligator's eye as effectively as a rifle. Viola lent me a little tape measure which, no doubt for shameless reasons, she kept in her stocking. With this I measured the implement before returning it to its cold store. Thirty nine centimetres long, with a diameter of twenty four centimetres in the middle and twenty five at the glans! Its dimensions made it a formidable weapon.

Meanwhile, Edmonde, realising that tears were to no avail, handed herself over to our black waiters in preparation for the sacrifice.

St Agatha

Medlar Lucan & Durian Gray

We first heard about Alberto G while attending a symposium on Chaos Magic in Cefalu. We were chatting with our friend René De Vere-Maudsley after his lecture on Egyptian burials in Victorian London, when we happened to mention that the next day was the feast of our favourite martyr, Saint Agatha – an occasion which we hoped to celebrate in suitably baroque style. René immediately became excited, and begged to introduce us to Alberto G's *Pasticceria dell'Oriente* in Catania – an establishment which he described as 'a vision of Lourdes in marzipan.'

On the road to Catania René told us more of Alberto. Born in poverty in Taormina, he had posed as a youth among leopardskins and Greek urns for the photographer Wilhelm Von Gloeden, that exquisitely perfumed purveyor of classical erotica to the nobility. He later moved to Catania, where he worked as a tout among the glittering carcasses of tuna and scabbard-fish in the street-market. His piercing blue eyes and muscular good looks soon attracted the attention of the wives of local potentates, and a flourishing career as a gigolo appeared to open up before him. But the Allied invasion of 1943 robbed him of his clientele. In Rome after the war he found employment as a stunt-man at *Cinecittà*, and was doubling for Charlton Heston in Ben Hur when a javelin entered his throat, nicking the carotid artery. Close to death, he was granted a vision of the martyred St Agatha, who stood before him with tears of pity in her eyes, offering her severed breasts to him on a platter. Alberto made a miraculous recovery and vowed to perform a ritual each year in honour of his saviour.

The *Pasticceria dell'Oriente* did not disappoint. Among hanging gardens of rose neon and chrome, the display cabinets revealed a lurid anatomical theatre of cannoli, cassate, puddings and creams – all lovingly shaped as organs of St Agatha. In the centre of the room, on an ornate silver stand, lay the *pièce de résistance*: a pair of pink dome-shaped blancmanges, each luxuriously nippled with a green glacé cherry.

Through the door came an eruption of voices as St Agatha's chariot, a vast devotional armoured car pulled by teams of grunting young bucks, rumbled past with cries of *Siete tutti devoti, tutti?*

Cettu! Cettu! roared the crowds lining the street.

Alberto walked in. Bare-chested, in the surgical white trousers of a pilgrim, he entered the room straight-backed, the light glinting from his polished head. From the counter he picked up a sharp knife, unnecessarily large for slicing blancmanges. Intoning a hymn in praise of St Agatha, he jabbed the point of the blade repeatedly into his chest. As the blood welled up from a series of penetrations, he leaned over the dishes of confectioneries, sprinkling them with crimson drops and moaning, *Io sono tuo martire. Io sono il pelicano.*

The Pelican straightened up and wavered uneasily before taking the knife to each of his nipples and carefully cutting around them until a circle of blood appeared and flowed like red milk in two lines down his chest. The room broke into solemn applause as the old man was led away and the sweet breasts of St Agatha, stained with his blood, were distributed among the faithful.

Saturday 3 February 2001
Into Catania for Saint Agatha. We begin by visiting the church of San Nicolò, an unfinished building with a jagged crown of black volcanic rock. Closed for years, it is supposedly used for satanic rituals. Next door is the university's Faculty of Letters, once a Benedictine convent, a huge *monstre gai* of

grey stucco, where the monks were accused of attempting to create paradise on earth.

On to the *Pescheria*, with fishmongers shouting like crazed preachers from pulpits of glistening silver sea-creatures. Beyond them greengrocers, salumieri, butchers with neatly bisected lambs hanging from rails above quivering piles of jellified meat stew known as *zuzu*. The decadence continues in a dried fruit shop selling dense black medallions of grape concentrate stamped with heraldic eagles, lions and shields.

The streets are packed. A great fever is in the air. St Agatha's day is approaching.

Sunday 4 February
The festival begins. There are queues to enter the dungeon where St Agatha was martyred. Outside, in the streets the faithful assemble according to their guilds (fishmongers, butchers, bakers, pastrycooks, etc.) each around a *candelora*. These are complicated wooden structures, half folk art half wedding cakes. Each *candelora* has heavy bars for carrying, which pass through a massive box surmounted by sculpted lions, eagles or kneeling dwarfs. These in turn support gilded theatrical stages where scenes from St Agatha's life are played out by miniature painted figures. St Agatha herself is topless, with two bloody circles where her breasts should be. Her torturers brandish iron forceps. Above them fly cherubs, holding out symbols of her martyrdom among wreaths of flowers and circlets of twinkling electric bulbs. Groups of *fedeli*, stocky young men in white night-shirts and black berets, sit around, chatting, smoking, talking into their mobile telephones.

Rosario leads us up to the fifth floor apartment of Dr Z____, retired Head of the Sicilian Tax Office. We take *limoncello* and cakes in his elegant rooms while waiting for the procession to begin. His balconies give a wide view of the entire urban scene. As well as the *candelore*, there are lumbering devotional chariots like silver-plated Sherman tanks, dragged by teams pulling on ropes that are three or four hundred metres long. These squeeze through the swarming streets while shouts of *Cittadini, cittadini, siete tutti devoti, tutti?* roll up to us like the smoke of sacrificial fires through the darkening air.

A Renaissance Dessert

David Madsen

During the carnival week last year, Leo and I attended a most
extraordinary banquet given by Lorenzo Strozzi, the banker,
brother of Filippo Strozzi, who is well known in Rome (and
perhaps beyond) for his epicurean inclinations; Leo came
dressed as a cardinal, wearing a silly sort of eye-mask of black
velvet. Nobody was supposed to know he was there, apparently,
but as Cardinals Rossi, Cibo, Salviati and Ridolfi were also
present, this absurd attempt at incognito was somewhat futile.

We were all led up a flight of steps to a door which had
been painted black, through which we entered a large hall,
entirely draped in black silk and velvet; in the middle of this
hall stood a black table on which reposed two black glass
flagons of wine and two human skulls, filled with the very
choicest viands.

'Do you think the poor man is depressed?' Leo whispered
to me.

'No. We're meant to be mystified, or a little frightened, or
perhaps both.'

After nibbling for a while, everyone was ushered into an
adjoining hall, even larger, which was blindingly, brilliantly lit
by innumerable candles and oil-lamps, some of the most
exquisite execution, in gold and silver, adorned with precious
stones. I caught Leo eyeing them enviously. We sat down at
the huge table, and after some moments were surprised – not
to say shocked – by a deep rumbling beneath our chairs; one
or two of the ladies swooned, and Cardinal Ridolfi, ridiculous
old actress that he is, leapt to his feet with a squeal of horror
and announced:

'The apocalypse has begun!'

In fact, it was the sound of a mechanical contrivance beneath the floor, which was so designed (cleverly, I concede, but all rather *de trop*) as to allow a great circular board to rise up from the room below, through the floor, until it was precisely level with the table at which we sat, and on it was heaped great dishes of victuals. Relieved more than anything else, several of the guests burst into applause. Lorenzo Strozzi allowed himself the faint trace of a smile, like a magician gratified at the success of his first trick, but knowing that there are even better ones to come. As indeed there were.

Servants placed a chased silver platter in front of each guest, who found, to his or her consternation, that what it contained was quite inedible. There were little cries of horror or delight or bewilderment; there was oddly forced laughter; some people began to look more than a little frightened.

'What have you got in yours?' I asked Leo.

He peered down at his plate and sniffed.

'It would appear to be half a pair of female undergarments,' he answered. 'Boiled.'

'I've got a raw sausage.'

'An empty eggshell!' a voice cried.

'A toad – oh Jesus – a *live* toad!' shrieked another, less enthusiastically.

'The heel of a shoe –'

'A kerchief, fried in batter . . .'

'Good God Almighty – a penis! No, no, wait a moment – ah! A blanched baby marrow, I think –'

Suddenly, the lights were extinguished. Quite how Strozzi managed it, I do not know; maybe there were servants hidden behind the drapes – in fact, now I come to think of it, this is the only way it *could* have been done. The great hall immediately rang with the shrill screams and shrieks of all the ladies, and Cardinal Ridolfi. Then we heard the slow rumble and shudder of the mechanism again, which was clearly being lowered, freshly loaded, and sent up a second time. After this, the candles were relighted (which took some time), and – behold! – the great table at which we sat was laden. This time the applause was strenuous and prolonged.

For the first course we were served vegetable soup with *stracciatelli*, and *potage à la royne*, which were accompanied by enormous slices of bread fried in oil and garlic and piled high with finely minced and seasoned partridge and pheasant, decorated with *funghi porcini*, artichokes deep-fried in the Jewish manner (Strozzi was a banker, after all), and baby onions. There was also *potage garni* accompanied by all manner of offal (which I heartily dislike, but in any case my Gnostic principles would not permit me to eat any of the meat.)

The second course consisted of venison broiled in stock, pies of every variety, pressed tongue, spiced sausages and salamis served with chopped melon and figs, and savoury egg flans. These delicacies were followed by huge roasts: more partridges and pheasants, larks (their tongues, basted in honey and orange with *basilico*, served separately), wood doves, pigeons, young chickens, and whole lambs. Then came a huge array of dishes made from butter, eggs and cheese – pies, flans, pastries, and so on; bowls of *melanzane* marinated in white wine and sprinkled lavishly with fragrant herbs, celery chopped with onions and peppers drenched in oil, also put in an appearance. The wines flowed as freely as a drunkard's piss.

After several hours of continuous eating, I was feeling quite faint; indeed, I could not imagine how so many of the other guests were still happily cramming themselves. Leo, unsurprisingly, chomped his way through the lot; however, he had not as yet farted (although I expected a real stinker at any moment), which was some small blessing. Lorenzo Strozzi, at the head of the table, finally rose to his feet a little unsteadily.

'Your Holiness – ah – Your Eminences, I meant to say, of course! – my dear and very *special* guests! I offer you now the climax, the apotheosis, the summit of this rather *unusual* evening.'

He clapped his hands, and four servants entered the hall, bearing on their shoulders a massive silver dish, in which was heaped what looked like half the cream in Rome; it was decorated more richly than Leo's tiara, with bright red cherries, brown pine kernels, thin green strips of angelica, all kinds of nuts and berries, and was wound about with a great length of dried leaves that had been dipped in gold. The entire assembled company (including myself, I readily admit) drew in its breath.

Strozzi went on, clearly drunk:

'Ah, but all is not what it seems to be, my very dear and *special* friends! No indeed. What you see before you is but the phantasm of the thing itself – the accidents which occlude and conceal the substance, as our good Tomaso d'Aquino would have said. You see, Your Eminences? I am not entirely unversed in the queen of sciences. Excuse me, I digress. Yes, invisible to your eyes, most cherished guests, is a delight more subtle, more – what shall I say, what term to employ? – more *sensuous* (for that must surely be the word!) than the simple sweetness which mere appearances promise. And let me give you a small clue, a tiny hint, so to speak, of the secret which is shortly to be revealed: I provide no implements for this, my final and most exquisite offering; you must use *only your tongues.*'

And with that, he collapsed back in his chair.

The dish was placed somewhat awkwardly in the centre of the table; for some moments we all sat and stared at it. Then Cardinal Salviati stood up, leaned as far as he could across the table, stuck out a greenish, corrugated tongue, and dipped the tip of it into the great mound of cream. He closed his eyes for a moment, licked his lips, then opened his eyes again and nodded.

'Very delicious,' he pronounced. 'Very delicious indeed. Flavoured with *grappa* and wild honey, if I am not mistaken.'

'Bravo, Eminence!' Lorenzo Strozzi cried drunkenly.

Embolded by Salviati's initiative, several of the gentlemen and two of the ladies did likewise; they giggled and nudged each other as they extended their tongues to taste their host's culinary 'apotheosis.' The technique, awkward though it was, was clearly catching on. It fell to Cardinal Ridolfi however, to finally expose the 'secret' of the extraordinary *dolce*; bending across the table and wiggling his tongue, he pushed it into the creamy mass only to withdraw it again with a piercing and womanly shriek.

'*It moved!*' he cried. 'God's bones, I tell you it moved! Ah! –'

There was a general commotion as it was observed that the great mound of decorated slop was indeed moving; it shuddered and wiggled, as if suddenly endowed with an alien life of its own. Clotted lumps of cream fell away, nuts and cherries flew off and showered onto the table. It seemed to be *growing*. Ridolfi by now was having an attack of the vapours, wiping his lips furiously with the back of his hand as though he had ingested poison; indeed, had this been a banquet given by Pope Alexander VI Borgia, whose memory still haunted curial slumbers, it might well have been.

Everybody was at the thing now, licking and scraping the cream off as fast as they could; people were stretched out across the table, plates were pushed aside or even fell to the floor; there was screeching and laughing and vulgar gestures. I do not think I have ever seen so many protruding tongues in my life, and it is a spectacle I care never to witness again; human beings look utterly ridiculous with their tongues sticking out. Leo should ban people doing it in all papal states. As a matter of fact, I had entirely forgotten about Leo: he was slumped in his chair, spellbound by the goings on. His eyes bulged and watered.

There was a young woman buried under that grotesque hillock of cream; furthermore, it quickly became obvious, as first a thigh was exposed, then a foot, a wetly glistening pink nipple, and finally a hairy pubic mound, that she was a very naked young woman. The cacophony of screaming and guffawing rapidly swelled in volume as people began to applaud. And still the tongues were at work, probing and wiggling and scraping lasciviously, lingeringly, across the smooth, pale flesh. Two men – one of them rather young for this sort of thing in my opinion – were licking at the same breast, contending for the stiff little nipple, occasionally looking into each other's eyes in a sly, knowing manner as they did so. Much to my surprise however, it was a lady (I use the term cautiously) whose face was buried deep between the shuddering thighs, sucking, slurping shamelessly, her long tongue darting rapidly in and out of the private opening hidden beneath the bush of black hair. I can well imagine what sort of cream she hoped to find down *there*. The young woman stretched herself out in the dish, still half-covered with rapidly liquifying slop; she writhed and groaned and fluttered her eyelids in a sexual ecstasy. The colloidal sludge oozed and squelched beneath her buttocks. Then she uttered a low moan:

'Ah . . . ah!'

The last two things I noticed were that the young man sharing a breast with a fellow diner had drawn out his quivering penis and was rubbing it surreptitiously up against a leg of the table, while the female devotee at the *other* end had pushed a cherry up into the hairy labial glory-hole which was so occupying her attention – presumably for the pleasure of sucking it out again.

'Your Holiness,' I said to Leo, 'it is time for us to take our leave.'

'Yes, you are right, Peppe. Yes, yes.'

The Art of Cooking a Murder Victim

Guillaume Lecasble

In our previous classes we have always tackled the recipe by first considering the essential question of the raw material: man or woman? Today, a different approach is needed as the first and most important thing is to source your murder victim. The state in which you salvage him or her will then determine the recipe. For example, strangulation would suggest something along the lines of stuffed duck.

Although you will be forced to adapt according to what you find, to maximise your chances of success the first step is to find a murder victim who corresponds to your tastes. To help you in this endeavour I have created a list of questions to ask the pathologist before travelling to the scene of the crime.

1. Is the victim a man or a woman?
2. How were they murdered?
3. Is the body battered or bruised?
   Always remember that presentation is fundamental to a recipe's success. One tastes a dish with the eyes, the nose and the ears as well as the mouth.
4. Has there been much loss of blood? Can any congealed blood be recovered? Remember the wonderful properties of congealed blood in the gratin we made at the start of the course. With regard to blood, we will be tackling suicides next week, and you will learn how unfortunate it is that often the veins are slashed in a bathtub of water. The blood becomes almost unusable, unless one reduces it heavily through boiling – and even then the results are risky. Some readers may be of the opinion that suicide is a

type of murder practised on oneself; I will tell you next time why I have chosen to distinguish suicide from murder victims. We already have plenty on our plate this week.

5. If the body has been carved up, into what cuts has it been divided, and how many?

6. Are there any pieces missing, and if so which?

7. In what position is the body?

8. The scene of the crime.

   If for example the victim was discovered in a newly seeded garden, you'll have to use the same approach as with a red pepper. However, the multiple orifices, body hair, nails etc., make it much more complex to de-seed a human body than a pepper. One of the reasons we have chosen cannibal cuisine is to avoid irritations of this sort often posed by more traditional recipes.

9. Never forget to check the age.

   No need for further explanation here. We've spent several session on the subject, and everything that has already been said applies equally to murder victims.

10. Was there any sexual contact, and what kind?

11. Any identifiable diseases?

    Skin diseases are visible to the naked eye; a pathologist will be able to give you good advice concerning others. Liver diseases tend to produce a bitter taste. The thing to avoid at all costs is the anxious individual – nervous bile is undetectable and spreads only at the end of the cooking process. Your meal will suddenly be fit only for the dustbin, leaving you empty-handed with guests to feed.

12. Clothes?

13. Social standing?

14. Was the victim afraid?

15. Did the victim smoke?

16. Did they drink?

17. Were they on drugs?

18. Is any silicone present? As with veal fed on hormone-enhanced diets, there are two schools of thought. Unlike the monsantists, the organic lobby is fiercely opposed to the consumption of silicone. On the one occasion I personally had the opportunity to eat a surgically-enhanced murder victim, the silicone was in the breasts. It may have been my imagination but the jelly-like consistency of the flesh seemed offset by a milky flavour. The life-giving breast had thus spiced up an otherwise bland dish. Some of my fellow guests spat out their first mouthful, so this may be a matter of taste.

If the answers you receive to these questions whet your appetite such that you wish to proceed, make sure to pose a few additional questions regarding the eyes, hair, nails, teeth and body hair. Remember our session on hair: it is extremely tasty, not to mention visually attractive, when frozen and then fried in very hot oil seasoned with a little garlic.

For today I have chosen to demonstrate the issues with a victim killed in his car. Let's go through the questionnaire point by point.

1. It is a man.
2. He was killed by a shot in the head. The resulting fusion of brain matter with blood lends a slightly sweet flavour, meaning that the head can be caramelised with a dash of vinegar and no need for added sugar.
3. The head has of course been damaged. We must therefore create a 'blackened' dish, as in Cajun cooking; as you know this allows for a normalisation of the appearance. However, be conservative with oven temperature; you don't want your victim to look charred.
4. In this case, yes, the head has bled a great deal. Calculate cooking time and temperature according to the amount of blood still present, thus ensuring that the flesh doesn't dry out. Tenderness is crucial.

5. The victim has not been carved up.
6. No part of the body is missing.
7. The victim fell onto the steering wheel, jamming the horn. Even in a lifeless body sound creates vibrations transmitted through the eardrum. This is very helpful for even distribution of flavour.
8. Scene of the crime: a 4×4 jeep, implying the victim was rich (answer to question 13). The leather upholstery may have perfumed his lungs, but in answer to question 15, he was a smoker. Of cigars – butts were found in the ashtray. Before cooking insert two small holes in the ribcage to drain the liquefied tar.
9. The victim was still young. Given his social status one can infer good nutrition and thus assume that any excess fat is 'good' fat. You will also notice that tennis had overdeveloped his right arm; he must have been right handed. Because of this, when carving you should give preference to the left side, especially for the more muscular cuts.
10. Irrelevant question. He was returning from the country-side and had been driving for six hours – enough time to build up any semen he may have spent. With regard to anal sex the victim was a virgin.
11. The victim had a small amount of psoriasis on his elbows. Nothing nasty. Before cooking, grate a little and keep to one side.
12. Good quality clothes, which will only have contributed to his well being. On to our own, therefore . . .
13. The big one: was he afraid? Examine his face. We're in luck, he had no time for fear. If he had, rest assured he'd have been good for nothing but the morgue.
14 & 15: Finally, he had taken no alcohol or drugs; more's the pity! There is nothing better than internal organs pickled in alcohol. Regardless of type, the marinating and preservation processes produce the unique taste of a kiss

following a glass of wine. As for drugs, they tend to mellow the general flavour.

We have now considered all the angles. I suggest you switch on the oven and get cooking.

'Blackened murder victim, served with grey matter gravy and elbow garnish.'

Decadent Death Styles

.

Death Styles

Jad Adams

> 'Death laughs, breathing close and relentless
> In the nostrils and eyelids of lust'

I've always liked that line from Swinburne and when my decadent friends started to die it seemed particularly apposite. We were, of course, the AIDS generation. I don't mean they all died of AIDS, though some did, but certainly the disease set a tone for youthful death from the challenges of sex, drugs, drink and despair.

Staying on the move, you pass a lot of gatekeepers and sooner or later one of them is going to bounce you out of the club forever. The thing about living fast and dying young is that you can be sure you are burning up your life, you just don't know in which form the grim reaper will appear to invite you for a dance.

So my friend David, a poet, died from nasopharyngeal cancer, related to drinking and smoking. But he could just as easily have died on the loo, his body finally giving up on the struggle of life, like my friend Barrie. Now, Barrie was a prolifically promiscuous homosexual flagellant who sometimes used intravenous drugs but being thusly a multiple risk for AIDS didn't mean that carried him off. He was just worn out with excess.

Our mutual friend Peter died injecting a dodgy drug but he didn't take much care of himself and he did indeed have the collection of illnesses called AIDS – the drugs just got there first. Not so his lover Hasani who worked at the BBC and whose day off was to sit in a cubicle in the public toilets on

Clapham Common with a flask of tea and a bag of sandwiches and provide sexual services gratis to any man who wanted them. When I last saw him alive his limbs were like brown pipe cleaners with his head a walnut on top.

Death styles of the poor and decadent, as the Goncourt brothers reflected in their diary of 1861 culminate in 'dying in shreds at the age of forty-two, without even strength left in them to suffer.'

> Ghosts go along with us until the end;
> This was a mistress, this, perhaps a friend.

Debbie bled out after falling over drunk in the bathroom and hitting her head, Maggie finally tired of her drugs and her men and took an overdose.

I remember one time having dinner with three other men, a film director, a singer and the director's lover. Within eighteen months the director and singer were dead, I never had the heart to enquire as to the lover's fate; sufficient for the day is the evil thereof. It may be of no consolation to their mothers, but at least they didn't get old and boring.

Some just slipped away and I don't know what space they are in. I am unaware, for example, if my chum the drunken classical scholar Patrick is in soul-space or earth-time but he lives in my memory which is all I need. He used to silence the company with the statement 'I am going to tell you a joke, I am going to tell you the oldest joke in the world.' When he had quiet he would begin 'Lupae nanus dicit . . .' and would continue to tell the entire story in Latin. If he is dead, which I suspect, I think he will have told that joke to the shades of Johnson and Dowson. And they will have laughed.

Primordial Soup

Christine Leunens

A woman in late middle-age was sitting on a weathered sack of charcoal, taking in the sun. Her hair was three sorts of blonde, and if this weren't enough variety, her roots were grey. She had on a grass-stained pair of trainers, a tight pair of jeans, a T-shirt and, from what I could see (and anyone else, quite easily) no bra. Her smile was empty, a rag-doll smile with black button eyes.

I assumed she was one of my neighbours and replied, 'Just some shopping, Ma'am. Salt and pepper are fine things, but one does need variety in life.'

Her smile transformed into a contortion of malice. 'You bit my man.'

I could not apologize before I knew whom she was talking about. 'Which one?' I asked, and not in the least insolently.

'You bite often?' she sneered and came at me with clenched fists. Like the neglected fruit of an overgrown garden, her breasts sagged under their own weight. Although they could feed a famished army, the man to whom she was referring had apparently not bothered to take a bite for many a year.

'My past samples do not concern you unless you have consumed your partner since? I did not think so. Goodbye.' I did not wish to dismiss her rudely, but her face answered my questions quicker than her speech did, and besides, I had my own cuisine to worry about.

'So you eat every dick you come across?'

'If you enjoy the same flesh over a prolonged period, I congratulate you. As far as I'm concerned, no piece has yet addicted me.'

She blocked my path.

'Now if you shall excuse me.' I pushed past her, but didn't get very far.

'You're not going anywhere,' she grabbed me, 'You bit my husband's ass bad!'

She was breathing heavily; a hiccup jarred her chest and I detected a trace of pork and beer.

'I do not wish to upset you, Madame, but your husband was given the gift of free will from Our Lord above, he consented willingly, I promise you, you shall find no signs of chains or thrashing if you examine him more thoroughly. He should cut the links off himself if serving as a woman's meal, other than his lawfully wedded wife's, tempts him so much.'

'He told me all 'bout how it happened, you prick-tease, you was jerkin' off a carrot in his face, you was playin' with a cherry like it was y'r tit, you were puttin' yer mouth on all kinds o'fruits an' lickin' 'em nasty, toyin' with every obscenity you could get yer dirty fingers on!'

As she pulled my hair, I stepped around in an ungainly little dance. 'I beg your pardon?!'

'Whadda ya think, yeah gotta go to university ta understand? You all think yer so high an' mighty, yer all ajecated an' smart, well lemme tell yeah, yer more a slut than I ever put my eyes on!'

'Let no man judge you in eating, Colossians, 2–16.'

'Don't you play no holy mouth with me, ya nasty cunt!'

'One [man] has faith to eat everything, but the [man] who is weak eats vegetables. Let the one eating not look down on the one not eating, and let the one not eating not judge the one eating, Romans 14:2, 14:3.'

'Shut yer mouth, you stinkin' sperm bag!' She gave my head another more forceful tug backwards; unfortunately, she was pulling the silver chain of my crucifix as well as my hair. 'Tell me how it all happened, I'm curious t'hear yer vursion. Tell me why ya picked 'im? You knew he had a big one, ya could smell it a mile away, couldn't ya? Was that yer criterion? You teased him 'til you was certain? You was just starin' at it in the mirror, dying t'have it, wasn't ya?'

'If truly you are intent on learning the particularities, Madame, since I was a child, I never was one to clear my plate, so I assure you, I couldn't care less how big the portion is.'

I never saw a face so sceptical when hearing the truth spoken. She looked down at my hair dress, crinkled her nose in disgust, and pulled my hair mercilessly. I was certain the silver chain was going to cut my throat, when it all of a sudden broke, and the tiny Jesus fell into the cleavage of my breasts.

'If you'll forgive me, Madame, I left something on the stove . . . and I really must be going . . . '

Grass seeds had been planted around the building, but the grass had not yet grown; normally we weren't allowed to be standing where we were. I looked down and saw my silver chain, long and fine, a shiny scar across the earth, a tiny food chain, a food chain Jesus was an integral part of.

'Don't give me no fuckin' cop-out! I asked you a question an' I wanna answer now!'

'Would you terribly mind restating it more specifically?'

'Why in hell did ya choose my husband?!'

'I assure you, I did not choose him. I did not even sample him. There is all of him still available for you.'

'You think he was good ta play with, an' now ya throw him back like scraps! Like a bone ta an ol' dog!'

'Scraps? I didn't even get a mouthful! If he came home stripped, it wasn't me!'

'Delinquent,' she kicked me before crossing the street as an old man peddled by, flag high on his three-wheeler like a proud tail.

I studied the shelf with care before making my choice: tarragon, allspice, capsicum, celery salt, grains of paradise, bay leaves, caraway seeds, juniper, mace, turmeric, coriander, garlic powder, oregano, nutmeg, cardamom, thyme, cloves, saffron, cumin, paprika, red pepper, thyme, sesame seeds, and dried parsley. I avoided looking at the cashier. I looked down at my bare and blistered feet instead. She rang the small bottles up and, one by one, rolled them down to the bag boy. I could feel her eyeing me like I was weird; maybe it was my teeth chattering, or my shifting from foot to foot.

When I returned, the hob was beaming with anticipation. The idea of cooking was succulent to me. I tore off my hair dress. It stuck to me and I felt like I was skinning myself. My whole body was perspiring, which proved useful, for the spices adhered more easily. I powdered my self instinctively, primitively, powerfully.

When I sat on the hob, the heat was like a magnet attracting my skin, adhering to it so thoroughly, it felt like being sucked into the metal disc. I did not scream, only my other self did, for it was weak just as flesh is known to be. I smelt meat quite soon, several meats at that, for sitting as I was, I'd offered the hob all seven, and as many different skins. The small triangles of fattiness at the junction of my thighs were most unlike the leanness of the red meats; the stringy, brown loop to the back yielded an earthy scent I could clearly distinguish from the buttery, lardy layer of the buttocks; the mild cheesiness of the labia, the fishiness of the mucous membranes, the warm, eggy, yeasty gases that came from the life-giving orifice were each quite unique. I had detected the particular aroma of fish, fowl, red meat, rabbit, pork, veal, and shellfish, when unfortunately the bouquet was spoilt by the smell of burning hairs. These were like onions, put in the pan too early, and now scorching, overpowering the dish. The snapping and popping were not everywhere uniform. Those dangling flaps which can be spread like a tiny quail's wings, whose edges were already crinkly like bacon, strangely, reacted the least, stuck too sadly to the burner to move, they turned a greyish-white. My buttocks, the most sedate of the mass, on the contrary, made a tremendous fuss. The tiny pockets of air behind the dented orange skin were liable to unexpected explosions, and the onslaught of greasiness threatened fire. My intimate folds shrunk before my very eyes. My juices ran down the front of the stove and onto the floor, between the other burners and down my legs and feet; some of it cooked as soon as it was freed, thickened, browned, blackened. The pain was atrocious, for my uncooked cells were still imbued with that force, pulling themselves away from inert food, holding tightly onto the miracle, the autonomy, the fuss, one calls life.

My head, heavy with thoughts, drooped dangerously towards the floor. I noticed a small flame had taken in the triangle of coarse hairs; it was dancing its everlasting hip-thrusting dance, celebrating its power to transform flesh to meat, life to food, pain to senselessness. The kitchen began to turn faster and faster. My head fell forwards, bringing the rest of my body down with it, down onto a pile of dirty dishes which broke, their fragments sticking into the last of me.

Alice, the Sausage

Sophie Jabès

Alice had seen the light: that was it, that was exactly what she wanted to be, a *salsiccia*, a beautiful and big *salsiccia*, extremely fragrant, smooth and fat. A sausage. Alice couldn't take her eyes off the streaky bacon she had just prepared for herself. Alice the sausage. Alice had finally found her way. She was lying there, in the sauce, in the middle of the lentils, smiling, pleasing and appetizing.

Alice went to stretch out on the sofa. The revelation was decisive, she had to meditate, weigh up the consequences of her discovery, establish a plan of action, concoct a strategy. The task was not going to be easy.

Alice dragged herself in front of the mirror. She smiled with childish, amazed delight. Her arms bloated, her stomach, swollen like a wine skin, her eyes drowned in the fat of her cheeks constituted so many pleasant surprises for her to evaluate with thorough precision. Those arms had to swell even more, puff up, stretch and become even podgier. There had to be no more difference between arms and fingers, or between thighs, calves, ankles and feet. All had to come together in one round form towards which all Alice's desire strained.

Alice's skin was soft. She worked at making it even smoother. Three times a day she slid across the floor, on the tiles from Ferrara. She rolled from left to right, right to left, roaring with laughter. It was a long time since she had laughed so much. She liked the contact of the cold floor beneath her thighs and forearms. She kneaded her body in that manner for hours on end. Her skin was turning blue, with red marks, resembling the marbling of the chipolatas bought in the market. Alice was delighted.

Alice was still hoping the telephone would ring. But it didn't. In fact, she was no longer in such a hurry to see the twins again. Deep down, she knew that they would reappear one day, enticed by the fat. She wanted to be ready, surprise them, amaze them, leave them breathless.

Alice had bought a parrot. It was a male macaw which murmured words of love and encouragement all day long. 'Go go tootsie wootsie,' it hurled when it saw Alice rolling on the floor. 'I love you, yeah yeah yeah,' it sing-songed with little clucks of satisfaction, delighting the young woman each time she was depilating. The parrot could also sing some tunes from *La Traviata* that he interlaced with obscenities, thus rendering something like, '*E troppo tardi* . . . show us your arse, sweetie.' Alice listened to it while eating pizzas, her mouth full and her hands greasy. She spent hours making him repeat, 'Alice the sausage, Alice the sausage.' The parrot looked at her with empty round eyes and intoned, 'Alice the sausage, the girl who fucks nice, Alice the sausage, the girl who sucks spice, Alice the sausage, are you getting the message?'

Alice often fell asleep on the sofa. The parrot carried on muttering 'heave-ho!', the cuckoo sounding the hours and half hours, amid the greasy wrappers, the bottles of Chianti and Coke, the piles of plates she refused to wash.

Alice left boxes of pizza, plates with sauce, leftovers of ice cream and squid fritters littered everywhere. It all blended cheerfully, and it stank like a pigsty. Alice delighted in that putrid smell. 'A sausage cannot be made with Hermès scarves,' she loved to repeat.

Alice slept more and more. She was awake for three hours a day at the very most. She rose, or rather, slid to the floor, crawled as far as the kitchen, devoured everything there was to devour, gave some seed to the macaw, which thanked her with moist eyes: 'Thank you, sausage,' looked with satisfaction at the progress of her swelling in the mirror and rolled back to bed.

Alice's skin became extremely smooth. Flavoured too. With basil. Parsley. Green peppercorns. She smelt of the herbs and spices she sprinkled passionately on her food. It was marvellous to behold. Her flesh was swelling, abundant, springy, or almost.

Alice went to so much trouble caressing herself with creams and potions patiently prepared, kneading herself, that it was as if her skin became lined with felt. Alice had started her depilations again. The sessions lasted longer, that was all. She now needed between ten and twenty kilos of lemons and as much sugar, very little water and lots of patience. Alice had plenty of that.

Every evening Alice inspected the results. Sometimes she lost heart. She collapsed on the sofa and contemplated her bruised legs with sadness. The task seemed impossible, the goal too far away. She cried, leaning on her Regency chest of drawers, ruminating with dread over the idea that she would probably never be a sausage. She looked at her life again. Those men to whom she had been as nice as possible, her father who used to sing in a raucous, albeit melancholic voice, her mother gone with her most generous lover. It all seemed so vain and useless. Her efforts, her sufferings, for nothing. For a few bruises and a few kilos too many.

Her anxiety overwhelmed her all the more. The pit deep in her stomach became more hollow and deeper still. More threatening. She swallowed big plates of *cannelloni*, heaped spoonfuls of chestnut cream and fell asleep like an angel.

Alice always had the same dream. She was on a beach, on the edge of a jetty, and there was an enormous chocolate cake topped with a pretty red cherry on the water. She wanted to get to the cake. A parrot came and landed next to her, cackling in her ear, 'Alice the sausage, Alice the sausage.' She could see her limbs change form, her legs and arms swell, her body become a big, chubby, white pudding with wings. She could then follow the parrot which took her near the much coveted dessert. As soon as she approached, the dessert sank in the water. As she left, it came back to the surface. The more she desired it, the more it seemed to defy her. She finally made up her mind and shot forward, trying to catch it. She landed a few centimetres from the cake. Only the cherry was left and from up close it looked all wrinkled.

Alice always woke up in a sweat, screaming. She had missed the cake, she had missed her life.

In order to soothe the wound which reopened, she dragged herself towards the fridge, finished off two plates of *lasagne* and a few slabs of milk chocolate. She found some *bocconcini, mozzarella, rosette* with *mortadella* and lentils with bacon.

Slightly calmer now, she went back to bed holding her bulging stomach.

She couldn't fall asleep. The cuckoo sneered. The parrot snored on its perch. Alice felt lonely and empty. With that strange feeling that she was going to take off if she didn't stuff herself. She had to eat.

There was not much left. Alice was acting crazy. Stale farmhouse loaves, old apples that had been left about, roasted chicken legs, slightly rancid. Alice found a tin of flageolet beans at the bottom of the cupboard. Alice hated those beans. She devoured them avidly. It was as if she had a vacuum cleaner in her stomach. She sucked in everything she could find, unsalted rusks, stuffed cabbage, olives, a jar of mustard, some fresh cream, gherkins, slabs of cooking chocolate. Nothing could fill the emptiness.

Alice went back to bed. She dreamt of *porchetta* and grilled lamb chops.

Days went by, nights too.

Alice hardly moved now. She ate straight from the bags the delivery men left at her door. She no longer had the strength to lift them.

She caressed her shapeless body. Weighed its roundness in her hands. Spent hours staring at the portrait her brother had drawn of her. To become imbued with it. Convinced that her wish was soon to be granted.

Alice, the sausage . . .

One horrible January morning, a cold, rainy and soulless day, Alice didn't wake up. Perhaps she felt like making the most of her reserves, like hibernating, we will never know, but the fact was that Alice didn't deign to open her eyes. The macaw called in vain, 'sweetie, tootsie wootsie, sausage,' but she kept her eyes closed.

It was on that same morning that, with a severe storm breaking outside, the twins chose to push the door open and pay their friend a visit.

At first they were taken aback by the smell. They almost left, but they had brought three kilos of lentils with them, it would have been a shame to leave before showing them to Alice.

So they came in, groping their way in a room plunged into total darkness, whispering:

'Alice, Alice, are you there?'

They couldn't see a thing, the parrot kept quiet. They thought Alice must be out and they would have to wait patiently on the sofa.

When they sat down they felt a kind of viscous but, at the same time, firm mass beneath them. They leapt to their feet.

'What's that?' they shouted, their heads bobbing.

Before their eyes was an enormous sausage, a kind they had never seen. A pink sausage marbled to perfection, a magnificent sausage.

'What a beauty!'

The twins had never dreamed of anything so beautiful. They immediately believed that Alice must have prepared that sausage for their dinner. Extremely proud to have thought to bring the lentils, they settled in the wicker chairs to wait for Alice, who wouldn't be long.

They didn't move. Alice didn't come back.

Could they leave without talking to her? That was out of the question.

They fell asleep.

When the twins awoke, hunger was gnawing dreadfully at them. Fulvio, being less timid, said aloud what Flavio had been thinking for quite a while.

'What about cooking some lentils and eating a bit of the sausage?'

'Without waiting for Alice?'

'You know her, she's so nice, she will be delighted to know we have eaten our fill.'

Hearing those words, Alice opened the fatty slit which was now her eye. The twins, after so many months of absence, were standing next to her, whispering about how nice she was. Alice was on the verge of tears, her happiness seemed too copious. Finally her efforts were to be rewarded. She understood of course that the twins wanted to eat her. It didn't matter, she realized that her life would take on its whole meaning. In that desire for her, there was an absolute gratitude, a boundless trust. Those twins, whom she had sucked so often and so patiently, were going to devour her . . . bit by bit. For the first time Alice felt an intense pleasure, close to ecstasy.

Fulvio and Flavio put the lentils on to cook, took a little penknife they kept to slice the bread and *porchetta* and started to cut the sausage.

Alice didn't scream. She was in pain but the moment was so exquisite, her happiness so intense. Here was the opportunity to be perfectly nice to the twins. The gift of herself finally took on its whole and entire meaning. She didn't utter a sound. At the third mouthful Alice passed out. It was never known if it was from pain or orgasm.

Fulvio and Flavio had a feast. Until that day they had eaten nothing so delicious. So mild. So well-flavoured. So unctuous.

So tasty. By the end of that winter day they had quietly relished the whole of Alice in a feast as unexpected as it was delicious.

Once the sausage and the lentils had been consumed they had a rest. Despairing of all hope of seeing their friend come back, they left her a note assuring her that the meal had been fantastic. They departed feeling light-hearted, promising to return soon to thank her.

When the twins came out into the street, the sky had cleared. There was one single cloud which looked down on them with affection as they passed. A cloud which wondered if the sausage meat had been unctuous enough, delicious enough, tender enough. The cloud smiled to see them so happy, but were they completely satisfied?

Even in heaven, Alice was trying to fathom out if she had been nice enough.

It was at that precise moment the parrot decided to speak. It had watched Alice's feast without opening its beak, but, moved by remorse, or regret, it finally let slip, between two bird sobs: 'Alice the sausage, Alice the sausage.'

It repeated those words till nightfall, without stopping, only ending when it dozed off on its perch, missing its owner and the seeds she used to dish out.

My Funeral

Louise Welsh

The old women are there, too old to give a damn,
They've brought along the kids, who don't know who I am
                                    Jacques Brel, *My Death*

I'm generally an austere soul. I 'drink gin to mortify my taste for fine vintages' and always choose someone I'm not sexually attracted to when being unfaithful. I do however have one decadent pastime – planning my own funeral. After all the prospect of being at the centre of one last party is the only consolation death holds.

For many years I flirted with the idea of copying Shelley's cremation. Burned on an open pyre on a beach in Italy by his poet brethren. I imagined the chief mourner plunging her hands into the flames to retrieve my finely formed skull as Lord George Byron reputedly did for his old chum's (it crumbled in his hands). Heart, lungs, liver I'd bequeath my organs to any mourner that desired them.

But then Scotland gained devolution, Donald Dewer was given a state funeral, and while I know there's many in line before me, I would relish the chance to stop the traffic one last time.

I've no illusions, I know I've lived too long to make a beautiful corpse, so there'll be no open coffin. Instead let some cherubic child carrying a picture of me slim and lithe at seventeen, head the parade. Behind her comes a New Orleans jazz band, every marching step a hesitation, every trumpet note mournful.

The dress code will be black, as dapper or scruffy as

personal style dictates, but shades are mandatory. All mourners must walk the long route round the city; I've no wish to make folk suffer so the infirm can be pushed in wheelchairs decorated with black crepe.

The arrival of my coffin should be as carefully timed as the star turn's entrance onto a variety stage. Once the crowd is warm, but before they're too drunk to appreciate the sheer majesty of my coffin, set atop an ebony coach led by black blinkered stallions with nodding ostrich plume headdresses. There will be no pious requests for *no flowers please* at my send-off. I want gangster wreaths with tributes spelt in flowers.

The general holiday will mean that from the badlands of the East to the genteel West End the streets will be lined with old and young, perhaps a few souls will even travel over from Edinburgh.

The dancing clubs and majorette troupes of Glasgow will have donned their devil costumes, topped their batons with plastic skulls and bring up the wake shaking their booties to the rhythm of the Maryhill women's drum group. No bagpipes please. And finally, a sombre line of Hell's Angels on Harleys each one topped by a black and red silk pennant will give a last glare to the crowd to remind them of who I am – was.

The picture gets hazy towards the end. I imagine other writers, friends and enemies, my publisher and agent among the throng and realise that I want to outlive them all. After all I know that once they've thrown me in the ground they'll all head to the pub and as the drink flows the conversation will soon drift from me to them . . .

The Last Word

Dear Rowan,

What the fuck does a mummy from Cambridge know about decadence?

You don't even fuck! I was on my way to a brothel the other day when I met you: 'Would you care to join me my darling?' I said. You looked at me as if I had just dribbled sherry trifle in front of starving Biafrans. 'Er, um, no thank you,' you stumbled. Whore licks? Off home for Horlicks more like.

What is the point of a woman who doesn't fuck? It's like a bank without money. A lighthouse without a light. Christianity without Christ. The only brilliant thing about women is the fact that they are guaranteed to have on them at any time, any place, a pair of tits for sucking and a cunt for fucking. But what of you? You quiver and shiver, but never deliver. Let me tell you baby, a woman who doesn't fuck, doesn't do anything else.

I wouldn't even object if you were a nun. Halibut. In decadence as in religion, the blasphemers operate shoulder to shoulder with the believers, enjoined by passion. It's the don't knows you want to watch out for, the in-betweens, the luke-warm. And because you, Rowan, are neither hot nor cold I will spew you out of my mouth.

It is intolerable. You pose as outré but you are about as decadent as the St Trinian's hockey team. You are a non swimmer working as a life guard. A sheep in sheep's clothing. A gong at a railway crossing clanging loudly and vainly as the train whooshes by.

In the 1830s, one gentleman, when charged with pushing his pregnant mistress into the Seine defended himself by saying, 'We live in an age of suicide; this woman gave herself to death.' That's decadence, Miss Pelling. Put your brat in an orphanage and come down here bitch and milk my fucking cock.

So fuck you – I'm not appearing in your crappy book. Every word in it is a lie, including 'and' and 'the'. You want me to be an electric eel in a pond of goldfish? Pah! My work is not companionable. And there is no such thing as co-starring with Sebastian. Especially with straight-to-video performers. Middleweight, middlebrow, middle-aged, middle-income, middle-class, middle-of-the-road, middle-England, middling twats.

All of you have learned to write but evidently can't read. If you could read your stuff you'd stop writing. If asked to sign your book, I would whip out my cock, and piss all over it. 'There. There's my fucking signature.' I would say.

In the absence of piss I have used ink.

HRL His Royal Lowness. Sebastian Horsley.

Dear Reader,

There are losers who borrow books from the library; there are more enterprising losers who have stolen them from the library (or the remainder bin) – but you, a loser who has actually bought this book?

Was it difficult wading through these shallows? Was its attack like being stoned to death with popcorn? Was it like watching a chicken try to fly?

You deserve everything you didn't get. Reading about decadence is like dancing about architecture. Writing describes the unlived life. Reading is a lonely and private substitute for experience.

And just what the fuck have you done? Have you fucked a 1000 prostitutes? Or sold your body to the lowest bidder? Have you run a brothel? Cut off the end of your own finger or come over your own sister? Deliberately electrocuted yourself or jumped out of an aeroplane on amphetamines? Surely you have you swum naked with the great white shark or been crucified with real nails? Have you been buggered by a mass murderer? Have you fucked an old lady? Or what about an amputee with no arms or legs? A limbless trunk full of your own spunk? Even a blow up doll would be a start. Have you played Russian Roulette? Or been shot at by a whore? Or what about eating a big bowl of your own faeces? Or even a big bowl of fuck? Surely you've made a million in a year and spent a million in a year? Or smoked £100,000 of crack? Injected heroin into your cock? Watched someone die? Overdosed your girlfriend? Jumped off a cliff? Had a shot in the dark, a shot in the arm, a shot in the head? Have you fucked in a church and prayed in a brothel?

No, I didn't think so. I have. The hand of God, reaching down into the mire, couldn't elevate me to the depths of depravity.

But you? What of you sad reader? Sitting there with your book. What can be explained with words is only the waves, the foam on the surface, but decadence has its place underneath the waves, in the silent depth of the unspeakable.

Wake up. A real man does not think of victory or defeat. He plunges recklessly towards an irrational death. By doing this, you will awaken from your dreams.

Your Mother's a prostitute and I shit on the corpses of all your past ancestors.

HRL His Royal Lowness. Sebastian Horsley

Appendix

Contributors

Jad Adams is a television producer and author. His books include *Madder Music, Stronger Wine*, the biography of Ernest Dowson.

Maria Alvarez is a journalist and writer. She lives in London. Her first novel, *Mirror, Mirror*, will be published by Fig Tree (Penguin) in February 2007 – if it makes her wealthy, she plans to employ Snowball.

Phil Baker is a writer and critic. He is the author of *The Dedalus Book of Absinthe* and is currently finishing a biography of Dennis Wheatley.

Belle de Jour is the nom de plume of a writer and high-class escort, whose infamous, award-winning blog of her London life was read by 15,000 people every day before being turned into a bestselling memoir: *Belle de Jour: The Intimate Adventures of a London Call Girl*. She has now retired from her night job.

Vanora Bennett grew up in London and lived in Moscow during the 1990s. She is the author of *The Tastes of Dreams*.

Anne Billson is older than the rocks among which she sits; like the vampire, she has been dead many times, and learned the secrets of the grave; and has been a diver in deep seas, and keeps their fallen day about her; and trafficked for strange webs with Eastern merchants. Anne Billson is a film critic, photographer and writer. She's the author of two novels: *Suckers* and *Stiff Lips*, and two books for the BFI on *The Thing* and *Buffy the Vampire Slayer*.

CONTRIBUTORS

Jeremy Bourdon was born in 1979 in Virginia. He lives in London and has had many unrequited loves.

Joe Boyd is one of the music industry's legendary record producers and the Executive Producer of the 1988 feature film *Scandal*. His memoir of the Sixties' music industry scene *White Bicycles: Making Music in the 1960s* was recently published by Serpents Tail. *UFO Club* appears courtesy of Serpent's Tail.

Stevie Boyd grew up in Belfast. After fighting in the punk wars he moved to Leeds in 1981 to be closer to Johnny Thunders. He is one of the writers included in the definitive guide to Northern Irish punk, *It Makes You Want to Spit* (available online now).

Brock Norman Brock is a soldier and a writer. For many years he served under Rowan on the *Erotic Review*. He is also a noted accordionist.

Mick Brown writes for the *Telegraph* magazine and is currently writing a biography of Phil Spector. His book on *Performance* is published by Bloomsbury.

Michael Bywater was born prematurely and has been compensating ever since. His motto is 'indolence is the virtue of . . .' oh finish it yourself. He is Taurean, protean, myopic and at heart an organist. Do not go up the winding stone stairs with him, whatever he may say. [Editor's note: but *do* read his recent acclaimed book *Lost Worlds* – as serialised on Radio Four – a glossary of the missing which weaves a web of everything we no longer have, published by Granta Books.]

Andrew Crumey is the author of five novels, including *Pfitz* and the award-winning *Music, in a Foreign Language*. Unusually for a novelist, he is a scientist by training and has a Ph.D in theoretical physics.

Dickon Edwards: writer, flaneur, lyricist, model, philosopher and member of the recording artistes Fosca. He can be found at www.dickonedwards.co.uk or running his club night, *The Beautiful and the Damned*, in North London's Boogaloo.

Malcolm Eggs is the editor of the essential guide to where to breakfast, http://londonreviewofbreakfasts.blogspot.com. Anyone who visits Britain without consulting this resource will starve.

Salena Godden's short stories and poems have been published in many anthologies and her memoir *Springfield Road* will be published by Harper Collins/Harpers Press in 2007/ 2008. Her performances have featured on BBC Radio 4's *Bespoken Word* and BBC Radio 3's *The Verb*. Renown in the 90s for 'taking poetry into clubs' and nicknamed Salena Saliva – she records, writes and performs in cult duo SaltPeter with Peter Coyte. They recently signed a record deal, launching with a single titled 'Everybody Back To Mine' and with an album to follow in February 2007. Sassy and a heady cocktail of Jamaican and Irish she lives in North London and has no pets, husbands or children.

Nick Groom is Reader in English and Director of the Centre for Romantic Studies at the University of Bristol. He is the author of *Introducing Shakespeare*, *The Forger's Shadow* and *The Union Jack: The Story of the British Flag*. He lives on Dartmoor, plays the hurdy-gurdy and does his utmost to support the local hostelry.

Lisa Hilton grew up in Cheshire but lives in the United States. She was a columnist for the *Erotic Review* and is the author of *Athénaïs* and *Mistress Peachum's Pleasure*.

Tom Holland is a writer, broadcaster and classical historian. He is the author of the hugely acclaimed books of popular history *Rubicon* and *Persian Fire*. He has written a series of lauded adaptations for Radio 4 of Herodotus's *Histories* and Virgil's *Aeneid*, to be followed by Homer's *Iliad* and *Odyssey* and he is the author of the novels *The Bone Hunter, Slave of My Thirst* and *Lord of the Dead*.

Sebastian Horsley lives in London, has fucked over 1,000 prostitutes and was fired as the *Observer's* sex columnist after causing a debate over anal sex.

J.K. Huysmans' most famous novel was *Against Nature* (*A Rebours*), and it was the novel which began the French decadent movement. This new translation is by Brendan King, who has translated Huysmans' *Là Bas, Marthe* and *Parisian Sketches* for Dedalus.

Robert Irwin has been described as Britain's most original novelist, he is also its leading Arabic scholar and divides his time between Kennington and Vauxhall. His six novels include *Prayer-Cushions of the Flesh* which has recently been made into a film by Magnus Irvin and Ray McNeil and is now available on DVD. For more details visit www.prayercushions.co.uk. Dedalus has published a film tie-in edition which includes fourteen pages of film stills and information about the film.

Sophie Jabès was born in 1958 and currently lives in Paris. She is the author of three novels. The excerpt from her first novel *Alice, the Sausage* has been translated from French by Paul Buck and Catherine Petit. It will be published by Dedalus in November 2006. *Alice la saucisse* copyright © Editions Gallimard 2005.

Alan Jenkins is a poet, critic and deputy editor of the *Times Literary Supplement*. He has published several collections of poetry including *Harm* 1994 (winner of the Forward Poetry Prize), *The Drift* 2000 (which was a Poetry Book Society Choice and short listed for the TS Eliot Prize) and *A Shorter Life* 2005 (short listed for the Forward Poetry Prize).

Stuart Kelly is a critic and the author of the *Book of Lost Books*.

Erich Kuersten has worked for the biggest art swindler in world history, is a mockumentary maker and ham actor. He is the editor of the Acidemic Journal of Film and Media (www.acidemic.com).

Hari Kunzru is the author of *The Impressionist* (winner of the Betty Trask Prize 2002 and shortlisted for the Guardian First Book Award and the Whitbread First Novel Award) and *Transmission*. He was named as one of Granta's Best of Young British Novelists, 2003.

Philip Langeskov is an editor and indolent. Born in Copenhagen in 1976, he last did a full day's work in 1984, at the age of eight, and has since been engaged in cultivating the grass that grows beneath his feet.

Hélène Lavelle has travelled widely, living in Russia and Japan (where she researched into the delights of the 'floating world'). She presides over an occasional salon of writers, artists, connoisseurs and explorers of the farther shores.

Guillaume Lecasble was born in 1954, he is an artist and film-maker. *Lobster* is his first novel (and it is published by Dedalus). *Lobster* copyright © Editions du Seuil 2003. *Lobster* and *The Art of Cooking a Murder Victim* have been translated by Polly McLean.

Christine Leunens was born in the USA but came to Europe to work as a fashion model. She is now a full-time writer and lives in Caen in France. Her first novel *Primordial Soup* was published by Dedalus in 1999.

Medlar Lucan & Durian Gray met while running their scandalous Edinburgh dining-club, the Decadent. Following exile in the Far East, they now live in El Periquito, a cabaret-brothel in Havana. They are the authors of *The Decadent Cookbook*, *The Decadent Gardener* and *The Decadent Traveller*.

Isabelle McNeill teaches French cinema and literature at the University of Cambridge and is a fellow of Trinity Hall. She is involved in the Cambridge Film Festival and has edited their Festival Daily paper for three years.

David Madsen is a philosopher and theologian. He is the author of three very decadent novels: *Memoirs of a Gnostic Dwarf*, *Confessions of a Flesh-Eater*, *A Box of Dreams* and a baroque cookbook, *Orlando Crispe's Flesh-Eater's Cookbook*. All his work is published by Dedalus.

Mark Mason is tall, dark and handsome. He watches a lot of football and is a bestselling novelist. His novels include *What Men Really Think About Sex* and *The Catch*.

Karina Mellinger worked in Italy and is now a full-time writer. Dedalus have published her novel *A Bit Of A Marriage*.

Octave Mirbeau (1848–1917) was an anarchist and writer. He is best known today for his novels *Torture Garden* (1898) and *The Diary of a Chambermaid* (1900), both published by Dedalus. *The Diary of a Chambermaid* was filmed both by Jean Renoir (1946) and Luis Bunuel (1964).

Christopher Moore following five years as a jobbing journalist and writer in London, left the UK in 2004 to lessen the chances of one day living in Surrey. He is now a jobbing journalist and writer in Paris in 2004 and has no plans to move to Saint-Germain-en-Laye.

John Moore is a former band member of The Jesus and Mary Chain and a founding member of the chillingly noir British indie band Black Box Recorder. He once made money importing absinthe, is a regular contributor to the *Idler* magazine, and has just completed his first novel.

William Napier is the author of the best-selling *Attila* trilogy and an international man of mystery.

Rowan Pelling is a journalist and broadcaster and the former editor of the *Erotic Review*. She grew up in a pub and went to a school for the daughters of missionaries, both of which establishments helped determine her downward spiral. She is currently writing a memoir of her days as an eroticist (which is due to be turned into a feature film). She lives in Cambridge with her husband and young son and, as Sebastian Horsley says, you can't get less decadent than that.

André Pieyre de Mandiargues (1909–1991) was a prolific storyteller, novelist and art critic. His short stories, 'Clorinde' and 'Moon Walker', are included in Michael Richardson's two volume study of surrealism, *The Dedalus Book of Surrealism* (1993) and *The Myth of the World: Surrealism 2* (1994). *Cow Shed* and *Portrait of an Englishman in his Chateau* are translated by J. Fletcher and copyright © Editions Gallimard 1979.

Jacob Polley has had two books of poems, *The Brink* and *Little Gods*, published by Picador. His website can be found at www.jacobpolley.com

Xavior Roide is an international pop star, member of Placebo and is one half of Spanky and Xavior, a theatrical/comedy act.

Nicholas Royle was born in 1963 in Manchester. He is one of Britain's finest novelists (*Antwerp* and *The Director's Cut* being essential reads for anyone) and an advocate of the short story.

Professor Nicholas Royle teaches at the University of Sussex, specialising in literary theory. He also writes short stories.

Elizabeth Speller is modelling herself on her name sakes: Elizabeth Bathory, Elizabeth of Austria, Lizzie Borden and

Bess of Hardwick. In this way, using only virgins diamonds in her hair, an axe and some compelling sexual techniques, she hopes to acquire age-defying beauty, an empire and several kings, the effective removal of interfering relatives, half a dozen wealthy husbands and extensive property in the north. In the meantime she has just published *The Sunlight on The Garden* (Granta).

Catherine Townsend grew up in the United States, she lives in London and is a sex columnist for 'The Independent'.

Helen Walsh grew up in Liverpool, moved to Barcelona at the age of 16 and worked in its red light district. Her first novel was *Brass*.

Louise Welsh was one of the *Guardian's* Best First Novelists of 2002, she is the bestselling novelist of *The Cutting Room, Tamburlaine Must Die* and *The Bullet Trick*.

Oscar Wilde was the world's wittiest decadent, and the leading advocate of 'art for art's sake' of his time. Wilde was convicted of gross indecency in 1895 and after his release in 1897 spent three years in self-imposed exile until his death in 1900.

John Wilmot, 2nd Earl of Rochester, was born in 1647 and was England's greatest libertine. His play *Sodom, or the Quintessence of Debauchery* is believed to have been the first piece of pornography ever printed. He died of a variety of venereal diseases at the age of 33.

Moments in Decadent History

The Beginning
God created Eve from Adam's rib to give him a playmate. Eve then went on to eat the apple and begin the decadence movement.

Sodom and Gomorrah
When things got back to front.

The decline of the Roman Empire with starring parts for Caligula (AD 12–41) Nero (AD 37–68) and Heliogabalus (AD 204–222) . . . setting a standard in decadent behaviour which has yet to be matched.

61 A.D. Titus Petronius Niger, Consul of Bithynia and Arbiter of Elegance at Nero's court, writes the world's first decadent novel, *Satyricon*. Its most famous chapter is 'Trimalchio's Dinner', at which a gluttonous millionaire displays the magnificence of his vulgarity. This is one of the founding texts of decadent gastronomy.

July 13th 939 Pope Leo VII dies from a heart attack, while engaged in strenuous sexual activity.

May 19th 1649 Oliver Cromwell establishes the Commonwealth of England and its colonies. For ten years all gaiety is outlawed, puritanical laws close the theatres and abolish the use of ritual and ceremony in religious services (the closest the majority of England's population ever come to beauty in their lives was through the Church). Cromwell elegantly defines the part of the English character that decadence would war against.

1659 John Wilmot, later the second Earl of Rochester, enters
Wadham College, Oxford, and 'becomes debauched'. Later he
delights the Restoration court as part of the Merry Gang,
along with Henry Jermyn, Charles Sackville, Earl of Dorset,
John Sheffield, Earl Henry Killigrew, Sir Charles Sedley,
William Wycherley, George Etherege, and George Villiers,
Duke of Buckingham. He sets himself up as 'Doctor Bendo',
assisting women with fertility problems (along the way
supplying much of the sperm himself). He dies in 1680 from a
combination of syphilis and other venereal diseases, though
not before leaving versions of himself in numerous novels,
plays and poems, as well as producing his own, mostly pornographic, canon.

April 23rd 1661 Charles II is restored as the monarch, jollity
is restored, horse-racing is again allowed and the theatres are
re-opened with actresses appearing on the English stage for
the first time. Sex re-appears in English life.

1680s And over in France, the Sun King is on the throne. The
'libertine' emerges, and embraces the pleasures of the flesh to
the exclusion of religion and monarchism. At this time, the
fictional address 'à Anconne, chez la veuve Grosse-Motte' (At
Incunt, in the house of the big-motted widow) is very
popular.

1689 Publication by Mr Joseph Streater of *The Farce of
Sodom or The Quintessence of Debauchery* by John Wilmot,
Earl of Rochester. The play to be sold by Mr Benjamin
Crayle, bookseller. The book is banned and burnt the next
year.

November 3rd 1718 The birth of John Montagu. The fourth
Earl of Sandwich has an ambivalent role in decadent history.
He required sustenance during a spell at the gaming tables and
ordered that his servant bring him a piece of meat between
two pieces of bread. The sandwich was invented. While the

sandwich has democraticised debauchery, providing fuel for countless generations to continue their ribald joys, it meant that the wealthy no longer provided the extravagant feasts that had been the mark of decadent entertaining since the time of Trimalchio.

May 1746 The founding of the Hellfire Club by Sir Francis Dashwood, later Chancellor of the Exchequer. The fourth Earl of Sandwich was a member. Their meetings were popularly believed to be blasphemous orgies, including the taking of communion from a naked serving girl's navel. Aleister Crowley would later appropriate the club motto of 'Fay ce que voudras'. (Do as thou wilt).

1782 Publication of *Les Liaisons Dangereuses*, Laclos' novel of sexual libertinism and corruption par excellence.

June 26th 1830 George IV, the former Prince Regent, dies after a life spent getting into debt, being bailed out by his father, and indulging his prodigious appetites: he is rumoured to have kept a lock of hair from each of his lovers; 7, 000 such envelopes were found on his death.

1835 The writer Théophile Gautier – the dedicatee of Baudelaire's *Les Fleurs du mal* – uses the phrase 'Art for art's sake' in the foreword of his novel *Mademoiselle de Maupin*, defining a way of life for decadents evermore.

October 7th 1849 The death of Edgar Allan Poe. Death has always defined the decadent, and Poe's death was as influential as his writing. Discovered unconscious in Baltimore, Poe lay in a coma for three days before waking to cry out 'Reynolds! Oh, Reynolds'. He died soon after. Charles Baudelaire was fascinated by Poe, and translated much of his work into French, which would be central to decadence as defined by French writers of the nineteenth century . The idea of Poe as a creative genius destroyed by materialism, cut down by philistines, become a powerful self-image for French 19th century decadents.

1857 Baudelaire's *Les Fleurs du mal* (*Flowers of Evil*) and Flaubert's *Madame Bovary* prosecuted for obscenity in France.

1860s Absinthe has become so popular in France that from café to cabaret, 5pm becomes 'l'heure verte'.

July 1873 After scandalizing polite Parisian society with their affair, Paul Verlaine and Arthur Rimbaud move to London. A year later, Rimbaud departs for Paris and in a jealous rage Verlaine shoots him in the wrist. Verlaine is imprisoned for two years and Rimbaud retreats to write *Une Saison en Enfer* (*A Season in Hell*). He then gives up writing poetry and becomes a gun-dealer in East Africa.

1876 Degas exhibits his 'Sketch of a French café', showing the actress Ellen Andrée and the engraver Marcellin Desboutin with a glass of absinthe in the Café de la Nouvelle-Athènes. It is booed, and put into storage. Under the name 'Absinthe' it is put on show in London in 1893, where the Victorians see it as shockingly degraded, and a blow to morality.

1877 Tuberculosis is defined by J.F. Cohnheim – decadents rejoice at the naming of their disease.

1884 The world meets *Des Esseintes*, the protagonist of *A Rebours* (*Against Nature*), in the first truly 'decadent novel of the industrial age'. Wilde imitated it for his *Picture of Dorian Gray* (1891), and Huysmans' masterpiece was damned as 'sodomitical' during Wilde's trial.

April 16 1894 The first issue of *The Yellow Book* is published. Founded by Henry Harland and Aubrey Beardsley but conceived with the help of Walter Sickert and John Lane, the publisher of Bodley Head, the literary magazine's home. It enjoyed modest success, but Wilde (who never contributed to it) made it infamous, after he was seen clutching a yellow volume on his arrest in 1895. It was erroneously assumed to be *The Yellow Book*, and Lane's offices were attacked. It ceased production the following year. During its three brief years, it featured articles by Max Beerbohm, Arnold Bennett, Baron Corvo, Ernest Dowson, Richard Le Gallienne, Charlotte Mew, Count Stenbock and Arthur Symons.

1895 Wilde's Trial: Oscar Wilde is sentenced to two years in prison for 'a love which dare not speak its name.' He is declared bankrupt, his wife divorces him and his two sons' surname is changed to Holland.

1915 D.H. Lawrence's novel *The Rainbow* is seized by the police and declared obscene. This makes his next novel *Women in Love* (1916) unpublishable until 1920 when it is published in New York after a failed action for obscenity. It is then published in London in 1921, where a reviewer describes it an 'analytical study of sexual depravity' and an 'epic of vice.' D.H. Lawrence thought it his best book.

March 1918 Through the efforts of Ezra Pound and Margaret Anderson James Joyce's *Ulysses* begins to appear in serial form in the *Little Review* in New York. Margaret Anderson has great difficulty finding a printer but eventually finds a Serbian printer who is indifferent to the four letter words which were then considered unpublishable.

May 1922 Joyce and Proust, Picasso, Diaghilev and Stravinsky meet for a night at the Majestic Hotel in Paris, where a dinner is being given in Stravinsky and Diaghilev's honour. There are cameo appearances from the lesbian dominatrix Princesse Edmond de Polignac, and the Bloomsbury envoy Clive Bell. Proust died six months later, and Joyce passed out at the table, shamed by his lack of evening dress.

1929 At an exhibition of D.H. Lawrence's paintings in

London 13 pictures are removed by the police and pronounced obscene.

1931–32 A bored Anais Nin is introduced to Henry Miller and promptly leaves her husband to be with the novelist. Involvement spreads to his wife, June Mansfield, and Nin documents this steamy and scandalous affair in her extensive diaries

1932–33 Random House buy the US rights from Joyce for *Ulysses* and agree to take the burden of the legal costs. Judge Woolsey of the United States District Court in New York ruled that Celts are, and have a right to be, hypersexual. He finds the intention and method of *Ulysses* legitimate, making the book for the first time freely available in English.

1960 Penguin publish the complete unexpurgated text of D.H. Lawrence's *Lady Chatterley's Lover*. They are prosecuted under the Obscene Publications Act 1959, and many eminent authors, including E.M. Forster, Richard Hoggart and Helen Gardner appear as witnesses for the defence. The prosecution barrister famously asked the jury if it were a book they would want their servants to read. This trial had a profound effect on both writing and publishing and ushered in the 'swinging' decadent sixties.

1963 The Profumo Affair rocks the British establishment as sex and spying come together in the biggest scandal for many years. John Profumo is forced to resign as Secretary of State for War, not for his actions in the bedroom but for misleading the House of Commons about the nature of his affair with Christine Keeler.

April 16th 1977 Studio 54 is opened by Steve Rubell and Ian Schrager and quickly becomes the home for hedonism, exhibitionism and all-round debauchery. In 1979, Rubell and

Schrager are arrested and charged for skimming $2.5million, and the club is closed with one final party, called 'The End of Modern-day Gomorrah', on February 4th, 1980. Later the club reopened, though with much-reduced levels of transgression, and is currently a theatre.

June 1983 The publishing house of Dedalus is founded at an orgy in a Camberwell coffee bar... The name is inspired by the creator of the world's first labyrinth and father of Icarus – whose plunge from the sky in a glittering cascade of feathers and molten wax is an inspiration to all decadents.

1990 An art gallery in Cincinnati is unsuccessfully prosecuted on charges of 'pandering obscenity' after staging Robert Mapplethorpe's *The Perfect Moment*, (which includes several sadomasochistic portraits).

1993 Gerry O'Boyle opens Filthy Macnasty's Whisky Café in London, and Pogues' frontman Shane MacGowan swiftly takes up residence, to be followed by various Sex Pistols, Bad Seeds, and novelists. While working at the pub, Pete Doherty and Carl Barat form the Libertines, and the good times roll. New owners, however, have opened a sister pub in Twickenham, somewhat undermining the legend.

August 1994 The K Foundation (Bill Drummond and Jimmy Cauty) burn one million pounds, in £50 notes, that was unrequired profit from their incarnation as the KLF. A film made of the bonfire – *Watch the K Foundation Burn a Million Quid* – was thought to have been destroyed, but a single print circulates in ghostly form.

1998 The flavour of the Belle Epoque returns to Britain when Hill's Absinth is imported from the Czech Republic. The importers later turn to an absinthe museum in France to recreate the original recipes, and La Fée Absinthe is born in 2000.

December 2004 A copy of the Earl of Rochester's play *Sodom, or the Quintessence of Debauchery* is sold at Sotheby's for £45,600.

2006 London erupts into a riot of nipple tassles as burlesque and cabaret clubs spring up throughout the city, with the Bethnal Green Working Men's club at the forefront.

Further Decadent Reading

Charles Peltz has made his personal choice of forty-five decadent books to read. The editors have supplied some information about their contents.

1. Arthur Machen – *The Hill of Dreams* (1907)

Possibly Machen's masterpiece, the semi-autobiographical *The Hill of Dreams* follows Lucian Taylor from his home in Wales as he struggles to make a living in London. A decadent classic written in 1897 but only published in 1907.

2. Arthur Machen – *Three Imposters* (1895)

These delicately interlinked tales frame Gothic horrors within the scenery of a morally degraded London, where three young men attempt to solve a mystery.

3. Jacques D'Adelsward Fersen – *Lord Lyllian* (1893)

Forced to flee Paris for Capri after a scandal that mirrored Wilde's, *D'Adelsward Fersen* fictionalised his infamous *Pink Masses* and the subsequent witchhunt in this bitingly satirical novel.

4. Edmund John – *Flute of Sardonyx* (1913)

Writing in the Uranian school, these desperately passionate odes to unsullied youth were published just before John died in Sicily.

4. Stefan Grabinski – *Dark Domain* (1993)

This collection of stories by the 'Polish Poe' were written

between 1918 and 1922. They cover all his predelictions: the psychological, the mythical, the world of trains and railways, with mysterious travellers reacting to the relentless, hypnotic impetus of mechanical travel and the demonic and the dark, disturbing world of human sexual desire. Translated by Miroslaw Lipinski for Dedalus in 1993, new edition in 2005.

5. Clark Ashton Smith – *Emperor of Dreams* (2002)

Smith created fantastic and dense worlds, and also dabbled in poetry, sculpture and painting. A friend of Lovecraft, his stories (only published in book form forty-one years after his death in 1961), are part of the weird fiction firmament.

6. Vincent O'Sullivan – *Master of Fallen Years* (1993)

This collection of psychological supernatural tales, named for O'Sullivan's favourite story, displays the New York writer's horror for human nature and justifies his position at the centre of Yellow Nineties decadence.

7. R. Murray Gilchrist – *The Basilisk and Other Tales of Dread* (2003)

Before writing extensively on the Peak District, Gilchrist created suffocatingly atmospheric ghostly tales, including The Crimson Weaver, a vampire story published in *The Yellow Book*.

8. Thomas Ligotti – *The Nightmare Factory* (1984)

A confessed devotee of H.P. Lovecraft, Ligotti here leads the reader down dark corridors, weaving horror and reflection to enviable effect.

9. M.P. Shiel – *Prince Zaleski* (1895)

Shiel's Zaleski, the original decadent detective, stalks humanity's despicable errors from his tower in a deserted abbey in these three tales of declining morality.

10. M.P. Shiel – *Shapes in the Fire* (1896)

Collection of grotesque horror and detective stories heavily influenced by Poe, overlain with images of decadent extravagance, these stories are unique in style and delivery and are among the most distinctive supernatural stories of the nineteenth century.

11. Salvador Dali – *Hidden Faces* (1944)

Dali's only novel – with illustrations by the artist – tracks a group of aristocrats in the 30s in their pursuit of pleasure, pain and decadent perfection.

12. Montague Summers – *Antinous* (1907)

Summers, a clergyman, eccentric and believer in werewolves, celebrated pederasty in this collection of poems, named for the lover of Hadrian.

13. Leonard Cline – *The Dark Chamber* (1927)

Trying to escape his tortured reality, and revisit his lost youth via various stimulants, Richard Pride trangresses the natural order and unleashes the primordial memory of humankind. Cline was in prison, awaiting trial, when his classic was published.

14. William Lindsay Gresham – *Nightmare Alley* (1946)

A sordid tale of carnival life, Gresham's first novel was in 1947 made into a film starring Tyrone Power and along the way introduced the word 'geek' (a sideshow performer who bites chickens' heads off) to widespread usage

15. Vernon Lee – *Hauntings* (1906)

AKA Violet Paget, the prolific author and contributor to *The Yellow Book*, Vernon Lee brought the femme fatale into Victorian literature with this landmark collection of supernatural tales.

16. Fr Rolfe – *Don Renato* (1963)

Rolfe worked on this historical romance, a mix of letters from Rolfe and the diary of a doomed seventeenth-century priest in Rome, from 1907–08, though it remained unpublished until 1963, largely due to Rolfe's never-ending amendments.

17. J.F. Bloxam – *The Priest and the Acolyte* (1894)

This short story of a priest's carnal love with his altar boy was at one time credited to Wilde, who denied authorship, describing it as 'at moments poisonous: which is something'.

18. G.S. Viereck – *The House of the Vampire* (1907)

With this novel of a young man's fear of losing his creativity – a novel crowded with homosexual undertones that clamour to become overtones – G.S. Viereck established his place as an early master of the vampire genre.

19. Gustav Flaubert – *Salammbô* (1862)

A novel set in Carthage after the first Punic War, is Gustave Flaubert's tour-de-force exercise in the exotic, the morbid, the luxuriant and the violent. Flaubert's fascination with child sacrifice, crucifixions and love unto death give his historical novel a feverish and fantastical quality. Yet it is all underpinned by the author's meticulous research into the history and archaeology of ancient Carthage.

20. Remy de Gourmont – *Histoires Magiques* (1894)

A collection of decadent short stories. He liked stories about femmes fatales and Francis Amery translated some of them for Dedalus under the title of *Angels of Perversity* in 1992.

21/22. Marcel Schwob – *Coeur Double* (1891) and *Le Roi au Masque d'Or* (1892)

Where Wilde's French ended, Schwob's began, and he corrected Wilde's errors in time for *Salome*'s first performance. *Coeur Double* was his first book of short stories, dark fantastical tales that he developed the following year in *Le Roi au Masque d'Or*, which features cruel counts, sickly maidens and mad scientists.

23. Barbey D'Aurevilly – *Les Diaboliques* (1874)

Six decadent stories which celebrate the seven deadly vices while showing no counterbalancing interests in the seven cardinal virtues. Dedalus published Ernest Boyd's translation in 1986, new edition in 1996.

24. Aubrey Beardsley – *Under the Hill* (1897)

A baroque romance containing snatches of pornographic fantasy, which Beardsley did not live long enough to complete and which was too ahead of its time to have been published in full in any case.

25. Élémir Bourges – *Le Crépuscule des Dieux* (1883)

A lurid novel in which the evil mistress of a French aristocrat encourages his three children to taste the fruits of their inherited degeneracy, leading to an orgy of incest, murder, suicide and traumatic insanity.

26. Jean Lorrain – *Monsieur de Phocas* (1901)

A leading proponent of dandyism, blatant in his homosexuality in an easily scandalised Paris, Lorrain gives us Monsieur de Phocas, a man falling relentlessly into the gap between reality and hallucination, grasping at easy but dangerous pleasure during his headlong and bloody descent. A *fin-de-siècle* classic translated into English by Francis Amery for Dedalus in 1994.

27. Jean Lorrain – *Nightmares of an Ether Drinker* (1895)

Lorrain again blurs his narcotic reality and poisonous cauchemar in this collection of tales, which, although fuelled by ether, contain within them foreshadowings of the author's mysterious death from the effects of the drug years later.

28. Renée Vivien – *Une Femme m'apparut* (1904)

The bolt of lightning was a wealthy American lesbian called Natalie Clifford Barney, the transfixed witness was the established Symbolist poet Vivien (born Pauline Tarn in London), the result was this account of the magnetic attraction between the two women, casting Barney as Atthis, who forced Sappho into suicide. Vivien died at 34, ravaged by alcoholism and anorexia.

29. Jean Lombard – *L'Agonie* (1888)

The agony in question is that of the clash between homosexual desire and the strictures of society, laid in out in full in this nearly entirely forgotten epic of desire and despair.

30. Maurice Maeterlick – *Serres Chaudes* (1889)

This was the first collection of poetry from the Belgian Nobel prize winner, and came about after an encounter with J.K. Huysmans. It clearly reveals the writer's turning away from Christianity, and the confusion that this rupture engendered. They were to remain his only original verses.

31. Edouard Dubus – *Quand les Violons sont Partis* (1892)

A crucial book of symbolist verse, sulphurously decadent. Much admired by fellow poets, Dubus was plagued by insanity, occult delusions and drug addiction, and, on release from an insane asylum, was found dead from a morphine overdose in the pissoir of Place Maubert in the Paris Latin Quarter, having published only this book and a short play in collaboration with fellow symbolist Ephraim Mikael.

32. Ernest Dowson – *Verses* (1896)

Ernest Dowson is the tragic poet of the Yellow Nineties. Tuberculosis and absinthe brought him an early death. *Verses* is his first collection followed by *Decorations* in 1899. His poems can be grouped into love poems, devotional verses and poems of ennui and world-weariness. Most of us know some lines by Dowson – 'gone with the wind' from *Cynara*. 'They are not long, the days of wine and roses' from *Vitae Summa Brevis*.

33. Georges Rodenbach – *Bruges-la-Morte* (1892)

Perhaps the greatest work of Belgian decadence, this novel celebrates the city of Bruges: its dark streets, its darker secrets, and the beautiful woman who wanders them. Is she the *doppelgänger* of Hugues Viane's dead wife, or is she haunting him as intimately as the city itself? Translated into English by Mike Mitchell for Dedalus in 2005.

34. Stanislas de Guaita – *La Muse Noire* (1883)

A co-founder of *l'Ordre Kabbalistique de la Rose Croix*, de Guaita wrote this collection of poetry after sensibly rejecting a career in the law for mysticism and the occult.

35. Robert de Montesquiou – *Les Chauve-Souris* (1892)

Rumoured to be the inspiration for Huysmans' *Des Esseintes* and Proust's *Baron de Charlus*, and captured in oils by Whistler, the Comte de Montesquiou-Fezensac was a dandy par excellence, flitting between high and low society, and producing poetry from time to time in private, lavishly produced editions, bristling with symbolism.

36. André Pieyre de Mandiargues – *Un Anglais decrit dans le chateau fermé* (1953)

This Englishman in his chateau is not a restrained man. Sexually and sadistically, he visits his desires upon the other inhabitants of the castle, with extreme violence and perversity. Translated for Dedalus by J. Fletcher in 1998 under the title *Portrait of an Englishman in his Chateau*.

37. J.K. Huysmans – *A Rebours* (1884)

The most significant study of a decadent personality in French Literature. Dedalus will publish a new English translation by Brendan King in 2008 under the title of *Against Nature*.

38. J.K. Huysmans – *Là-Bas* (1891)

The classic tale of Satanism and sexual obsession in nineteenth-century France. Translated for Dedalus by Brendan King in 2001, new edition in 2006.

39. Octave Mirbeau – *Le Jardin des Supplices* (1898)

To Mirbeau: 'Ah, yes! the Torture Garden! Passions, appetites, greed, hatred, and lies; law, social institutions, justice, love, glory, heroism, and religion: these are its monstrous flowers and its hideous instruments of eternal human suffering. What I saw today, and what I heard, is no more than a symbol to me of the entire earth. I have vainly sought a respite in quietude and repose in death, and I can find them nowhere.' Translated into English by Michael Richardson for Dedalus in 1995 as *Torture Garden*.

40. Hans Heinz Ewers – *Alraune: The Story of a Living Creature* (1911)

A Satanist fantasy inspired by the works of Poe and de Sade which was a bestseller in Germany.

41. J.G. Ballard – *Vermillion Sands* (1973)

This book collects Ballard's stories about Vermillion Sands, an artists' colony marooned in a languid future of unlimited leisure, high technology, and mysterious, jewel-eyed women. Half-sentient buildings drift in and out of the encroaching desert, art projects threaten the nature of reality, and the inhabitants pursue their obscure enthusiasms, all against the numbing blue skies and the desolate sands. In common with many of Ballard's books, it's emotionally cold, but full of sharply brilliant ideas and vivid, over-saturated images.

42. M.J. Harrison – *The Ice Monkey* (1983)

Creepy short stories in dank, occult London

43. Count Stenbock – *Studies in Death* (1893)

A decadent short story collection from the most exotically enigmatic and cursed character of the 1890s, who Arthur Symons described as ' inhuman and abnormal; a degenerate, who had I know not how many vices'.

44. Maurice Rolliinat – *Les Névroses* (1883)

After a false start in realism, Rollinat joined a fringe decadent group and turned his attention to death, the fear of it and the attraction of it, in this book of poems, subsections with titles such as souls, lusts, refuges, spectres, darkness.

45. Iwan Gilkin – *La Nuit* (1897)

A true poet of the night, the Belgian Gilkin was much inspired by Baudelaire and Lautréamont for this collection of poems.

For non-fiction decadent reading we suggest you try Mario Praz's *Romantic Agony* (1933).

The Decadent Handbook Survey:
The 20 Most Decadent People Alive

Dedalus asked 1,000 men and women who they believed to be the most decadent people alive to mark the publication of *The Decadent Handbook*. They were allowed to nominate up to ten individuals. The results are as follows:

1. Pete Doherty
2. Keith Richards
3. Shane MacGowan
4. Kate Moss
5. Paris Hilton
6. P Diddy
7. Courtney Love
8. DBC Pierre
9. Mick Jagger
10. Michael Jackson
11. Hugh Hefner
12. Elton John
13. Colin Farrell
14. Russell Brand
15. Prince Charles
16. John Leslie
17. Pete Burns
18. Rt Hon Baroness Thatcher
19. Lindsay Lohan
20. Sebastian Horsley

Pete Doherty was head and shoulders ahead of any other nominee with his name suggested by over two-thirds of the voters. As one respondent wrote: "Doherty wins it for me – there's a difference, for me, between decadence and straight-forward hedonism (Keith Richards), and between being decadent and being grotesquely ostentatious (P Diddy). Doherty retains an air of innocence."

The editors were astonished by the passionate response to our survey. Most people feel very strongly about who rightly has some claim to be described as 'decadent' and who does not. For many people true decadence is all about people who seek extreme experiences without any reference to personal safety or social mores – like Doherty. For others it's about people who are profligate while in some sort of public office. That's why Margaret Thatcher and Prince Charles turned up on the list.

It's interesting to see that people who behave outrageously are largely lionized by society. The people who nominated Doherty and Keith Richards, Kate Moss and Courtney Love, are huge fans of them. Most people's lives are so dictated by domestic and financial worries that they feel glad someone somewhere is totally off the rails. It's as if people who behave decadently are doing it for all of us.

Worthy Nominees Who Failed to Make the Short-list:

President Bush of America was nominated by some voters because, as one correspondent wrote, "he spends the earth's resources as if they were his own."

Also nominated was President Nizayov of Turkmenistan, "Surely no one else today is indulging themselves on the scale of Prezident Nizayov, Turkmenbashi 'Father of Turkmeni-stan.' He has built ice palaces in the desert, made reading his work compulsory, and renamed Wednesday after his mother. His image is superimposed on every TV channel, and a giant golden statue of him in the centre of the capital rotates constantly to catch the sun."

Since being nominated President Nizayov has died but we felt his achievements still deserved a mention.

And Boris Johnson was backed by twelve voters because: "He has such reckless disregard for his own professional wellbeing."